PRAYING THE MASS

A Guide to the New English Translation of the Mass

PRAYING THE MASS

The Prayers of the Priest

Jeffrey Pinyan

author@PrayingTheMass.com
www.PrayingTheMass.com

Contents

Acknowledgements

Once again, I am in the debt of Rev. John Zuhldorf ("Father Z") and Rev. Tim Finigan: the former for his enlightening commentaries on the prayers of the Roman Missal, and the latter for his warm review of the first volume and his gracious foreword in this second volume.

The Notre Dame Liturgy Center (liturgy.nd.edu) has a set of video catecheses on the new translation, which were of great value; I thank in particular Msgr. Bruce Harbert and Rev. Paul Turner. Another valuable online source is Msgr. Charles Pope's "The Mass in Slow Motion" series on the Archdiocese of Washington's web site (blog.adw.org). In addition to those fine resources, the series of twelve articles on "The Spirit of the Liturgy" for the Year for Priests published by ZENIT news agency were a source of inspiration and learning during my research.

The hands holding the Host above the chalice on the cover belong to Rev. Martin Miller, a priest of Opus Dei at Princeton University. I thank him for his contagious attitude of reverence when celebrating Holy Mass.

I was able to find the time to write the first volume of this series due to the financial crisis of 2008-2009: I was only working a four-day work week at my full-time job. I thank God that I am no longer on furlough, but I have had to try harder to find time to write this second volume, so I thank my wife Kristin for her patience and encouragement. I thank my parents for their support and for sharing my excitement at this endeavor.

I thank my brother, Rev. Charlie Pinyan, who first inspired me to read *Sacramentum Caritatis*, the Apostolic Exhortation of Pope Benedict XVI that led me to study the liturgy of the Roman Rite. Finally, I thank His Holiness Pope Benedict XVI for his writings about the liturgy that have served my liturgical formation well.

This book is dedicated to all the ordained saints of the Church.

Foreword

In *The Spirit of the Liturgy*, Cardinal Ratzinger urges that the vestments worn by the priest at Mass should make it clear that he is not there as a private person but in the place of Christ. He is there to make way for the action of God that will take place in the sacred Liturgy. The priest must therefore celebrate the Mass devoutly and attentively, taking care to use the words and the gestures of the liturgy as prescribed by the Church in such a way that he himself, as well as the people, are nourished by them and led to participate in the sacred mysteries fully, actively and consciously.

In this volume Jeffrey Pinyan takes the trouble not only to offer a rich commentary on the spoken prayers of the priest, but also to consider the vestments and ritual gestures that accompany them. Lay people will be greatly helped by his explanation of the meaning of the different parts of the Mass that are said by the priest. Priests will also find here much material for reflection on their celebration of the Mass: this would be a helpful book to have at hand for a retreat or a day of recollection. The two sets of questions for reflection at the end of each chapter show how this book can be used by both clergy and laity to deepen their participation at the Mass.

At various points, appropriate comparisons are made with the Extraordinary Form of the Mass, in the spirit of that mutual enrichment which Pope Benedict called for in *Summorum Pontificum*. I believe these will be especially helpful for those who only know the Ordinary Form of the Mass but would like to be better informed about the Extraordinary Form and its relationship to the form of Mass that they usually attend. The fact that the Extraordinary Form is considered sympathetically in a guide to the new English translation of the Mass is itself a sign of the liturgical peace that is beginning to break out: that "interior reconciliation at the heart of the Church" which Pope Benedict wished to accomplish.

The new ICEL translation of the Mass will be coming into use later this year. This significant change to the English Mass presents an opportunity for catechesis on the Holy Eucharist and on the sacred

Liturgy itself. Jeffrey Pinyan has taken this opportunity seriously, in a sincere concern to assist both priests and laity to worship God with greater understanding, and to "become thoroughly imbued with the spirit and power of the liturgy." Even this goal is not the end-point of the book: the greater understanding is intended to lead to a deeper praying of the Mass, a richer engagement with the presence of Christ in His mysteries, and a greater openness to receive the grace that He wishes to give us.

Fr. Timothy Finigan

INTRODUCTION
What is "praying the Mass"?

POPE ST. PIUS X SAID THAT "the Holy Mass is a prayer itself, even the highest prayer that exists." For this pope of the early twentieth century, it was never a matter of praying *at* Mass, but of praying *the* Mass. The Eucharistic liturgy (known as the Mass in the West, and the Divine Liturgy in the East) is the highest form of prayer because it is the prayer of Jesus Christ to God the Father. This liturgy is called "divine" because it is principally the work of God, not of man (*Catechism* 1069), although we are invited to participate in it, just as we are invited to become "partakers of the divine nature." (2 Pet. 1:4) The Church participates in this prayer because she is the mystical Body of Christ, Who in turn is the Head of the Church.

This definition of the liturgy as the prayer of Christ can be found in the first document of the Second Vatican Council, *Sacrosanctum Concilium*, the Constitution on the Sacred Liturgy (SC). The liturgy is "an exercise of the priestly office of Jesus Christ" and "an action of Christ the priest and of His Body which is the Church." (SC 7) The same sentiment can be found sixteen years earlier, in the first major modern papal writing on the liturgy, *Mediator Dei* (MD) by Ven. Pope Pius XII:

> The sacred liturgy is … the public worship which our Redeemer as
> Head of the Church renders to the Father, as well as the worship

which the community of the faithful renders to its Founder, and through Him to the heavenly Father. It is, in short, the worship rendered by the Mystical Body of Christ in the entirety of its Head and members. (MD 20)

The liturgy is an action of Christ, and the Church is His Mystical Body, so every member of that body participates in the liturgy; and because the liturgy is a priestly act, every member participates in a priestly capacity. But the Church, as a body, is composed organically and hierarchically (cf. 1 Cor. 12:12-20), so her members do not all exercise this priesthood in the same way.

Priesthood and Participation in the Mass

Through the sacrament of Baptism, all Christians share in the **baptismal priesthood**. (cf. *Catechism* 1268; MD 88) This is also called the **common priesthood**, but "common" here does not mean "base" or "plebian." It means "communal" or "universal," because it is shared by all. The laity exercise this priesthood in the Mass as the Body of Christ, but they also exercise this priesthood outside church walls, where they "work for the sanctification of the world from within," seeking the kingdom of God "by engaging in temporal affairs and by ordering them according to the plan of God." (Vatican II, *Lumen Gentium* [LG] 31)

There is a second participation in Christ's priesthood, one that is carried out by priests. Just as the baptismal priesthood is entered into through the sacrament of Baptism, the **ordained priesthood** is entered into through the sacrament of Holy Orders (ordination); it is also called the **ministerial priesthood**, because the priest ministers (serves) at the altar. (cf. *Catechism* 1120) The priest celebrating Mass is *in persona Christi capitis*, "in the person of Christ the Head" of the Body – not as a mere representative of the Body, but as a representative of Christ the Head. (*Catechism* 1348; MD 93) Even though these two priesthoods "differ from one another in essence and … in degree," they are related to one another, and "each of them in its own special way is a participation in the one priesthood of Christ." (LG 10)

There are real distinctions between the faculties and responsibilities of the ordained and the laity in the liturgy. C.S. Lewis described the beauty and wisdom of such a hierarchy: "Not as when stones lie side by side, but as when stones support and are supported in an arch, such is

His order." (*Perelandra*, p. 184) Despite all their differences, these two priesthoods do share some common elements. All the faithful are called to true participation in the Mass – participation that the Second Vatican Council described as *plenam* (full), *consciam* (conscious), and *actuosam* (active or actual). This participation is often manifested by gestures, postures, and verbal prayers or responses. Sometimes, however, this participation is *not* accompanied by an external act; when the Gospel is being proclaimed by a deacon, for example, everyone else (including the priest) is *listening*. This listening is active even though those listening are not visibly "doing something." Everyone must be receptive to the Scriptures, whether he is the one speaking them aloud or the one listening to them in silence.

Most of the prayers (including those that vary from day to day) and many gestures belong to the priest celebrant. The foremost of these is the Eucharistic Prayer, during which the bread and wine become the Eucharist, the Body, Blood, Soul, and Divinity of Jesus Christ. The laity can come to a better understanding of the liturgy, learn how to join their personal prayers and intentions to the prayers of the priest, and gain a greater appreciation of their priests, by paying attention to these prayers and actions of the priest; this understanding will lead them closer to the ideal of full, conscious, and active participation.

This *conscious* participation requires "that the faithful come to [the liturgy] with proper dispositions, that their minds should be attuned to their voices, and that they should cooperate with divine grace." To make this possible, it is the responsibility of pastors to "ensure that the faithful take part fully aware of what they are doing, actively engaged in the rite, and enriched by its effects." (SC 11) It is one thing to know what we are doing, but another to know why we are doing it. It is one thing to make an external gesture, but another to have the gesture authentically manifest our internal devotion. Simply put, we need to have an accurate idea of what we are participating in, what the Mass *is*. Paying attention must be supplemented by liturgical instruction or catechesis.

Liturgical Catechesis

The Second Vatican Council linked authentic participation to liturgical instruction:

In the restoration and promotion of the sacred liturgy, this full and active *participation* by all the people is the aim to be considered before all else; for it is the primary and indispensable source from which the faithful are to derive the true Christian spirit; and therefore pastors of souls must zealously strive to achieve it, by means of the *necessary instruction*, in all their pastoral work. (SC 14)

Authentic liturgical participation must be learned, which means we must be taught. But this need for instruction is not limited to the laity:

Pastors themselves [must] become thoroughly imbued with the spirit and power of the liturgy, and undertake to give instruction about it. A prime need, therefore, is that attention be directed, first of all, to the liturgical instruction of the clergy. (SC 14)

The Council did not consider it sufficient simply to simply reform the liturgical rites. The reform desired by the bishops included reforming the people as well, by means of pastoral instruction.

The Mass, although its principal purpose is the worship of God, also "contains much instruction for the faithful" in its prayers, and the visible signs and symbols employed in the liturgy "signify invisible divine things have been chosen by Christ or the Church." (SC 33) In his homily at the close of the 2008 Eucharistic Congress, Pope Benedict XVI issued a challenge to the Church to study the liturgy, the "great mystery" in which "every sentence, every gesture has its own meaning and conceals a mystery."

The study of the liturgy, within the Church's rich tradition, is the aim of this book and its companion, *Praying the Mass: The Prayers of the People*. But this study is not only directed at the head, toward mere intellectual comprehension; its goal is a *spiritual* understanding of the Mass as one cohesive prayer. In 1979, Ven. Pope John Paul II wrote about catechesis that

sacramental life is impoverished and very soon turns into hollow *ritualism* if it is not based on serious knowledge of the meaning of the sacraments, and catechesis becomes *intellectualized* if it fails to come alive in the sacramental practice. (*Catechesi Tradendae* 23)

A genuine understanding requires that the laity (and the priest) know what the prayers of the priest are, because these prayers are "addressed to God by the priest … in the name of the entire holy people and of all present" (SC 33), so that the whole congregation can pray the Mass *with* the priest. Pope St. Pius X said that you must follow with eye, heart and mouth all that happens at the altar. Further, you must pray with the priest the holy words said by him in the name of Christ and which Christ says by him. You have to associate your heart with the holy feelings which are contained in these words and in this manner you ought to follow all that happens on the Altar. When acting in this way you have prayed Holy Mass.

The New Translation: A Sacral Vernacular

In 2002, the third edition of the *Roman Missal* was promulgated in Latin. Since that time, various commissions have been working to create vernacular translations. The guiding document from the Church on how these translations should be developed is *Liturgiam Authenticam* (LA), the fifth instruction from the Church on the proper implementation of the Constitution on the Sacred Liturgy. Among the concerns voiced in this instruction is that some vernacular translations had certain "omissions or errors" that have prevented the Church "from laying the foundation for a fuller, healthier and more authentic renewal." (LA 6)

In late 2008, a new English translation of a portion of the third edition of the *Roman Missal* was approved by the Holy See. This part is called the "Ordinary" (or "Order of the Mass") because it is made up of those parts of the Mass that do not change from day to day and week to week.[1] By the end of 2010, the complete translation had been approved. Before the translation can be effectively employed, though, there needs to be a suitable period of catechesis. The anticipated date for the use of the new English translation in the United States is Advent of 2011, to provide time for clergy and laity to become familiar with the changes before they start saying and hearing them in the liturgy.

The first thing that many people will notice about the new English translation is the quality or character of the language used. The Church "consecrates" (sets apart) the vernacular for use in the liturgy by using it in a particular way. The new translation has an elevated style that will require an adjustment in how it is prayed and how it is listened to. The liturgy demands "a kind of language which is easily understandable, yet which at the same times preserves [the] dignity, beauty, and doctrinal

---

[1] The parts that change from one Mass to the next are called the "Propers." This book focuses on the Order of the Mass, not the Propers.

precision" of the Church's prayers. (LA 25) The Church calls this a "sacral vernacular," a sort of sacred dialect that is "characterized by a *vocabulary, syntax* and *grammar* that are proper to divine worship." (LA 47) This vocabulary uses more doctrinally precise words in place of imprecise words (e.g. "incarnate" instead of "born"), and employs a greater variety of expression, such as not always using the word "love" to translate the Latin words *caritas* and *dilectio*. In certain cases, transliteration is used, as in the case of *consubstantialis* being rendered as "consubstantial" instead of "one in being" in the Nicene Creed. Because many of the prayers of the Mass are spoken (or sung) aloud, they differ in style from texts that are read quietly to one's self. Some qualities of this style include "a solemn or exalted tone, alliteration or assonance, concrete and vivid images, repetition, parallelism and contrast, a certain rhythm, and at times, the lyric of poetic compositions." (LA 59)

Overall, because the new English translation is more faithful to the underlying Latin text, the translation has a noticeable "Latin" character. This might seem foreign or artificial to those who think that Americans need an "American way" of praying and that the British need a "British way" of praying, instead of using a "Latin way" of praying. That criticism misses an important point, though: we celebrate the Roman (Latin) Rite. No matter what vernacular language this Rite is translated into, it remains the Roman Rite, which means it will retain the Roman style of prayer, a style that includes word choice and "tone." Modern English translations of the Divine Liturgy of St. John Chrysostom sound Byzantine; so too the English translation of the Roman Rite should sound Roman.[2]

Another general characteristic of the new translation is greater clarity in references to Scripture. One excellent example is the acclamation said by the priest as he shows the Eucharist to the congregation, just before he receives it. In the old translation he said, "This is the Lamb of God who takes away the sins of the world. Happy are those who are called to his supper." The new translation renders this as "Behold the Lamb of God, behold him who takes away the sins of the world. Blessed are those called to the supper of the Lamb." In addition to matching the

---

[2] This is not always easy to accomplish: Latin is a very concise language, packing a lot of meaning into a few words, and English cannot always mimic that quality.

Latin text better, this new translation lets the words of Scripture shine through: the first sentence comes from St. John's Gospel (John 1:29), and the second sentence comes from the book of Revelation. (Rev. 19:9) The new translation more clearly connects the sacred banquet of Holy Communion with the marriage banquet of the Lamb and His Bride, the Church.

Why is there a new translation? The underlying reason is to improve our liturgical prayer. The liturgy is "the privileged place for catechizing the People of God" (*Catechism* 1074), and we must be receptive to the spiritual riches contained in the prayers and rites of the Mass. The new translation seeks to draw out these riches by quoting Scripture more accurately; by using words with greater doctrinal precision to show the unity between the "law of prayer" (*lex orandi*) and the "law of belief" (*lex credendi*); by using language that reminds us of God's grandeur, majesty, transcendence, and power; and by better representing our great Catholic liturgical heritage. We should not expect this external change in our liturgical prayer to bring about an internal change overnight, but the longer we use this new translation, the greater we will notice its effect on our experience of prayer, both public and private.

Liturgical Fidelity

While I am not writing a rubrical[3] guide nor a commentary on the *General Instruction of the Roman Missal*, I do mention the gestures and postures the priest makes, because these gestures and postures are bodily prayers that manifest externally the proper internal spiritual disposition. As Pope Benedict XVI wrote in his 2007 Apostolic Exhortation following the 2005 Synod on the Eucharist, because the art of proper celebration of the liturgy is the best way to ensure the actual participation of the people, "the best catechesis on the Eucharist is *the Eucharist itself*, celebrated well." (*Sacramentum Caritatis* 64; cf. 38) For that reason, I strongly advocate fidelity to the prayers and rubrics as found in the Missal, both by priests and congregations, so that the spiritual realities being celebrated are not obscured by the words said or the actions performed. At the same time,

---

[3] Rubrics (from the Latin *ruber*, "red") are the parts of the Missal printed in red ink; they instruct the priest or the people to make certain gestures, assume certain postures, or speak in an audible or inaudible voice. The parts of the Missal in black ink are the words to be prayed.

priests should avoid a cold and mechanical rubricism: "when the liturgy is celebrated, something *more* is required than the mere observation of the laws governing valid and licit celebration." (SC 11)

The Constitution on the Sacred Liturgy said that no person, "even if he be a priest, may add, remove, or change anything in the liturgy on his own authority." (SC 22) This not only ensures that no one adds anything improper to the Mass, or removes essential elements from it, it also ensures that the congregation will not be caught off guard by unexpected words from the priest.[4] The alteration of liturgical prayers by a priest can provoke the laity to change their responses as it suits them. This ultimately disrupts the stability of the liturgy, distorts its authentic meaning, and leads to liturgical disunity from one parish to the next, and even from one celebration to the next within the same parish.

There are two general questions about (or even objections to) rules governing liturgical prayer. The first is this: why do we use prayers and gestures that do not always correspond to what we are actually thinking and feeling at the time? The second follows from it: why don't we make up prayers extemporaneously and spontaneously, "as the Spirit moves us"? These are two valid questions and deserve pastoral responses.

As to why we use prayers and gestures that do not always match our personal dispositions, a 1954 essay by Anglican liturgical theologian F.H. Brabant provides a satisfying explanation:

> All liturgical acts – whether they make use of words [or] actions… – have a double function: one directed Godwards, expressing in outward form the thoughts and feelings of the worshippers, the other directed manwards, teaching the worshippers *how they ought to think and feel* by setting before them the Church's standard of worship. … That is why the Liturgy not only expresses what we feel; it also *teaches us what we ought to feel.* ("Worship in General" in *Liturgy and Worship*, pp. 12-13)

When we do not feel particularly repentant, the season of Lent still puts us into an atmosphere of penitence. Even when we are not particularly joyous or exuberant, the *Gloria* and the *Alleluia* still ring out our praise of

---

[4] I am referring specifically to situations where the priest says something and the congregation responds: if the priest changes his words, the congregation might not know when he is finished, leaving them confused in timing their response. This can distract the congregation from an attitude of prayer, focusing their attention on the mechanics of the Mass instead of its mystery.

the Lord. Even when we cannot grasp with our minds – and even when our hearts strain to believe – the substantial and Real Presence of Christ in the Eucharist, our bodies can still kneel before Him in reverence and awe and remind our souls of the mystery we are encountering.

Why do we use prayers and gestures that have been prescribed for us by the Church, instead of ones composed and selected by the local community, or thought up at the spur of the moment? One reason is that, while the Church is home to a diversity of liturgical Rites, and there is permission for options and local variations in certain cases, too much "local flavor" eventually leads to a real lack of catholicity (universality) and unity to what should be the same form of the Roman Rite.

A second reason to use the words the Church provides, and a rather practical one at that, is that these words have been carefully chosen to accurately convey the faith. The last thing we need in our worship of God is to respond "Amen" to prayer that openly invites heresy!

In his book on liturgical worship, *Beyond Smells and Bells*, Anglican Mark Galli gives a third reason to be wary about spontaneous language. After pointing out that many of the words we hear today come from advertising and marketing executives who use them to manipulate us, Galli writes that it is no real surprise that many people are put off by liturgical words that they perceive to be manufactured and stiff. People want "authentic" language:

> In our desire to be real, we start thinking that authenticity is another word for spontaneity, as if everything we say at the spur of the moment is more true, more sincere than words we craft carefully. ... Indeed, sometimes what we blurt out thoughtlessly is actually what we mean and feel. But more often than not, what we blurt out is ill-considered and something we either need to qualify or apologize for. *(Beyond Smells and Bells*, p. 113)

In the face of crafted language designed to deceive or manipulate, Galli writes that the liturgy does not "abandon crafted language" altogether, but shapes it "so that it reveals reality." The result is liturgical poetry:

> Poetry at its finest moments subverts our best attempts at hiding from reality. ... The poetry of liturgy has just this power. The liturgy contains words that have been shaped and crafted over the centuries. It is formal speech. It is public poetry. As such it reaches into us to reveal not only the unnamed reality of our lives but the God who created us. "In worship the voice of the Church

calls up thoughts and feelings often far beyond us," wrote [F.H. Brabant], "yet to which something in us faintly but firmly responds." (*Beyond Smells and Bells*, pp. 113-114)

English and Latin

Both this book and *The Prayers of the People* include the Latin words of the Mass along with the new English translation. Why?

Latin is still the liturgical language proper to the Roman (Latin) Rite.[5] Contrary to popular opinion, the Second Vatican Council did not call for the wholesale replacement of Latin with the vernacular in the Mass. What the Council did say is that, while the vernacular may be introduced into the liturgy, "the use of the Latin language is to be preserved in the Latin rites" (SC 36) and that "steps should be taken so that the faithful may also be able to say or to sing together in Latin those parts of the Ordinary of the Mass which pertain to them." (SC 54) Even Gregorian chant, which is not part of the typical experience in the vast majority of English-speaking parishes, was strongly endorsed in the Constitution, which described it as proper to the Roman liturgy (*"liturgiae romanae proprium"*) and said it should have the principal place (*"principem locum"*) in liturgical celebrations. (SC 116) Months before the Council convened, Bl. Pope John XXIII promulgated an Apostolic Constitution, *Veterum Sapientia*, praising the Latin language as universal, immutable, and non-vernacular (qualities making it specially suited for use in the liturgy), mandating its study, and affirming its retention in the life of the Church.

The Latin texts of the prayers are included in this book as a help for both laity and priests. If you have seen the Mass celebrated on EWTN, you will note that in addition to the congregation praying the Our Father in Latin, the words the priest says to introduce this prayer are also sung in Latin. By including the Latin text with the English translation in this book, the laity can be prepared for what they might hear if they attend a Mass in which Latin is used to some extent; priests can also familiarize themselves with the Latin and the new translation at the same time, should they want to begin slowly introducing Latin into the Mass.

---

[5] Accordingly, in the decree on priestly formation from Vatican II the Council Fathers considered the "study of the liturgical language proper to each rite" a necessary component of the education of seminarians. (*Optatam Totius* 13)

Ordinary and Extraordinary

The new English translation is of the **Ordinary Form of the Roman Rite**. The term "Ordinary Form" originates in an Apostolic Letter issued by Pope Benedict XVI in July of 2007. This letter, *Summorum Pontificum*, addressed issues concerning the older liturgy of the Roman Rite, the liturgy as it was celebrated before and during Vatican II. This older form of the liturgy has gone by many names: the 1962 Missal, the Pian Missal (named after Pope Pius V), the Traditional Latin Mass, the Tridentine Mass, the pre-Vatican II Mass, the Gregorian Rite (named for Pope St. Gregory the Great), and so on. The newer form of the Mass is also known by many names: the 1970 Missal, the Pauline Missal (named after Pope Paul VI), the post-Vatican II Mass, the *Novus Ordo*, and so on. These titles all vary in degree of accuracy.[6]

The Pope's Apostolic Letter made it permissible for any priest of the Roman Rite to celebrate Mass according to the older form.[7] The Pope also sent an explanatory letter to bishops along with *Summorum Pontificum* in which he provided consistent terminology – "extraordinary form" and "ordinary form" – for referring to the older and newer forms of the Roman Rite. These letters also drew attention to the need for a proper frame of reference for the interpretation of the documents of the Second Vatican Council as well as the liturgical development that followed it. Two years earlier, in his Christmas address to the Roman Curia, Pope Benedict XVI differentiated between two contrary approaches to the interpretation of the Council:

> On the one hand, there is an interpretation that I would call "a hermeneutic of *discontinuity and rupture*;" it has frequently availed itself of the sympathies of the mass media, and also one trend of modern theology. On the other, there is the "*hermeneutic of reform*," of *renewal in the continuity* of the one … Church. …
>
> The hermeneutic of discontinuity risks ending in a split between the pre-conciliar Church and the post-conciliar Church. … The hermeneutic of discontinuity is countered by the hermeneutic of reform, as it was presented first by Pope John XXIII in his speech inaugurating the Council. … [He said] that the Council wishes "to

---

[6] For example, the "pre-Vatican II Mass" continued to be celebrated after the conclusion of the Council, and the "Pauline Missal" has been revised by Ven. John Paul II and Benedict XVI.

[7] These books, although promulgated by Bl. Pope John XXIII in 1962, have since undergone slight revisions under Pope Benedict XVI, so the term "1962 Missal" is no longer accurate.

transmit the doctrine, pure and integral, without any attenuation or distortion."

The Pope later clarified this terminology in *Sacramentum Caritatis*, in which he equated "hermeneutic of reform" with "hermeneutic of continuity." Briefly stated, the premise of the hermeneutic of continuity is this: because the Church cannot oppose her own teaching, there can be no doctrinal opposition between the two forms of the Roman Rite. Liturgical reform, which has occurred throughout the Church's history, does not imply a change in the substance of the faith.

What is the significance of this "hermeneutic of continuity" and the Extraordinary Form for this book, which focuses on the Ordinary Form of the Mass? In an effort to show the unity between the two forms of the Roman Rite, I refer to the prayers in the Extraordinary Form (where they have been changed in the Ordinary Form) to provide a spiritual interpretation in continuity with the Roman Rite's liturgical tradition. A prime example is found in Chapter 5, on the Offertory Prayers.

"On Earth as it is in Heaven"

The first time that the word "worship" appears in the Old Testament in a context of sacrifice, it is used with words of distance: "go yonder and worship" (Gen. 22:5) or "worship afar off." (Ex. 24:1) In the Church's liturgy, and especially in her Eucharistic liturgy, we are indeed involved in a sacrifice that took place "yonder" in space (except for those Catholics in Jerusalem) and in time (a couple thousand years ago). But the liturgy also brings us into contact with a sacrifice that is "afar off" in a way that transcends space and time: the liturgy carried out in the heavenly Temple by the angels and saints, with none other than Jesus Christ Himself as the high priest. This is taught in the letter to the Hebrews and in the Constitution on the Sacred Liturgy from the Second Vatican Council:

> But you have come to Mount Zion and to the city of the living God, the heavenly Jerusalem, and to innumerable angels in festal gathering, and to the assembly of the first-born who are enrolled in heaven... (Heb. 12:22-23)

> In the earthly liturgy we take part in a foretaste of that heavenly liturgy which is celebrated in the holy city of Jerusalem toward which we journey as pilgrims, where Christ is sitting at the right hand of God, a minister of the holies and of the true tabernacle; we sing a hymn to the Lord's glory with all the warriors of the

heavenly army; venerating the memory of the saints, we hope for some part and fellowship with them; we eagerly await the Saviour, Our Lord Jesus Christ, until He, our life, shall appear and we too will appear with Him in glory. (SC 8)

The Second Vatican Council very clearly associated our participation at Mass with that eternal worship of God in Heaven, where Jesus is seen as "a Lamb standing, as though it had been slain" (Rev. 5:6), that is, still bearing the wounds He endured in His crucifixion. This ancient concept has been understood more or less clearly over the centuries. Even before Vatican II, Ven. Pope Pius XII said much the same thing:

May God ... graciously grant to us all that during our earthly exile we may with one mind and one heart participate in *the sacred liturgy which is*, as it were, *a preparation and a token of that heavenly liturgy* in which we hope one day to sing together with the most glorious Mother of God and our most loving Mother, "To Him that sitteth on the throne, and to the Lamb, benediction and honor, and glory and power for ever and ever." (MD 209; cf. Rev. 5:13)

Pope Pius XII also sought to remind his bishops (and through them, the whole Church) of these awesome realities encountered in the Mass: that the altar from which we receive the Eucharist is a participation in the "heavenly table" (MD 120), that our singing of psalms and hymns should "rise to heaven like the bursting of a thunderous sea" to join with the song of the saints and angels (MD 194), and that the sacrifice of the Eucharist, "re-presenting and renewing the sacrifice of the cross," is offered to God daily on earth as well as eternally in Heaven. (MD 205)

This teaching did not fall on deaf ears, neither before nor after the Second Vatican Council. A 1967 instruction on sacred music explained that when liturgical worship is celebrated in song, its hierarchical and communal nature "is more openly shown ... and the whole celebration more clearly prefigures that heavenly liturgy." (*Musicam Sacram* 5) In his 1998 address to bishops from the United States, Ven. Pope John Paul II spoke about active participation in the liturgy as being participation in "the liturgy of Creation, the liturgy of Heaven."

Bishop R. Walter Nickless of Sioux City, Iowa, taught his flock in his 2009 pastoral letter on continuing renewal in the Church (*Ecclesia Semper Reformanda*) that God "graciously comes to us ... to raise us up ... to the heavenly liturgy, where we worship in union with all the angels and saints. ... Thus we enter the heavenly sanctuary while still on earth, and worship God in the full manner that He laid out for us!" Deriving from this meeting of Heaven and earth in the liturgy, he went on to say that "how we worship – the external rites, gestures, vessels, music, indeed, the building itself – should reflect the grandeur of the heavenly liturgy."

In the chapters that follow, this participation in Heaven's liturgy through our earthly worship will hopefully be made clearer to you – and through you, to your family, your friends, and your parish.

Praying the Mass

If this book is neither a rubrical guide for priests nor a personal missal for use by the laity during the Mass, what is it? It is a "mystagogical catechesis" on the Mass. The aim of all liturgical catechesis is to initiate people into the mystery of Christ "by proceeding from the visible to the invisible, from the sign to the thing signified, from the 'sacraments' to the 'mysteries.'" (*Catechism* 1075) This form of catechesis is known as "mystagogy," and it was extremely prevalent in the early centuries of the Church.

Ven. Pope John Paul II wrote about this type of catechesis in his 2004 Apostolic Letter *Mane Nobiscum Domine* (MND):

> Pastors should be committed to that "mystagogical" catechesis so dear to the Fathers of the Church, by which the faithful are helped to understand the meaning of the liturgy's words and actions, to pass from its signs to the mystery which they contain, and to enter into that mystery in every aspect of their lives. (MND 17)

Pope Benedict XVI, in his response to the Synod on the Eucharist, also addressed the need for mystagogical catechesis:

> The Synod of Bishops asked that the faithful be helped to make their interior dispositions correspond to their gestures and words. Otherwise, however carefully planned and executed our liturgies may be, they would risk falling into a certain ritualism. ... The Synod Fathers unanimously indicated [a] mystagogical approach to catechesis, which would lead the faithful to understand more deeply the mysteries being celebrated. (*Sacramentum Caritatis* 64)

He then outlined three key elements of mystagogical catechesis, echoing the three steps described earlier by his predecessor:

1) **interpreting** the liturgical rites in the light of salvation history
2) **explaining** the signs and symbols used in the rites
3) **relating** the rites to all the dimensions of Christian life.

The Mass is an encounter with mystery, but that does not mean we should not try to study and understand it, although we should not expect to understand it completely. This book is designed to help answer the questions "Why is the priest saying this?", "What does it mean?", and "What does it mean to me?" I seek to "crack the bone of the words and look at the marrow," in the words of Rev. John Zuhlsdorf. The liturgical texts are annotated with Scripture references, many of which are given fuller treatment. Attention is given where the translation has changed.

Hopefully this book will give you a greater understanding of the words, postures, and gestures said and performed by the priest[8] during the prayer of the Mass. You will learn the biblical origins for the various movements in this great symphony of prayer. Each chapter begins with a verse from the Old Testament and a verse from the New Testament related to the part of the Mass being examined, presents the parts of the Mass as an experience of spiritual prayer, and ends with two sets of questions (one for priests, another for laity) to lead you into further contemplation by **interpreting**, **explaining**, and **relating** the rites. The inexhaustible treasure trove of spiritual riches contained in the Mass will be opened more readily to you, and you can grow in holiness as the Church's liturgy takes on new meaning in your life.

The whole Mass is a prayer of worship and an encounter with the mystery of God. When you pray the Mass, then you will be doing more than just "going to Mass," you will be worshiping God: you will learn how to "love the Lord your God with all your heart, and with all your soul, and with all your strength, and with all your mind." (Luke 10:27)

---

[8] This book is subtitled "The Prayers of the *Priest*," but not *all* the words covered in this book are necessarily those of a priest or bishop. Some of the words are said by deacons, some can be said by a cantor or a choir, and some can be said by a reader or instituted lector.

The Lord will take his zeal as his whole armor,
and will arm all creation to repel his enemies.
(Wisdom 5:17)

Put on the whole armor of God,
that you may be able to stand against the wiles of the devil.
(Ephesians 6:11)

1

Preparing for Prayer

I GREW UP IN NORTHERN New Jersey, and my family attended Mass at the parish of St. Luke's in Ho-Ho-Kus. I was an altar boy there for several years, but it was only recently, while visiting the pastor, that I noticed a bronze plaque on the sacristy wall, above a sink. The words on this plaque were Latin, but I was able to piece together its meaning based on a few cognates and a smattering of Latin vocabulary:

DA DOMINE VIRTUTEM MANIBUS MEIS
AD ABSTERGENDUM OMNEM MACULAM
UT SINE POLLUTIONE MENTIS ET
CORPORIS VALEAM TIBI SERVIRE

It means, "Give, O Lord, virtue to my hands, to be cleansed from all stain, that I might serve you without corruption of mind or body." These words are above the sacristy sink because they are the words of the traditional prayer spoken by the priest as he washes his hands during his preparation for Mass.

While certain elements of Catholic worship are reminiscent or evocative of daily life, they are at the same time set apart from secular or profane associations: they are consecrated for divine purposes, often by means of prayers and blessings. So it is with the seemingly mundane (that is, worldly) chore of "getting dressed" for Mass. The priest does not *just* wash his hands; he does not *just* toss on a clean alb and secure it with a rope; he does not *just* grab whatever stole and chasuble suits his mood. Instead, the preparatory actions of the priest are accompanied by prayers that speak of a spiritual battle and a heavenly mystery unfolding here on earth in the life of the priest.

Why does the Church "dramatize" such preliminary activities? The answer can be found on a sign on another sacristy wall, in Emmitsburg, Maryland. There, in the Basilica of St. Elizabeth Ann Seton, the priest sees these words: "Priest of God, celebrate this Mass as if it were your first Mass, your last Mass, your only Mass." This is a solemn reminder to the priest to be aware of the sacred mysteries dispensed at his hands, and to pay attention. Mass should not be celebrated casually, but with due reverence and devotion. The sanctuary is not a stage for the priest, nor is the altar a prop. The priest is not an entertainer and the Mass is not a show. The priest, as a minister of Christ the High Priest, was ordained to renew and offer, sacramentally, the once-and-for-all sacrifice of Christ. The words in the sacristy of the Basilica, like the words in the sacristy in St. Luke's church, are meant to remind the priest of this profound truth.

Vestments and Vesting Prayers

The Old Testament describes the liturgical worship of God carried out by Israel, and liturgical worship did not disappear with the advent of the New Covenant in Christ's blood. In fact, St. John's apocalyptic vision of the heavenly liturgy describes Jesus dressed in priestly attire standing in the midst of priestly furnishings, a sign of continuity between the Old and New Covenants: "Then I turned to see the voice that was speaking to me, and on turning I saw *seven golden lampstands*, and in the midst of the lampstands one like a Son of man, clothed with *a long robe* and with *a golden sash* across his breast." (Rev. 1:12-13) Jesus is also seen wearing a golden crown. (cf. Rev. 14:14) He sees God seated on a heavenly throne appearing "like *jasper* and *carnelian*" and surrounded by "*twenty-four* elders, clad in *white garments*, with *golden crowns* upon their heads." (Rev. 4:3-4) At the end of the book of Revelation, John sees the new city of Jerusalem descending from Heaven and he identifies twelve particular stones that adorn its walls. (cf. Rev. 21:10, 19-20)

All of these details are related to the worship of God as carried out by Israel before the Temple was destroyed in A.D. 70. God commanded Moses to have holy garments made for Aaron (the high priest) and his sons (the other priests): "a breastpiece, an ephod, a *robe*, a coat of checker work, a turban, and a *sash*." (Ex. 28:4) On the turban was set a *golden crown*. (cf. Ex. 29:6) The Israelites were also to make a golden lampstand (what is called today a menorah) holding seven lamps to be in the tent of worship. (cf. Ex. 25:31-37) King David arranged Aaron's descendents, the priests of Israel, into *twenty-four* divisions. (cf. 1 Chr. 24:1-19) These priests wore robes of fine *white* linen. *Twelve precious stones* were embedded in the breastplate of Aaron, the high priest; these stones almost exactly match the stones seen by John in his vision. (cf. Ex. 28:17-20) The first stone was *carnelian* (also called sardius), the last stone was *jasper*.

What does all this mean for *new* covenant worship? In the letter to the Hebrews, we read that Israel served God in "a copy and shadow of the heavenly sanctuary" (Heb. 8:5) while Jesus has entered "the sanctuary and the true tent which is set up not by man but by the Lord." (Heb. 8:2) This comparison is explained further in Hebrews 9. The new covenant in Christ's blood replaces the "copy and shadow" with the sacrament, a tangible reality that makes present what it signifies. The vision of Jesus in high priestly attire vindicated Israel's worship, showing that it did point to a true heavenly reality. While the vestments worn by the priest in Catholic worship are not sacraments, they *are* sacramentals[1] and signs of the heavenly liturgical worship of God that is made present in the Mass.

The liturgical vestments of the Church have developed slowly over time, just as her liturgical rites have developed. The use of liturgical clothing in Judaism probably accounts for the retention of vestments reserved for worship in the Church, but the early Christians did not wear Jewish vestments. Instead, they adopted the secular manner of dress in the Greco-Roman world, distinguishing vestments from secular clothing primarily by their quality and decoration. Even when the Greco-Roman

---

[1] Sacramentals are "sacred signs which bear a resemblance to the sacraments" and better dispose us "to receive the chief effect of the sacraments." (*Catechism* 1667)

style changed, the Church retained her ancient vestments with few substantial alterations; they remain as a testament to the antiquity of our liturgical worship.

In the Roman Rite, there are several sacred vestments worn during the Mass as signs of the ministerial office of certain members of the Body of Christ. (*Code of Canon Law*, 929) The common vestment to all ordained and instituted ministers is the **alb** worn with a **cincture** around the waist (unless the alb is made to fit without it). Beneath the alb, if the clothing at the neckline (including the Roman collar) is not concealed, an **amice** should first be put on. Over the alb is the **stole**, worn over both shoulders for priests, but only over the left shoulder (bound at the right hip) for deacons. The vestment proper to a priest celebrant is the **chasuble**, worn over the alb and stole. The vestment proper to a deacon is the **dalmatic**, worn over the alb and stole. There is another vestment, the **maniple**, which is required in the Extraordinary Form of the Mass but was made non-obligatory in 1967; its status in the Ordinary Form is a matter of some dispute, and its inclusion in this book is primarily for its catechetical and spiritual value. Acolytes, lectors, altar servers, and other lay ministers may wear the alb and cincture (and perhaps the amice as well), but they may not wear the maniple, stole, dalmatic, or chasuble, which belong only to the ordained. (GIRM 119)

Over time, the sacred vestments accrued various interpretations. An eighth-century Greek document provides a symbolism for all the priestly vestments. In the West, similar works of interpretation were written in the ninth century in Gaul (modern France). The first layer of symbolism was moral: the vestments symbolized the virtues to which their wearers aspired (e.g. humility, chastity, charity). The second layer, which was not very widespread, interpreted the vestments allegorically: they were the armor of the priest, a warrior of God, waging a spiritual battle at the altar.

By the twelfth century, vestments acquired a third, dogmatic layer of symbolism: the priest is Christ's representative, and his vestments refer to certain dogmas pertaining to Christ (the Incarnation, His two natures, His virtues, etc.). The dogmatic symbolism lacked references to His Passion and death; these did not appear until the thirteenth century in a fourth layer of symbolism, which could be called "representative." This type of symbolism became very popular because it was the easiest to express and to understand: each vestment represents something Christ wore during His Passion and death, from the shroud placed over His head to the cords that bound Him. The priest is thus visually configured to Christ, Whose ministry he carries out.

Along with these interpretations, vesting prayers were developed for the priest to say as he put on each vestment. The vesting prayers of the Roman Rite evoke to varying degrees the Scriptural imagery of being dressed with the "armor of God." (Eph. 6:11)[2] The sacred vestments are meant to remind the priest (and the congregation) of the sufferings that Christ endured, because they are analogous to the garments He wore during His Passion; they also mystically signify the virtues that enable the priest to fulfill his ministry in faithfulness to God. The four types of symbolism – moral, allegorical, dogmatic, and representative – can be woven together to create a rich tapestry that can produce great spiritual fruit for the priest or layman who contemplates it.

While the modern *Roman Missal* contains prayers of preparation and thanksgiving for the priest, it does not contain these vesting prayers (which are, however, found in the Missal for the Extraordinary Form). Still, the whole Church, especially her ordained ministers, would benefit from the use of these prayers, which is still permitted. They are included in this book to prompt this consideration.

Washing the Hands

Before anything else, the priest[3] washes his hands, not in imitation of Pilate (cf. Matt. 27:24), but of the Levitical priesthood. (cf. Ex. 30:19) It is analogous to Moses removing his sandals before the burning bush: the priest acknowledges that he is approaching "holy ground." (Ex. 3:5)

Da, Dómine, virtútem mánibus meis ad abstergéndum omnem máculam; ut sine pollutióne mentis et córporis váleam tibi servíre.

Give virtue to my hands, O Lord,	*Ps. 29:11*
to be cleansed from all stain,	*2 Sam. 22:21; Jas. 4:8*
that I might serve you without corruption of mind or body.	*1 Tim. 4:12*

---

[2] Four passages referring to spiritual armor are Wisdom 5:17-20; Isaiah 59:17; Ephesians 6:10-17; and 1 Thessalonians 5:8.

[3] These prayers, up to and including the prayer for the stole, are said by both priests *and* deacons.

With this prayer, the priest does not ask for his hands to have the power to cleanse from sin, but rather he asks God to cleanse his hands from the stain of sin, so that he may celebrate the Mass with pure intentions. This first prayer, said before the priest has put on any vestment, orients his mind and heart toward virtue and purity.

The priest will wash his hands once or twice more, in the course of the Mass: at the end of the Offertory and possibly during the ablutions after Holy Communion.

Amice

After washing his hands, the priest puts on the amice. The amice (from the Latin *amicire*, meaning "to cover") is a square of white linen wrapped around the shoulders close to the neck and tied in place. It serves to cover up the priest's clothing at the neck, even his clerical attire; if the alb would cover this area completely, the amice is optional.

There has been some speculation about the original purpose of the amice. It may have helped to keep the celebrant's throat and neck warm, so that his voice might stay clear for speaking and singing. It was used as a hood during the Middle Ages, especially by monks; it would be worn covering the head until the priest reached the altar, at which point he would pull it back and it would rest on his shoulders (a use continued by certain religious orders today). Another explanation is that it protected the fabric of the chasuble from the priest's perspiration. Whatever its functional origin, it has received significant symbolic value.

As he puts on the amice, the priest prays:

**Impóne, Dómine, cápiti meo gáleam salútis,
ad expugnándos diabólicos incúrsus.**

Place upon my head, O Lord, the helmet of salvation,   *Isa. 59:17; Eph. 6:17*
that I may overcome the assaults of the devil.   *Eph. 6:11*

The amice is a symbol of the "helmet of salvation," which is the virtue of hope. (cf. 1 Th. 5:8) Having hope cover his head means that the priest should have his mind occupied with the things of Heaven and the care of souls, free from the fleeting worldly cares that can so easily distract him. His thoughts should be fortified against needless worry by confidence in God and hope in His promises. It should be no wonder that priests, who work for the salvation of souls, would be subject to "the assaults of the devil," who would want to deprive him of peace in his soul, heart, and mind – especially during the celebration of Mass.

The amice also represents Christ's humanity, humility, and death. As it was once worn as a hood, it is a sign of Christ's humanity that He took up, veiling His divine glory. It is a sign of His humility during the Passion, when He endured being blindfolded and struck. (cf. Mark 14:65; Luke 22:64) Furthermore, after He died on the cross, He was wrapped not only in a bodily shroud (cf. Matt. 27:59) but also with a cloth around His head. (cf. John 20:6-7) The amice, then, evocative of the death of Christ, calls the priest to die to himself and live for Christ (cf. Gal. 2:20), the supreme exercise of humility.

The virtue of humility, following the example given by Christ, is indispensible for the priest; this was reaffirmed in the Vatican II Decree on the Ministry and Life of Priests, *Presbyterorum Ordinis* (PO): "Among the virtues that priests must possess ... none is so important as a frame of mind and soul whereby they are always ready *to know and do the will of him who sent them* and not their own will." (PO 15) Humility disposes the priest's will to recognize his own limitations and boundaries, and confess his dependence on God. Humility also calls the priest to understand his true relationship to his neighbor; he must be willing to serve all, from the richest to the poorest, remembering that ministry "to one of the least of these" (Matt. 25:40) is ministry to Christ. Humility is closely bound to charity, by which we love God above all else for His own sake, and we love others for God's sake.

Archbishop Timothy Dolan of New York City alluded to the need for humility during his 2009 ordination of five men to the priesthood; he said that we must praise God "that their ordination is God's doing, not ours; that this is a pure gift from God, not an earned trophy; that His call trumps our curriculum vitae." In ordination, priests receive extraordinary powers, and they tend to attract more respect (or at least more attention) than the average person. Without the virtue of humility, a priest would forget Who made him who he is: indeed, no priest is a self-made man! It is by "this humility and by willing responsible obedience [that] priests conform themselves to Christ" (PO 15), Whose ministry they carry out.

Alb

Next, the priest puts on the alb (from the Latin *albus*, meaning "white"), a long white garment that covers the whole body, from the neck to the ankles. The origin of the alb as a liturgical vestment is an ancient Roman garment worn under a tunic or cloak. The priest prays:

Deálba me, Dómine, et munda cor meum;
ut, in Sánguine Agni dealbátus, gáudiis pérfruar sempitérnis.

Purify me, O Lord, and cleanse my heart, so that,   *Ps. 51:7-9*
washed in the Blood of the Lamb, I may enjoy eternal bliss.   *Rev. 7:14*

The alb, being white, symbolizes the purity and innocence of baptism, and the proper disposition of the soul for Mass. The bright whiteness of the alb ought to represent the interior purity of the soul.

The color white is evocative of the divine glory of Christ: at the Transfiguration, He appeared in garments described by the Evangelists as "dazzling white" (Luke 9:29), "glistening, intensely white" (Mark 9:3), and "white as light." (Matt. 17:2) Mocking Christ's innocence, Herod dressed Christ in a "white garment" (Luke 23:11, DR[4]) when he sent Him back to Pilate. The newly baptized are dressed in white (often an alb for adults) to signify that in Baptism they have "put on Christ." (Gal. 3:27; cf. Rom. 13:14; Eph. 4:24; Col. 3:10)

The prayer speaks of being "washed in the Blood of the Lamb," a direct reference to the book of Revelation. The Lord promises that the worthy "shall walk with me in white" and that whoever "conquers shall be clothed like them in white garments." (Rev. 3:4-5) St. John sees more white garments and white robes (cf. Rev. 3:18; 4:4; 6:11), as well as saints dressed in robes of "fine linen" (Rev. 19:8) that are symbols of their "righteous deeds."

> After this I looked, and behold, a great multitude which no man could number, from every nation, from all tribes and peoples and tongues, standing before the throne and before the Lamb, *clothed in white robes*, with palm branches[5] in their hands, and crying out with a loud voice, "Salvation belongs to our God who sits upon the throne, and to the Lamb!" ...

---

[4] This is the Douay-Rheims translation; the Latin Vulgate reads *veste alba*.
[5] The palm branch is usually used in iconography to identify the depicted saint as a martyr. It also represents victory over death and Christ's royal triumph. (cf. John 12:13)

Then one of the elders addressed me, saying, "Who are these, clothed in white robes, and from where have they come?" I said to him, "Sir, you know." And he said to me, "These are they who have come out of the great tribulation; they have *washed their robes* and *made them white in the blood of the Lamb.*" (Rev. 7:9-14)

While other blood stains garments red, the precious blood of the Lamb cleanses and purifies them, making them white.

Cincture

The priest fastens the alb around his waist with a cincture (from the Latin *cingere*, meaning "to gird"), although this is optional if the alb is made to fit close to the body; but as with the amice, the spiritual import of the cincture should not be overlooked. The cincture is a rope serving as a belt or girdle, like the "golden sash" that St. John saw Christ wearing around his breast. (Rev. 1:13) As the priest ties the cincture, he prays:

Præcínge me, Dómine, cíngulo puritátis, et exstíngue in lumbis meis humórem libídinis; ut máneat in me virtus continéntiæ et castitátis.

Gird me, O Lord, with the cincture of purity,	*Eph. 6:14*
and extinguish in my loins all fleshly desires,	*Gal. 5:16; Col. 3:5; 1 Pet. 2:11*
that the virtue of continence and chastity	*1 Th. 4:3*
may abide within me.	

The cincture is a symbol of the virtues of continence (abstinence from sexual activity) and chastity (purity in sexual conduct). In an age where immodesty in dress pervades our schools, workplaces, and churches, and prime-time television is filled with sexually suggestive images, these virtues are especially important to Latin Rite priests who, ordinarily, are unmarried men.[6] In this way, the cincture is an emblem of the need for bodily mortification.

Mortification is a form of Christian asceticism, the practice of self-discipline and penance to overcome sinful tendencies and grow in virtue.[7] The word comes from the Latin *mortificatio*, which means "a killing; a

---

[6] While the Latin Church, as a rule, only ordains unmarried men as priests, the Eastern Churches have retained the discipline of ordaining married men as priests, although neither the East nor the West permits priests to marry *after* they have been ordained. There have been a small number of married priests in the Latin Rite in recent history, owing to the 1980 "pastoral provision" of Pope John Paul II that can permit a married minister of some other Christian community (e.g. the Anglican or Lutheran communions) to be ordained a priest after converting to the Catholic faith.

[7] St. Paul cautions that mortification *could* be taken to the unwise extreme of "self-abasement and severity to the body" without a spiritual goal of "checking the indulgence of the flesh." (Col. 2:23)

putting to death." St. Paul wrote of the practice to the Romans: "*put to death* the deeds of the body" (Rom. 8:13) and "make no provision for the flesh, to gratify its desires." (Rom. 13:14) To the Corinthians, he wrote: "*I pommel my body* and subdue it, lest after preaching to others I myself should be disqualified." (1 Cor. 9:27) And to the Colossians, the same: "*Put to death* therefore what is earthly in you." (Col. 3:5)

It was a primary theme in Paul's letter to the Galatians, in which he repeatedly contrasted living in the flesh *apart* from Christ with living in the flesh *subjected to* and *renewed in* Christ:

> I have been *crucified with Christ*; it is no longer I who live, but Christ who lives in me; and the life I now live in the flesh I live by faith in the Son of God... (Gal. 2:20)
>
> Are you so foolish? Having begun with the Spirit, are you now ending *with the flesh*? (Gal. 3:3)
>
> Walk by the Spirit, and *do not gratify the desires of the flesh*. For the desires of the flesh are against the Spirit, and the desires of the Spirit are against the flesh; for these are opposed to each other, to prevent you from doing what you would. (Gal. 5:16-17)

Paul reaches the summit of this teaching by professing plainly that "those who belong to Christ Jesus have *crucified the flesh* with its passions and desires." (Gal. 5:24) This crucifixion of the flesh, putting the flesh to death so that it may be brought to new life in Christ, is an identification of each Christian with Jesus in crucifixion; it takes on a deeper meaning for priests who are conformed in a special way to Christ by ordination.

Although the term "mortification" has fallen out of fashion in recent decades, it was mentioned in the Vatican II decree on the priesthood: "priests consecrated by the anointing of the Holy Spirit and sent by Christ must *mortify the works of the flesh* in themselves and give themselves entirely to the service of men." (PO 12) Pope Paul VI, writing on penance in 1966, explained and promoted mortification to all Christians:

> True penitence, however, cannot ever prescind from physical asceticism as well. Our whole being, in fact, body and soul ... must participate actively in this religious act whereby the creature recognizes divine holiness and majesty. The necessity of the mortification of the flesh also stands clearly revealed if we consider the fragility of our nature, in which, since Adam's sin, flesh and spirit have contrasting desires. This exercise of bodily mortification – far removed from any form of stoicism – does not

imply a condemnation of the flesh which sons of God deign to assume. On the contrary mortification aims at the "liberation" of man, who often finds himself, because of concupiscence, almost chained by his own senses. (*Paenitemini*, II)

The communion fast – abstaining from food or drink (except for water and medicine) for an hour before receiving Holy Communion – is a form of mortification that teaches us to order our physical hunger toward our spiritual hunger for God's sustenance in the Eucharist.

The priest speaks of being "gird" with the cincture. The expression "gird your loins" is a Biblical phrase that means "make yourself ready." This was done by tucking one's garment, usually a robe or tunic, into the girdle (belt) so that it would not impede physical movement. God used the phrase when instructing Israel on how they should eat the Passover meal (cf. Ex. 12:11) and when commissioning prophets. (cf. Jer. 1:17) Jesus used it when He admonished His disciples to be vigilant and ready, saying "Let your loins be girded and your lamps burning." (Luke 12:35) The phrase has a military connotation as well, because the girdle also held the sheath for a soldier's sword. (cf. 2 Sam. 20:8; Nah. 2:1) It is primarily in this context that St. Paul uses the imagery of wearing truth as a belt, speaking about the spiritual warfare that the Christian wages against the powers of evil: "Stand therefore, having fastened the belt of truth around your waist." (Eph. 6:14)

The cincture calls to mind the cords with which Christ was bound at His arrest and scourging. (cf. Matt. 27:2; John 18:12) The priest, because of the sacramental character he received at his ordination, acts *in persona Christi* when he administers the sacraments of the Church; he is thus "bound" to Christ, and can expect persecution and ridicule rivaling that received by his Master. (cf. John 15:20)

Maniple

Another traditional vestment is the maniple (from the Latin *manipulus*, meaning "bundle" or "handful"), used in the Extraordinary Form. It is like a small stole for the left forearm. As he fastens it, the priest prays:

Mérear, Dómine, portáre manípulum fletus et dolóris; ut cum exsultatióne recípiam mercédem labóris.

May I merit, O Lord, to bear the maniple of weeping and sorrow, *Ps. 126:6* that with joy I might reap the rewards of my labors. *Ps. 126:5*

27

This curious vestment probably derives from the handkerchief worn by orators on their arm, called a *mappula*. It was also known as a *manipulus*, because it was folded together and held in the hand like a small bundle. It was used, as you might imagine, for wiping away perspiration and tears from the face; over time, it took on a sacred character inspired by its use.

Rev. Mauro Gagliardi of the Office of Liturgical Celebrations of the Supreme Pontiff wrote an article on vestments for ZENIT news service's series "The Spirit of the Liturgy" in which he explained that "medieval ecclesiastical writers regarded the maniple as a symbol of the toils of the priesthood," which is why the prayer associated with it refers to the vestment as "the maniple of weeping and sorrow." He goes on to say that "in the first part the prayer references the weeping and sorrow that accompany the priestly ministry, but in the second part the fruit of the work is noted." The prayer was inspired by Psalm 126:5-6, where the word "sheaves" or "bundles" is translated in the Latin text of the Bible as *manipulos*; the verses are: "May those who sow in tears reap with shouts of joy! He that goes forth weeping, bearing the seed for sowing, shall come home with shouts of joy, bringing his sheaves with him."

The maniple represents the sorrows that Christ endured. As far as His Passion is concerned, the maniple (along with the cincture and stole) represents the cords that bound Him while He was scourged. For the priest, it symbolizes contrition and penance, as well as the sorrows and cares (and even fatigue) that he must patiently bear as he serves God and His Church with his "hands full" (*manus plenae*) of good works. But in response to that life of self-sacrifice, the maniple is also a symbol of the rewards of priestly ministry, as the vesting prayer reveals. Perhaps the words of Baruch apply most to this particular vestment:

> Take off the garment of your sorrow and affliction, O Jerusalem, and put on for ever the beauty of the glory from God. Put on the robe of the righteousness from God; put on your head the diadem of the glory of the Everlasting. (Bar. 5:1-2)

Stole

Next comes the stole (from the Latin *stola*, meaning "garment"), a long and narrow vestment like a scarf, worn around the neck. This vestment comes from the one worn by Roman magistrates when exercising their official duties (as a judge wears black robes on the bench). The stole usually has a small cross sewn into it at the middle, which is kissed in an act of reverence before it is put on. The prayer for the stole is:

Redde mihi, Dómine, stolam immortalitátis, quam pérdidi in prævaricatióne primi paréntis et, quamvis indígnus accédo ad tuum sacrum mystérium, mérear tamen gáudium sempitérnum.

Restore to me, O Lord, the stole of immortality,	*Rom. 2:7; 1 Cor. 15:53*
which I lost through the transgression of our first parents,	*Wis. 2:23-24*
and, unworthy as I am to approach your sacred mysteries,	*Luke 17:10*
may I yet attain to eternal joy.	*Sir. 2:9; Isa. 61:7*

In mentioning the "stole of immortality," the prayer refers to one of the preternatural gifts with which our first parents were endowed. When God created Adam and Eve, He made them incapable of suffering death, but this gift was lost when they transgressed the command by which God tested their obedience. (cf. Gen. 3:3, 22) This bodily immortality will be restored to us in the resurrection (cf. Luke 20:36; Rev. 21:4) in which we will "attain to eternal joy." Because it is a sign of immortality, it reminds the priest of the immortal and eternal God, the One who instituted the "new and *eternal* covenant" that he celebrates at the altar.

The stole is worn by ordained ministers during administration of the sacraments as a symbol of the authority of their clerical office, as well as of the obedience and faithfulness with which they should carry out their duties. It is not just a sign of his own clerical authority, but a reminder that he must be obedient to God's authority and His divine law in the fulfillment of his duties.

The stole, like the cincture, is evocative of the cords that bound Christ during His trials, so it is also a symbol of the burdens that come with ordained ministry. It can be associated with the "yoke of Christ," as it hangs over the shoulders of the priest, but that association is more often made with the vestment that goes over the stole, the chasuble.

Chasuble

For the priest, the next vestment is the chasuble (from the Latin *casula*, meaning "little house"), a large garment that covers the others, with a hole in the center for the priest's head. As he puts on the chasuble, the priest prays:

29

Dómine, qui dixísti: Iugum meam suáve est et onus meum leve: fac, ut istud portáre sic váleam, quod cónsequar tuam grátiam. Amen.

O Lord, who said, "My yoke is easy and my burden is light": *Matt 11:30*
grant that I might bear it well,
so as to receive your grace. Amen. *Rom. 5:2; Heb. 12:15*

The chasuble, more than the stole, is the symbol of the "yoke" of Christ. A yoke is a beam that attaches two animals (often oxen) together to allow them to pull a load, such as a plow.

God freed His people Israel from the yoke of slavery they endured in Egypt. Their Exodus foreshadowed the Exodus (cf. Luke 9:30-31) on which Christ leads us by His crucifixion: "For freedom Christ has set us free; stand fast therefore, and do not submit again to a yoke of slavery." (Gal. 5:1) Christ frees us from the yoke of sin and offers us His own in return: "Take my yoke upon you, and learn from me; for I am gentle and lowly in heart, and you will find rest for your souls. For my yoke is easy, and my burden is light." (Matt. 11:29-30) It is important to remember that a yoke is never carried alone: we are either yoked to Satan by sin, or we are yoked to Christ. The yoke of Christ is above all a duty to love one another, and "this is the love of God, that we keep his commandments." (1 John 5:3; cf. John 14:15; 15:17) The chasuble represents Christ's yoke: the virtue of charity, that is, love of God for His sake and love of others for God's sake. The priest cannot love God nor his fellow man by his *own* strength; he needs God's grace. The priest cannot bear the yoke of charity alone; he needs Christ alongside him to help him.

In addition to writing about the "armor of God" in military terms in his letter to the Ephesians, St. Paul told the Colossians to be clothed in the virtues. First he tells them to strip themselves naked of vices: "put them all away: anger, wrath, malice, slander, and foul talk from your mouth." Then he tells them how to dress themselves: "put on the new man," whose nature is "compassion, kindness, lowliness, meekness, and patience." He also tells them to let their hearts be ruled by "the peace of Christ" and to let "the word of Christ" dwell in them. (Col. 3:8-16) All the priest's vestments are meant to evoke these virtues of the new man.

Over all these virtues, Paul tells them to "put on love, which binds everything together in perfect harmony." (Col. 3:14) This divine love is represented by the chasuble. It is worn over the stole, signifying that authority must be "covered" by love; that is, authority must be carried out with love, for, as St. Paul taught, if we have not love, we are nothing. (cf. 1 Cor. 13:2) It is worn over the other vestments because "love is the fulfilling of the law" (Rom. 13:10), because love exceeds all other virtues and brings them to perfection. The love of God must completely cover the priest and be his inspiration in all his work.

The chasuble is evocative of the seamless tunic worn by Jesus at His crucifixion. (cf. John 19:23-24) In the *Catena Aurea* ("golden chain") of St. Thomas Aquinas – a compilation of Scripture commentary – Church Fathers and other commentators on Scripture saw the tunic, which the soldiers could not tear apart, as a symbol of the Body of Christ and the Church. To St. John Chrysostom, the tunic that was "woven from top to bottom" is an allegory for Christ's divinity ("woven from top," that is, Heaven) and humanity ("to bottom," that is, earth, in His Incarnation), which are united in one Divine Person. To St. Augustine, the tunic is the unbreakable unity of the Church over the whole world; it is also the bond of charity that retains that unity, as God *is* love, and the tunic is woven from above. Theophylactus interpreted the tunic as Christ's body, which was "woven from above" when the Holy Spirit overshadowed the Virgin Mary and she conceived the Son of God. He went one step further, alluding to the Eucharist, saying that this body is indivisible although it is distributed for us to receive in Communion, because each fragment of the Precious Body is the whole substance of Christ.

The chasuble also signifies the purple cloak Jesus was dressed with in derision. (cf. John 19:2) But whereas that cloak and the crown of thorns were used by the soldiers to mock Christ's kingship, the chasuble, usually the most elegant and decorated of all the vestments, shows true honor to His kingship. Purple is also a color of penance (as we see during Lent) and so it speaks of the sadness and sacrifice of the Passion. These two concepts, kingship and sacrifice, are united in the chasuble: Christ's kingship is, among other things, one of service in love, and the crucifixion shows us the lengths to which that love drives Christ to serve.

Dalmatic

The deacon does not wear a chasuble, but instead a dalmatic.[8] It is a short-sleeved tunic that came to Rome from Dalmatia, which is where it received its name. The prayer for the vesting of the dalmatic is:

Indue me, Dómine, induménto salútis et vestiménto lætítiæ; et dalmática justítiæ circúmda me semper.

Endow me, Lord,
with the garment of salvation and the vestment of joy, *Isa. 61:10*
and with the dalmatic of justice ever encompass me. *Sir. 27:8*

The dalmatic symbolizes the joy and happiness that are the fruits of dedication and service to the Lord.

The shortness of the sleeves is a reminder of the "practical" purpose of the deacon (cf. Acts 6:1-4), that he should be unencumbered in his ministry to the people. The shape of the dalmatic is a closer match to the tunic that Christ wore at His crucifixion, so it represents the deacon's participation in the suffering of Christ, as well as in the service of Christ.

Preparatory Prayers

The priest's preparation for Mass does not consist only of vesting. The Church considers a prayerful disposition in her priests so important that it is a matter of canon law: "A priest is not to omit dutifully to prepare himself by prayer before the celebration of the Eucharist, nor afterwards to omit to make thanksgiving to God." (*Code of Canon Law*, can. 909) The *Roman Missal* contains a selection of traditional preparatory prayers for priests for this very purpose.

In an article for ZENIT's "The Spirit of the Liturgy" series, Rev. Paul Gunter, OSB describes the priest's private preparation in this way:

> When the Introductory Rites occur, various actions, invisible to the congregation, have already taken place. These not only set the scene for the holiest of holies, but also distinguish in a priest's life the manner in which he arrives at his appointment at the altar so that the demands of the world shall not jar against the recollected sacredness the celebration of holy Mass requires.

---

[8] Although the dalmatic *may* be omitted out of necessity or on account of a degree of lesser solemnity (cf. GIRM 119b, 338), it is praiseworthy to refrain from omitting it. (cf. *Redemptionis Sacramentum* 125) The dalmatic is always worn by deacons in the Extraordinary Form of the Mass.

In the Missal provides three prayers for priests: one of St. Ambrose, one of St. Thomas Aquinas, and one to the Blessed Mother, all of which are profoundly Eucharistic and penitential.[9] There is also a "Statement of Intention" that is recommended for the priest to pray regularly to keep him ever aware of the importance and purpose of celebrating Mass.

Prayer of St. Ambrose

The priest begins by expressing "fear and trembling" (Phil. 2:12) in approaching the banquet of the Lord as a sinner, and recognizing that he does not rely on his merits, but on the Lord's "goodness and mercy." Throughout the prayer, he asks for God's protection, healing, salvation, mercy, and compassion, so that he might receive the Body and Blood worthily and with due reverence.

The priest ends by asking that his reception of Holy Communion be efficacious:

> And grant this this sacred foretaste of your Body and Blood
> which I, though unworthy, intend to receive,
> may be the remission of my sins, the perfect cleansing of my faults,
> the banishment of shameful thoughts, and the rebirth of right sentiments;
> and may it encourage a wholesome and effective performance
> of deeds pleasing to you,
> and be a most firm defense of body and soul
> against the snares of my enemies.

The fruits of Holy Communion are many: a deepening of our union with Christ, a strengthening and renewal of grace, the remission of venial sin, the strength to resist mortal sin, and an increase of charity to serve God and our fellow man. (cf. *Catechism* 1391-1397) The prayer of St. Ambrose reminds the priest of God's graciousness in bestowing these benefits through the Eucharist.

Prayer of St. Thomas Aquinas

This prayer calls upon God as the "physician of life," the "fountain of mercy," the "light of eternal brightness," and the "Lord of heaven and earth," while confessing to be sick, unclean, blind, poor, and needy. The priest asks God to heal, wash clean, enlighten, enrich, and clothe him. Then the priest prays that he might receive the "bread of Angels" with

---

[9] The prayers of St. Ambrose and St. Thomas are also appropriate for the laity to pray.

reverence, purity, faith, penitence, and charity, and to truly receive the Blessed Sacrament in Its reality and power.

Participation in the Eucharist is the fulfillment of the call to be one body in Christ (cf. *Catechism* 1396); this prayer, then, ends with the hope that by receiving the Body of Jesus Christ, born of the Virgin Mary, the priest might be received by Christ into His Mystical Body, the Church.

Prayer to the Blessed Virgin Mary

Finally, the prayer to the mother of our Lord asks for her spiritual presence and consolation during the Mass. In it, the priest asks Mary, "as you stood by your most dear Son while he hung on the Cross, so, in your kindness, may you be pleased to stand by me" at the altar, calling to mind the essential unity between Christ's sacrifice on Calvary and the sacrifice of the Eucharist at Mass.

Statement of Intention

The final preparatory prayer is the "Statement of Intention," which dates back to Pope Gregory XIII (A.D. 1572-1585).

> My intention is to celebrate Mass
> and to consecrate the Body and Blood of our Lord Jesus Christ
> according to the Rite of the Holy Roman Church,
> to the praise of Almighty God and all the Church triumphant,
> for my good and that of all the Church militant,
> for all who have commended themselves to my prayers
> in general and in particular,
> and for the welfare of the Holy Roman Church.
>
> May the almighty and merciful Lord grant us joy with peace,
> amendment of life, room for true repentance,
> the grace and consolation of the Holy Spirit
> and perseverance in good works. Amen.

The "Church triumphant" and "militant" in this prayer are references to two of the three states of the Church, with "penitent" or "suffering" being the third. These states relate to our battle with sin: those who are enjoying the glory of God in Heaven have triumphed over sin; we on our earthly pilgrimage are the "militant" who wage a daily battle against sin; and those who have died in Christ but require further purification from sin (which the Church calls Purgatory) are the "penitent" or "suffering" Church. (cf. *Catechism* 954, LG 49) Although the Church suffering is not mentioned in this prayer, they do benefit from the offering of the Body and Blood of Jesus Christ, as will be explained in Chapters 5 and 6.

This statement of intention is a sort of elaboration on the response of congregation to the priest's *Orate, fratres* at the end of the Offertory: "May the Lord accept the sacrifice at your hands, for the praise and glory of His name, for our good and the good of all His holy Church."

The *General Instruction of the Roman Missal* says that the priest "must serve God and the people with dignity and humility, and by his bearing and by the way he says the divine words he must convey to the faithful the living presence of Christ." (GIRM 93) All that the priest does before the beginning of Mass should remind him of his "dignity and humility" as a priest carrying out the sacred ministry of Jesus Christ, and conform him to "the living presence of Christ" that he is to manifest to all the faithful.

The vestments aid the priest by visually separating him from the secular or profane. (In a similar manner, the new translation serves to separate us from secular and profane language in our worship of God.) The outward sign of his clothing points to the inward transformation that took place at his ordination; they impress upon him and those who see him the dignity of the ministerial priesthood. The vestments serve to remind the priest that the center of attention in the liturgy is not himself, but Christ; and that the priest is not there as a private person, but that he stands in place of Christ. In the words of Joseph Cardinal Ratzinger, "What is merely private, merely individual, about him should disappear and make way for Christ." (*The Spirit of the Liturgy*, p. 216)

The priest, in wearing the sacred vestments, conforms himself to the words spoken by St. John the Baptist about Jesus: "He must increase, but I must decrease." (John 3:30) The vestments "hide" the priest and draw our attention to Christ. To help the priest in this regard, the vesting prayers place upon his lips words of humility before God: he prays to be protected, purified, and restored by God.

Finally, the preparatory prayers remind the priest that he is a sinner in need of God's gracious mercy, so that he enters into the celebration of the Mass and the offering of the Eucharist with a spirit of thanksgiving, reverence, and awe. This whole rite of preparation is meant to instill in the priest a deep sense of (and respect for) his identity. The next chapter will show that this identity is not manifested only by sacred clothing, but also by sacred actions.

Questions for Reflection: Priests

1) **Interpret**: In Wisdom 5:17-20 and Isaiah 59:17, God is depicted as Israel's warrior-champion. Not only does He fight for and protect His people, but He also "arm[s] all creation to repel his enemies." (Wis. 5:17) What does it mean for you to be "armed" by God, to be protecting His people?

2) **Interpret**: How was St. John the Baptist decreasing so that Jesus could increase? What obstacles do you need to overcome to let Jesus increase in your ministry as a priest?

3) **Interpret**: Jesus spent great amounts of time in prayer, often in solitude. His Passion began with fervent prayer in the Garden of Gethsemane. Why was preparatory prayer so important to Him, and why should it be important to you?

4) **Explain**: The stole can be almost completely hidden from view under the chasuble. Is this cause to wear it outside the chasuble or to omit it altogether? What is the value of a hidden sign?

5) **Explain**: The vestments are not all functional as they once were. What might the consequences be of vestments falling into disuse? What value is there in retaining vestments that no longer serve a strict functional purpose?

6) **Relate**: St. Paul writes that our enemies are not flesh and blood; we fight a spiritual war against Satan and his angels. The weapon of the priest in this battle is "the sword of the Spirit, which is the word of God." (Eph. 6:17) How do you prepare to preach? Do you train with "the sword of the Spirit"?

7) **Relate**: Do you exhort your congregation to prepare themselves spiritually for Mass? How can you increase their ability to enter into divine worship aware of the mysteries they will encounter?

Questions for Reflection: Laity

1) **Interpret**: Why would God have decreed special vestments for priests in the Old Testament?

2) **Interpret**: In the Old Testament, God is sometimes portrayed as Israel's warrior-hero, arrayed in armor and ready for combat: He is the "Lord God of hosts." What battle was in the minds of Israel then? What battle does the New Testament reveal?

3) **Explain**: Even though the sacred liturgical vestments originated in the secular dress of Greco-Roman culture, the vestments did not keep up with the changes in fashion. Why might that be?

4) **Explain**: The newly baptized are dressed in white (sometimes an alb) to signify their participation in Christ's purity. What garment of Christ's is represented by the alb? What else of Christ's should all the baptized be prepared to share in as well?

5) **Relate**: All the sacraments are meant to be preceded by some form of preparation. How do you prepare for the Mass? How can the priest's prayers guide you in approaching the Eucharist with love and reverence?

6) **Relate**: Priests wear special clothing when they celebrate Mass. How do you dress? Do the clothes you wear at Mass have any particular spiritual significance for you?

Then Aaron lifted up his hands toward the people and blessed them.
(Leviticus 9:22)

Jesus led them out as far as Bethany, and lifting up his hands he blessed them.
(Luke 24:50)

2

Ceremonial Actions

I N THE PREVIOUS CHAPTER, we read words from St. Paul on mortifying our bodies. But St. Paul also wrote about glorifying God with them. (cf. 1 Cor. 6:20) We are to offer our bodies to God as "a living sacrifice, holy and acceptable," our "spiritual worship." (Rom. 12:1) This worship is possible because our bodies have become "temple[s] of the Holy Spirit." (1 Cor. 6:19) St. Paul even encourages young women and men to remain unmarried so that they may focus their attention to being "holy in body and spirit." (1 Cor. 7:34) In all that he did, even to the point of martyrdom, Paul wanted, by his body, to courageously honor Christ. (cf. Phil. 1:20)

Bl. John Henry Cardinal Newman, a nineteenth century convert from the Anglican faith, was a firm believer in bodily worship:

> Our tongues must preach Him, and our voices sing of Him, and our knees adore Him, and our hands supplicate Him, and our heads bow before Him, and our countenances beam of Him, and our gait herald Him. ("The Visible Temple", *Parochial and Plain Sermons*, p. 1365)

In the Catholic Church, as Cardinal Newman realized, worship of God is "Incarnational," because God has taken a human body and walked upon the earth in human flesh. Our spiritual disposition is expressed bodily; this is worship "in spirit and truth." (John 4:24; cf. *Catechism* 1146, 1179) Cardinal Ratzinger wrote in *The Spirit of the Liturgy* that

> without the worship, the bodily gesture would be meaningless, while the spiritual act must of its very nature … express itself in the bodily gesture. … When someone tries to take worship back into the purely spiritual realm and refuses to give it embodied form, the act of worship evaporates, for what is purely spiritual is inappropriate to the nature of man. (p. 191)

The priest expresses his devotion and carries out his liturgical ministry with his hands, his lips, his eyes, his whole body.

Hands

Ever since the days of Jacob (and probably even before then), blessing was passed on from father to son by the laying on of hands:

> And Israel stretched out *his right hand* and laid it *upon the head* of Ephraim, who was the younger, and his left hand upon the head of Manasseh. … *So he blessed them that day*… (Gen. 48:14, 20)

God is said to work great wonders for His people "by a mighty hand and an outstretched arm." (Deut. 4:34; cf. Ex. 6:6; 1 Pet. 5:6) The "hand" of God is a symbol of His power, and He has granted His power to bless to the hands of His priests. (cf. *Catechism* 699)

The priestly blessing of the Mosaic covenant was often bestowed by the high priest lifting his hands over the people; Aaron (cf. Lev. 9:22) and Simeon (cf. Sir. 50:20-21) did this, and Jesus, the high priest of the *new* covenant, did it as well. (cf. Luke 24:50-51) Priests laid their hands on an animal's head to consecrate it to the Lord as a sacrifice (cf. Lev. 4), and also on the head of a man to consecrate him, not as a bloody sacrifice, but as a servant of the Lord, a *living* sacrifice. (cf. Num. 27:18-23) In the New Testament, we see Jesus lay his hands on the sick to heal them (cf. Mark 7:23; 8:23) and on the dead to revive them. (cf. Matt. 9:18) Jesus also prayed over children in this way. (cf. Matt. 19:13)

The Acts of the Apostles attests that the Holy Spirit was conferred on Christians by the laying on of hands. (cf. Acts 8:14-17; 19:5-6) This sacred gesture was also used to commission missionaries (cf. Acts 13:2-3) and to ordain men as deacons, priests, and bishops. (cf. Acts 6:5-6; 1 Tim. 4:14; 5:22; 2 Tim. 1:6) The epistle to the Hebrews classifies "the laying on of hands" as "elementary doctrine" (Heb. 6:1-2), so it seems to have been common knowledge in the early Church that the gesture of laying hands on a person was an Apostolic tradition with true sacramental power.

During the Mass, the priest makes several gestures with his hands: holding them together, holding them out to his sides, opening and closing them at the words "The Lord be with you," extending them over the bread and wine during the part of the Eucharistic Prayer called the *epiclesis*, raising them over the people for the solemn blessing, striking his breast, and making the Sign of the Cross. These deserve some further explanation.

Rev. Romano Guardini and Cardinal Ratzinger identified the same symbolism in the posture of **holding the hands together**, palm to palm:

> When we stand in God's presence in heart-felt reverence and humility, the open hands are laid together palm against palm in sign of steadfast subjection and obedient homage. ... These hands ... are laid, as it were, tied and bound together between the hands of God. (Rev. Guardini, *Sacred Signs*, p. 17)

> This [gesture] comes from the world of feudalism. The recipient of a feudal estate, on taking tenure, placed his joined hands in those of his lord – a wonderful symbolic act. I lay my hands in yours, allow yours to enclose mine. This is an expression of trust as well as fidelity [that] finds its true meaning in the relationship of the believer to Christ the Lord. This, then, is what is meant when we join our hands to pray: we are placing our hands in His, and with our hands we place in His hands our personal destiny. Trusting in His fidelity, we pledge our fidelity to Him. (*The Spirit of the Liturgy*, pp. 204-205)

This gesture also implies being collected or composed: it is used at the words "Let us pray" and at the end of a prayer. It is appropriate for the faithful to use this posture of holding their hands in prayer.[1]

During the presidential prayers, the priest stands with his **arms outstretched** and his palms facing up, known as the *orans* posture (Latin for "praying"). This ancient gesture of supplication and intercession was carried over from Judaism into Christianity. King Solomon used the gesture in supplication before the altar in the Temple: "Now as Solomon

---

[1] Holding the hands together with fingers interlocked is also common among the laity, although this is not prescribed for the priest.

finished offering all this *prayer and supplication* to the LORD, he arose from before the altar of the LORD, where he had knelt *with hands outstretched toward heaven*." (1 Kgs. 8:54) The intercessory character of this posture was portrayed by Moses during a battle with the Amalekites:

> Moses said to Joshua, "Choose for us men, and go out, fight with Amalek; tomorrow I will stand on the top of the hill *with the rod of God in my hand*." So Joshua did as Moses told him, and fought with Amalek; and Moses, Aaron, and Hur went up to the top of the hill. Whenever Moses held up his hand, Israel prevailed; and whenever he lowered his hand, Amalek prevailed. But Moses' hands grew weary; so they took a stone and put it under him, and he sat upon it, and Aaron and Hur *held up his hands, one on one side, and the other on the other side*; so his hands were steady until the going down of the sun. (Ex. 17:9-12)

This posture has a Christological meaning: Moses holding his staff in his hands stretched out (presumably above his head), with a man on his left and on his right, was seen as a *type* (a symbolic predecessor) of the Sign of the Cross by several Church Fathers.[2] God truly did deliver us from bondage and redeem us "with an outstretched arm" (Ex. 6:6) on the cross. Cardinal Ratzinger explains the symbolism:

> For Christians, arms extended ... remind us of *the extended arms of Christ on the Cross.* ... By extending our arms, we resolve to pray with the Crucified, to unite ourselves to his "mind." (Phil. 2:5) In the arms of Christ, stretched on the Cross, Christians see a twofold meaning. In his case too, in his case above all, this gesture is the radical form of worship, the unity of his human will with the will of the Father, but at the same time these arms are opened toward us – they are the wide embrace by which Christ wants to draw us to himself. (John 12:32) *Worship of God and love of neighbor* – the content of the chief commandment, which sums up the law and the prophets – *coincide in this gesture*. To open oneself to God, to surrender oneself completely to him, is at the same time – the two things cannot be separate – to devote oneself to one's neighbor. This combining of the two directions of love in the gesture of Christ on the Cross reveals, in a bodily and visible way, the new depth of Christian prayer and thus expresses the inner law of our own prayer. (*The Spirit of the Liturgy*, pp. 203-204)

Christ with His arms outstretched on the cross demonstrated the depth of His love for and obedience to His Father, and simultaneously the

---

[2] See St. Irenaeus, *Adversus Haereses* IV, 33; Tertullian, *Adversus Judaeos*, 10; St. Cyprian, *Treatise XI*, 8 and *Treatise XII*, II, 21; St. John Chrysostom, Homily XIV, 4; St. Augustine, *De Trinitate*, IV, 15.

depth of His love for *us*. When the priest prays with his arms held out and his hands facing Heaven, his bodily posture shows his absolute trust in God (to Whom the prayer is offered) and his solicitude for His people (for whom he is praying).

When the priest greets the faithful (such as by the words "The Lord be with you" or "Pray, brethren...") he **opens and closes his hands**. In *Ceremonies of the Modern Roman Rite* by Rev. Peter J. Elliott, this gesture is described as "an expression of peace and an invitation to prayer and recollection." (CMRR[3] 188) It is a presidential gesture, not a familiar one; it is inappropriate for the congregation to mimic the priest's gesture when responding "And with your spirit." [4]

During the part of the Eucharistic Prayer known as the *epiclesis*, the priest **holds out his hands over the bread and wine**. This gesture is an invocation of the Holy Spirit and is reminiscent of the Old Testament gesture of setting apart a victim for sacrifice. (cf. Lev. 16:21; CMRR 191)

A similar gesture is made when the priest bestows a solemn blessing on the people, **raising his hands over the congregation**. This too is an invocation of the Holy Spirit, although without the sacrificial overtones. This gesture of blessing was used by the high priests Aaron (cf. Lev. 9:22) and Jesus. (cf. Luke 24:50)

During the *Confiteor* (the first form of the Penitential Act), the priest **strikes his breast** at the words "through my fault, through my fault, through my most grievous fault." The congregation does the same. The priest also makes this gesture during Eucharistic Prayer I (the Roman Canon), as he says "To us, also, your servants, who [are] sinners." This is a sign of penitence and sorrow for sin. It was a common gesture of mourning in Israel (cf. Luke 23:48), and it was used by the tax collector who was truly contrite. (cf. Luke 18:13)[5]

---

[3] *Ceremonies of the Modern Roman Rite* is a manual for clergy and others involved in the liturgy. It is not a magisterial document (like the *General Instruction of the Roman Missal*), but it is a trustworthy compendium on liturgical matters that draws heavily upon authoritative Church documents.
[4] "In eucharistic celebrations deacons and non-ordained members of the faithful may not ... use gestures or actions which are proper to the same priest celebrant." (*Ecclesia de Mysterio*, art. 6, n. 2)
[5] This gesture is covered in greater detail in Chapter 4 of *Praying the Mass: The Prayers of the People*.

Sign of the Cross

The priest traces the Sign of the Cross from his head to his torso, from his left shoulder to his right. The priest also blesses the congregation with this gesture. If a deacon is going to read the Gospel, he approaches the priest for a blessing, and the priest makes the Sign of the Cross over him. The Book of the Gospel also has a cross traced upon it before the Gospel is read. The priest or deacon reading the Gospel traces the cross on his forehead, lips, and heart – as does the whole congregation. The priest also makes a Sign of the Cross over the bread and wine during the Eucharistic Prayer immediately after the epiclesis.

The Sign of the Cross is rich with symbolism. Through its words, it professes our faith in the Trinity, a God Who does not exist in isolation but in eternal communion, even before He created anything. Through the gesture itself, it is the sign of the sacrifice of Christ, the price that He paid for our redemption. It proves to us how much God loves us, that "while we were yet sinners Christ died for us." (Rom. 5:8) It orients us toward self-sacrifice for love of God, imitating Christ. (cf. Eph. 5:1-2)

In the thirteenth century, during the reign of Pope Innocent III, priests were instructed to make the Sign of the Cross "with three fingers, because the signing is done together with the invocation of the Trinity." The first three fingers – the thumb, index finger, and middle finger – are held together as a symbol of the unity of the Trinity, three Persons in one God; the other two fingers are curled into the palm, symbolizing the descent of Christ from Heaven to earth and the unity of His two natures, divine and human. This is still done in the Eastern rites of the Church. In the Roman Rite, the priest makes the Sign of the Cross with all his fingers joined together (CMRR 193), commonly understood to signify the five wounds Christ received during His crucifixion (His two hands, His two feet, and His side).

The Sign of the Cross is a testimony to both the Passion and the Resurrection, and the words of the prayer contain a profession of faith in the Trinity: "in the sign of the Cross, together with the invocation of the Trinity, the whole essence of Christianity is summed up." (*The Spirit of the Liturgy*, p. 178)[6] In the words of Maurice Zundel, in his 1939 catechetical

---

[6] This gesture is covered in greater detail in Chapter 2 of *Praying the Mass: The Prayers of the People.*

and scriptural reflection on the Mass:

> With what reverence, therefore, fervour and opening of heart and
> mind, with what profound wonder and joyful gratitude, with what
> unhasty deliberateness and complete recollection, we should make
> the sign of the Cross, always and everywhere, but with an even
> more intimate recollection, as we enter upon the Divine Liturgy.
> (*The Splendour of the Liturgy*, p. 23)

Because of the importance of such a gesture, it should never be made
carelessly.

Voice

In the first three verses of the Bible, we read that God creates by means
of His Spirit and His Word: "The Spirit of God was moving over the
face of the waters. And God *said*, 'Let there be light.'" (Gen. 1:2-3) It is
not so much a matter of God "speaking" as we consider speech – after
all, God is Spirit, and vocal chords are matter. What is significant is that
God is described so often in anthropomorphical terms long before it
ever occurred to the writers of Scripture that God would take on human
flesh. God has a finger (cf. Ex. 31:18), a whole hand (cf. 1 Sam. 5:11), a
face (cf. Gen. 33:10), ears (cf. Sir. 21:5), and a mouth. (cf. Matt. 4:4)

It is from the "mouth" of God that His words come forth, as would
be expected. Whether it was perceived by ears or by a heart of faith, the
word of the Lord was revealed to prophets, whose job it was to relay that
received word faithfully to the audience God intended. It is with the
voice of men, then, that the word of God is proclaimed. On a few truly
awesome occasions, God the Father spoke from Heaven in a way
perceptible to more than one man: at the baptism of Jesus in the Jordan
River (cf. Matt. 3:16-17), at His transfiguration (cf. Matt. 17:5), and just as
Jesus announced that His hour had finally come. (cf. John 12:27-30) In
Jesus Christ, God in the flesh, the *Word*-made-flesh, we are permitted to
see the finger, the hand, the face, the ears, and the mouth of God. And
from this mouth will come words of grace that perfect nature: "This is
my body. ... This is my blood." (Matt. 26:26-27)

In the Mass, the priest lends his mouth and his voice to Christ: he
does not say this, "This is *his* [Christ's] Body," but "This is *my* Body."
Through the voice of the priest we hear the voice of Christ: the priest "is
not now speaking from his own resources but in virtue of the Sacrament

that he has received, *he has become the voice of Someone Else*, who is now speaking and acting." (*The Spirit of the Liturgy*, pp. 172-173)

There are two voices that the priest uses during the Mass. One is normal and clear, used for the principal prayers and for the dialogue with the congregation. (GIRM 32) There may be variations in this voice depending on what is being said: the Gospel is not proclaimed in the same manner as an oration, which is not spoken in the same manner as the homily. (GIRM 38) The priest's voice is an important factor in the faithful's comprehension of the Mass and its prayers. In his recent essay, *Pastoral Ramifications of Liturgical Texts*, Rev. Paul Turner says that a priest "needs to sink himself into [a prayer's] meaning and express it with his voice, his face, his hands and his life," lest his voice "not match the exultation or sorrow of the prayer."

The texts of the Mass that are proclaimed aloud are meant not only to be spoken, but *sung*. Singing or chanting the prayers and readings is an ancient liturgical tradition, and while it requires a certain talent and practice, there are very simple melodies for many parts of the Mass, some of which you have probably used (or heard used) without knowing they are Gregorian chants. If you are familiar with singing the dialogue before the Preface of the Eucharistic Prayer (perhaps on Christmas or Easter), you have probably sung Gregorian melodies.

The other voice is a "low voice" (*sotto voce*), essentially a whisper, which is used for his personal prayers[7] (such as the prayers of preparation before receiving Communion); this voice is not meant to be heard by the congregation. These personal prayers, unlike the presidential prayers of the priest, are not said "in the name of the Church" but rather "in his own name, asking that he may exercise his ministry with greater attention and devotion." (GIRM 33) These prayers are not optional, but the fact that the congregation does not hear them is a matter of contention for some, who argue that these prayers should either be said aloud or simply omitted. The source of contention concerning these prayers is the place and purpose of silence in the liturgy.

---

[7] There are more of these prayers in the Extraordinary Form than in the Ordinary Form, and the words of some of these prayers have been revised in the Ordinary Form. Each of these prayers is treated in detail in its proper place in this book.

Silence

Indeed, silence – the counterpart to words spoken (or sung) aloud – is a very important part of the liturgy. Its majesty is often made known to us only by some unexpected noise that interrupts it. (*The Splendour of the Liturgy*, p. 40)

Even before Mass it is recommended that there be an atmosphere of reverent silence inside the church "so that all may dispose themselves to carry out the sacred action in a devout and fitting manner." (GIRM 45) We move from the hustle and bustle of the noisy world outside to the calm and collected quiet inside the church. Rev. Elliott calls silence "the best preparation for the celebration of the liturgy." (CMRR 233) Maurice Zundel calls the liturgy a "school of silence [that] teaches us to listen. And to listen is possibly the highest form of obedience and love." (*The Splendour of the Liturgy*, p. xi) This is because the word "obedience" comes from the Latin *obedire*, made up of a prefix *ob-* and the verb *audire*, which means "to hear." When we listen in silence, we learn what we ought to pray.

The purpose of silence depends upon the point in the Mass at which it occurs. During the Penitential Act, or after the words "Let us pray," there is silence for recollection; after a reading from Scripture or the homily, there is silence for meditation and reflection on what we have just heard; after receiving Communion and before the Post-Communion prayer, we observe a period of silence in which to offer prayer and thanksgiving to God in our hearts. (GIRM 45)

Cardinal Ratzinger was greatly concerned about the perception and reception of silence in the liturgy of our day. While the Mass involves responding to God through song and prayer,

> the greater mystery, surpassing all words, summons us to silence. It must, of course, be a silence with content, not just the absence of speech and action. We should expect the liturgy to give us a positive stillness that will restore us. (*The Spirit of the Liturgy*, p. 209)

In the liturgy, silence can never be "just a pause," he says, where we let our guard down and are assaulted by innumerable thoughts and desires; instead, it must be an opportunity for recollection and peace. This is not the case when silence is manufactured or treated mechanically, as if there must be a five-second pause after the lector has sat down and before the cantor stands up. For silence to be fruitful, it must not be a break in the action of the liturgy, but "an integral part of the liturgical event." (*Ibid.*)

For this to be a liturgical reality, rather than mere liturgical theory, silence must not be treated as just a period of waiting, but there must be an internal response to the external fact of silence; the silence must be filled with internal content. Cardinal Ratzinger continues:

> Then something happens inwardly that corresponds to what is going on outwardly – we are disposing ourselves, preparing the way, placing ourselves before the Lord, asking him to make us ready for transformation. *Shared silence becomes shared prayer*, indeed shared action, a journey out of our everyday life toward the Lord, toward merging our time with his own. (*Ibid.*, p. 211)

This recognition of silence as "active" and as something shared requires liturgical catechesis, according to Cardinal Ratzinger:

> Liturgical education ought to regard it as its duty to facilitate this inner process, so that in the common experience of silence the inner process becomes a truly liturgical event and the silence is filled with content. (*Ibid.*)

The Quiet Prayers of the Priest

With this understanding of silence, we can better grasp why the Mass includes quiet prayers for the priest. The silence that surrounds these prayers is not an interruption in the liturgy; it is not the case that it is improper for the priest to pray something that the congregation cannot hear, nor that the priest should be praying something personal while the congregation "waits" for him to finish.

Cardinal Ratzinger addresses these quiet prayers in *The Spirit of the Liturgy*, and he explains their importance and purpose by reflecting on the identity of the priest in the liturgy:

> Those who hold a sociological or activist view of the priest's duties in the Mass frown upon these prayers, and, whenever possible, they leave them out. The priest is defined in a narrowly sociological and functionalistic way as the "presider" at the liturgical celebration, which is thought of as a kind of meeting. If that is what he is, then, of course, for the sake of the meeting, he has to be in action all the time. But the priest's duties in the Mass are much more than a matter of chairing a meeting. The priest presides over an encounter with the living God and as a person who is on his way to God. The silent prayers of the priest invite him to make his task truly personal, so that he may give his whole

self to the Lord. They highlight the way in which all of us, each one personally yet together with everyone else, have to approach the Lord. (pp. 212-213)

By that last sentence, Cardinal Ratzinger means that the congregation's participation in the liturgy is not placed on hold while the priest says his personal prayers. Instead, the congregation can participate, in a sense, in the quiet prayers of the priest, and derive spiritual benefit from them.

For example, while the priest is praying the *Lava me* ("Wash me, O Lord…") in a low voice as he washes his hands during the Offertory, the congregation should not simply be watching him, but neither should they be distracted from this liturgical act, even if there is a chant or hymn being sung at the time. The congregation should know what the priest is praying, how it relates to the act of washing his hands, and how to make the priest's prayer – inaudible though it is – a part of *their* prayer; or, as Rev. Gagliardi explains it, "only in the measure that we understand and internalize the liturgical structure and the words of the liturgy, can we enter into an interior harmony with them." These quiet prayers "permit the priest who prays them, and the faithful who participate in the silence that accompanies them, to be conscious of the *mysterium fidei* in which they participate and so to unite themselves to Christ regarding him as God, brother and friend."

Rev. Gagliardi earnestly invites priests not to skip these prayers, nor to "transform them from prayers of the priest to prayers of the whole assembly, reciting them aloud like all the other prayers," because the theology on which they are based and which they express "is different and complementary to that which is behind the other prayers. This theology is manifested in the silent and reverent way in which they are prayed by the priest and accompanied by the other faithful."

Sung Prayer

Virtually every part of the Mass that is spoken aloud – the orations, the dialogues, even the readings from Scripture – can be sung; a sung liturgy is the ideal. Priests should take every care "that singing by the ministers and the people is not absent in celebrations that occur on Sundays and on holy days of obligation" because of the great importance that the Church attaches to the sung celebration of the liturgy. (GIRM 40) The

Church draws attention to Holy Week and the Paschal Triduum as days specially suited to the singing of the liturgy. (*Paschalis Sollemnitatis* 42)

Sacred music is not an add-on, but is in fact an integral element of the liturgy. (113) Pope St. Pius X explained that its purpose is to clothe the liturgical texts with a suitable melody so as to render greater glory to God, and by doing so to make them more effective in their ability to move us to devotion so that we are better disposed to receive the graces that come to us from celebration of the Holy Sacrifice of the Mass. (*Inter Sollicitudines* 1) The type of sacred music that is proper to the Roman Rite is Gregorian chant; the Second Vatican Council affirmed that it has primacy of place in the Roman liturgy. (SC 116) As mentioned earlier, you are probably familiar with Gregorian chant by sound, even if not by name.

Incense

The use of incense in Israel's worship was ordained by God at Mount Sinai. Moses was instructed to build an altar on which incense would be burned daily. (cf. Ex. 30:1-8) Burning incense produces a sweet-smelling cloud that represents both our prayers rising to God, and their being pleasing and acceptable to Him.

More than three-dozen times in the Pentateuch (the first five books of the Bible) burnt offerings are said to produce a "pleasing odor" to the Lord. It is not that God in Heaven had a nose with which to smell the smoke, nor that the smoke passed through our atmosphere and reached into some "heaven" in outer space. Just as God can use material things to communicate His grace to us (like water and oil in the sacraments), He can allow us to use material things to communicate our love to Him. It can be hard to imagine how the burning of animals could be a "pleasing odor" to God – perhaps it was for the people's sake that God instituted the burning of incense as well – but the intention behind the sacrifice was what pleased God so greatly.

However, after the reign of King Solomon, Israel was split in two, and both the northern and southern kingdoms fell into the worship of false gods. When they burned incense it was no longer pleasing to God, Who saw through it as an attempt to cover up the foul stench of their disobedience: "Bring no more vain offerings; incense is an abomination to me. ... I cannot endure iniquity and solemn assembly." (Isa. 1:13) Yet the Lord also spoke through the prophet Malachi that "from the rising of the sun to its setting my name is great among the nations, and in every place *incense is offered to my name*, and a pure offering; for my name is great among the nations, says the LORD of hosts." (Mal. 1:11) This prophecy was repeatedly interpreted by the Church Fathers as being fulfilled in the Church which reaches out to all the nations and in which the "pure offering" (the Eucharist) is perpetually offered to God, amid incense that once more pleases Him.[8]

Incense also allows our other senses to participate in our worship of God. The odor of burning incense engages our sense of smell. Our sense of hearing is edified particularly in the Eastern Rites of the Church, where chain of the censer has bells attached to it, so that every time that incense is used – and it is used quite liberally in the Eastern Rites – there is not only a delightful aroma, but a fervent ringing. This is sometimes achieved in the Roman Rite as well, by letting the censer clink against its chain as it is swung.

Incense is mentioned only a few times in the New Testament: in the Gospels, we read that St. Zechariah (father of St. John the Baptist) was chosen by lot to burn incense in the Temple when the angel Gabriel appeared to him (cf. Luke 1:8-12), and that frankincense was one of the gifts brought by the magi to the child Jesus. (cf. Matt. 2:11) Incense is also mentioned in passing in the letter to the Hebrews, as the particulars of Temple worship were described. (cf. Heb. 9:4) But it is in the book of Revelation that incense is portrayed in a truly Christian context:

> And when he had taken the scroll, the four living creatures and the twenty-four elders fell down before the Lamb, each holding a harp, and with golden bowls full of *incense*, which are *the prayers of the saints*... (Rev. 5:8)

> And another angel came and stood at the altar with a golden censer; and he was given much *incense* to mingle with *the prayers of*

---

[8] See the *Didache* XIV, 3; St. Justin Martyr, Dialogue with Trypho, XLI and CXVII; St. Irenaeus, *Adversus Haereses* Book IV, 17 and Fragments of Lost Writings XXXVII; St. Athanasius, Festal Letter 332, 4 and Letter 339, 11; *Apostolic Constitutions* Book VI, 23 and Book VII, 30; St. John of Damascus, *De Fide Orthodoxa* Book IV, 13. The Council of Trent (1562) also quoted Malachi 1:11 as pertaining to the Holy Sacrifice of the Mass. (cf. Session XXII, I)

all the saints upon the golden altar before the throne; and *the smoke of the incense* rose with *the prayers of the saints* from the hand of the angel before God. (Rev. 8:3-4)

These three verses show the fulfillment of what the psalmist had written several centuries earlier: "Let my prayer be counted as incense before you..." (Ps. 141:2)

This is why the Catholic Church uses incense in her liturgies. Not because incense on its own has any value before God, but because of what that incense represents. (GIRM 75) During the Mass, incense can be used to bless the altar and crucifix during the entrance procession, to bless the Book of the Gospels, to bless the bread and wine during the Offertory, and to show reverence to the Host and chalice during the Eucharistic Prayer as each is elevated after their consecration.

What is more, St. Paul admonishes Christians to "walk in love, as Christ loved us and gave himself up for us, *a fragrant offering* and sacrifice to God." (Eph. 5:2) He even speaks of Christians as being "the aroma of Christ to God" in the world. (2 Cor. 2:15) Lastly, he calls all gifts of self-sacrifice "a fragrant offering, a sacrifice acceptable and pleasing to God." (Phil. 4:18) This is why not only bread and wine are censed at the Offertory, but the priest, his ministers, and the whole congregation: we are all set apart for holiness, all "a fragrant offering" to the Lord!

Posture

Throughout the course of the Mass, the priest adopts four postures: standing, sitting, bowing, and genuflecting. Each posture pertains to his participation at that time: standing to pray, sitting to listen, bowing in humility, and genuflecting in awe of the Real Presence of Jesus Christ in the Blessed Sacrament on the altar.

Standing

Standing for prayer is an ancient posture, practiced in Jewish worship and continued in Christianity. It was the posture of Hannah (mother of the prophet Samuel) as she prayed for a son (cf. 1 Sam. 2:26) and of the three Jewish youths whom King Nebuchadnezzar had thrown into the furnace for refusing to worship his idols. (cf. Dan. 3:25) It was still customary in the first century, as Jesus mentions standing for prayer three times in the Gospels. (cf. Matt. 6:5; Mark 11:25; Luke 18:11-13)

Standing is the posture of intercession and mediation. Moses stood on the hill at Rephidim, interceding for Israel to win the battle against Amalek. (cf. Ex. 17:8ff) Although Jesus is usually described as sitting at the right hand of the Father, St. Stephen, the first martyr, sees Him standing at His Father's right hand, signifying His constant intercession for us in Heaven. (cf. Acts 7:55; Rom. 8:34; Heb. 7:25) Standing is also the posture of confidence before God: Jesus says "watch at all times, praying that you may have strength to escape all these things that will take place, and *to stand before the Son of man*." (Luke 21:36) This posture is also one of readiness, "the sign of vigilance and action" showing "the respect of the servant in attendance, of the soldier on duty." (*Sacred Signs*, p. 22) For all these reasons, the priest stands for prayer: at his chair or at the altar, on behalf of the Church or in his personal prayers, over the offerings of bread and wine or over the congregation. The priest stands for the entirety of the Eucharistic Prayer, while the congregation kneels at least from the epiclesis through the consecration; even the deacon kneels during that part of the Eucharistic Prayer. (GIRM 179)

The priest also stands (with everyone else) when the Gospel is read as a sign of respect. We stand for the Gospel (as opposed to the other readings) because although the whole Bible is the word of the Lord, in the Gospels we hear the Word, Jesus Christ Himself, speaking.

After the Gospel, when the priest[9] instructs the congregation with a homily, he does so "standing at the chair or at the ambo itself or, when appropriate, in another suitable place." (GIRM 136)[10] When a *bishop* preaches at Mass, "unless he decides that some other way is preferable, the Bishop should preach *while seated at the chair*, wearing the miter and holding the pastoral staff." (*Ceremonial of Bishops* 17)

Why does the bishop preach while sitting down? (Not because he is tired, although liturgies celebrated by bishops *do* tend to run longer.) The precedent for this comes from Jewish tradition, the "seat of Moses." In Exodus 18:13, we read that "Moses sat to judge the people." It was the custom to judge cases – and more generally, to teach or preach – sitting

---

[9] The homily may also be given by a deacon (cf. GIRM 66, 94), but it is unclear as to whether he may preach from his chair, which "does not hold the same liturgical weight" as the chair of the bishop or priest. (Rev. Paul Turner, *Let Us Pray*, p. 77)

[10] The ambo is the place (sometimes called a lectern or pulpit) from which the readings are given.

down. (cf. Matt. 23:2) Jesus sat to teach on numerous occasions: in the Temple (cf. John 8:2; Matt. 26:55), in synagogues (cf. Luke 4:20-21), on the ground (cf. Matt. 5:1), and even in St. Peter's boat. (cf. Luke 5:3) (It was customary for the *teacher* to sit and the *students* to stand.) The chair of the bishop, his *cathedra*, from which we get the word "cathedral," is a sign of his teaching authority. This is why it is traditional for bishops to preach while sitting at their chair.

Sitting

Although standing was the standard posture for worship, we do know that there was some sitting in the Church's liturgy even in its earliest days. St. Paul wrote about people sitting near one another (cf. 1 Cor. 14:30), and St. James admonishes those who would reserve seats of honor in the assembly to the rich, neglecting the poor. (cf. Jas. 2:2-4)

Sitting is the posture of listening and recollection. The priest sits during the Liturgy of the Word until the Alleluia, when he stands along with everyone else. If he is not giving the homily, he sits while another priest or deacon does so. He stands to intone the Creed, and does not sit down again until after Communion Rite is completed.

Bowing

A bow can be a sign of respect, of reverence, or of humble submission. Its first appearance in Scripture is when Abraham receives a visit from the Lord, appearing as three men: Abraham "bowed himself to the earth." (Gen. 18:2) Bowing was a staple of Middle Eastern hospitality. It also appears in Scripture as an act of worship, such as when Abraham's servant "bowed his head and worshiped the LORD" in response to God's faithfulness to Abraham. (Gen. 24:26)

In the liturgy, there are two forms or degrees of bowing: a bow of the head and a bow of the body (bowing from the waist, known as a "profound bow"). (GIRM 275) The priest is directed to make several bows during the liturgy, and specific instances will be addressed in each chapter. Generally, though, the priest bows his head whenever the three Divine Persons are named together ("the Father, the Son, and the Holy Spirit"), and at the name of Jesus as well. This practice, based on the words of St. Paul that "at the name of Jesus every knee should bow" (Phil. 2:10), was established as liturgical law by Pope Gregory X in 1274:

Each should fulfill in himself that which is written for all that *at the name of Jesus* every knee should bow; whenever that glorious name is recalled, especially during the sacred mysteries of the Mass, *everyone should bow the knees of his heart*, which he can do even *by a bow of his head*. (Second Council of Lyons, Constitution 25)

The priest also bows his head at the name of the Blessed Virgin Mary and at the name of the saint(s) being honored that day. These bows of the head should also be made by the congregation.

The priest makes a profound bow to the altar several times during the Mass. He also does so during the Creed (at the words "by the Holy Spirit was incarnate of the Virgin Mary, and became man" in the Nicene Creed, and at the words "who was conceived by the Holy Spirit, born of the Virgin Mary" in the Apostles' Creed); the congregation should make this bow as well. On two occasions mentioned below, this bow during the Creed is replaced by a genuflection.

The deacon makes a profound bow before the priest when asking for his blessing to pronounce the Gospel. Lectors and others who enter the sanctuary during Mass also make a profound bow to the altar.

Genuflecting

While the priest does not ordinarily kneel during the Mass (one exception is in the reading of the Lord's Passion, after Christ's death), he does make a few genuflections; in the Extraordinary Form, though, the priest makes many more genuflections. This posture is sometimes confused with kneeling, because the word "genuflect" comes from the two Latin words *genu* ("the knee") and *flectere* ("to bend"), literally meaning "to bend the knee," which sounds a lot like kneeling. A genuflection is the lowering of one knee (usually the right knee) to the ground.[11] A double genuflection is the lowering of both knees to the ground; kneeling is a prolonged double genuflection.

Genuflection is an act of adoration reserved for the Eucharist,[12] and for the crucifix during its veneration on Good Friday and Holy Saturday. In addition, the profound bow (honoring the Incarnation) made by all during the Creed is replaced by a genuflection on the two solemnities

---

[11] If you are unable to do so, another sign of reverence such as a profound bow is acceptable.

[12] Double genuflection (kneeling) is the traditional (and still acceptable) posture for receiving Holy Communion, being a fitting expression of reverence and adoration.

commemorating the Incarnation: the Annunciation of our Lord (March 25) and the Nativity of our Lord (December 25). (GIRM 137)

The priest genuflects to the Blessed Sacrament either three or five times in the Mass, depending on where the tabernacle is situated in the church. If the tabernacle is located in the sanctuary, he genuflects to the Eucharist upon approaching the sanctuary at the beginning of Mass and after leaving the sanctuary at the end of Mass; otherwise, he bows to the altar. Two genuflections are made after the consecration of the Precious Body and of the Precious Blood (in the Eucharistic Prayer). The other genuflection is made just prior to the priest receiving Communion.

Orientation[13]

Perhaps the most commonly misunderstood element of liturgical worship in the Ordinary Form of Roman Rite – second only to the use of Latin – is the direction that the priest faces during the Mass. If you are familiar with the Extraordinary Form of the Mass, you are well aware that for the majority of the Mass, the priest is not facing *toward* the people, but *away* from them. This orientation has been described in numerous ways, some of which are inaccurate and misleading: some say the priest has his back to the people (or worse, has turned his back *on* the people) or that he is facing the wall, others that he is facing the altar or the tabernacle.

First, if the priest "has his back to the people," then the same must be said of all the people in the church (except those sitting in the back), but I know of no one who takes offense at the fact that the people sitting in front of him are not looking at him. Just because the priest is not facing the people does not mean he is being rude or is ignoring them. Those who see the gesture as the priest "turning his back *on* the people" are simply deriving the wrong symbolism – one of moral injustice – from this posture. Second, if the priest is "facing the wall," then the same should be said of the whole congregation. Yes, the congregation is also facing the priest and the altar, but they are facing the wall beyond the priest and altar as well. Third, many modern churches are built such that when the priest is "facing the altar" he is *also* facing the people, so this

[13] This section is greatly inspired by two essays by Cardinal Ratzinger: "Eastward- or Westward-Facing Position? A Correction" (in *Feast of Faith*, pp. 139-145) and "The Altar and the Direction of Liturgical Prayer" (in *The Spirit of the Liturgy*, pp. 74-84).

description is not very specific. Fourth, the tabernacle is not necessarily on or behind the altar, so the priest is not necessarily facing it; and once more, the tabernacle should not be the focus of the priest's attention at Mass. (Ratzinger, *Feast of Faith*, p. 139)

All these descriptions focus on the wrong center of attention. What is the *proper* center of attention during the Mass? The Mass is a prayer to God; the "direction of the Eucharist [is] from Christ in the Holy Spirit to the Father." (*Feast of Faith*, p. 140; cf. *Catechism* 1073) This means that liturgy should be directed spiritually *ad Deum*, that is, "toward God." Ancient Christian tradition has manifested this spiritual orientation[14] by facing *ad orientem*, to the east (whereas Jewish worship faces Jerusalem).

Why the east? As they say in real estate: location, location, location! The east is the direction of the rising sun, which is a biblical symbol of Christ (the practice is not pagan); thus, the east is associated with His Incarnation, Resurrection, Ascension, and Second Coming.

The Incarnation

God is often identified with light in both the Old and New Testaments: the psalmist calls God "a sun and shield" (Ps. 84:11) and St. John says that "God is light and in him is no darkness at all." (1 John 1:5) So too Christ is likened to light and the sun, especially in His Incarnation, the first coming.

St. Jerome, in his commentary on the book of the prophet Ezekiel, saw the east gate of the Temple in Ezekiel's vision as a sign of the Virgin Mary's womb. Ezekiel saw that "the glory of the God of Israel came from the east" (Ezek. 43:2) and that "no one shall enter by it" except the Lord. (Ezek. 44:2)[15] This Scripture was interpreted as a prophecy of the Incarnation, so its association with the east is particularly important.

The prophet Isaiah foretold a time when a child would be born who be called "Wonderful Counselor, Mighty God, Everlasting Father, Prince of Peace" (Isa. 9:6) and who would sit on the throne of David and have a never-ending kingdom. Of that day Isaiah said "The people who walked

---

[14] The word "orientation" comes from the Latin *oriens*, meaning "the east; sunrise," which in turn comes from the verb *orior*, meaning "to rise."

[15] That this gate "shall remain shut" was seen by many early Church writers (e.g. Tertullian, St. Methodius, St. Ambrose, St. Augustine, St. Jerome, St. John of Damascus) as a prophecy of Mary's perpetual virginity, that she bore no other children besides Jesus.

in darkness have seen *a great light*." (Isa. 9:2) St. Matthew tells us that this was fulfilled by Jesus' preaching throughout the regions of Zebulun and Napthali. (cf. Matt. 4:12-16; Isa. 9:1)

The prophet Malachi foretold that the "sun of righteousness" would rise. (Mal. 4:2) The Advent hymn "O Come, O Come Emmanuel" [16] also invokes Christ as the *Oriens*, the "Day-Spring" or dawn. The Canticle of Zechariah (the *Benedictus*, Luke 1:68-79), which the father of St. John the Baptist proclaimed upon the birth of his son, ends by describing God's mercy being manifested as "the dawn [*oriens*] from on high" that would "shine on those who dwell in darkness," alluding to the Incarnation.

Finally, St. John the Evangelist refers to Jesus as the "light" in the prologue of his gospel (cf. John 1:4-9), and Jesus spoke of Himself in the same way. (cf. John 8:12; 9:5; 12:46)

The Resurrection

Christ's crucifixion can be associated with the setting of the sun: the sun was darkened (cf. Luke 23:45), Golgotha is on the west side of Jerusalem, and Jesus was buried in the evening. (cf. Matt. 27:57)

But the Church finds in the rising sun (the *oriens*, the east) a natural symbol of the Resurrection. (*Feast of Faith*, p. 140) Jesus rose from the dead at or just before sunrise. (cf. Luke 24:1; John 20:1) His Apostles captured a glimpse of His resurrected glory at His transfiguration when "his face shone like the *sun*, and his garments became white as light." (Matt. 17:2) St. Paul quotes an early Christian baptismal hymn in his letter to the Ephesians: "Awake, O sleeper, and arise from the dead, and Christ shall give you *light*." (Eph. 5:14)

The Ascension

St. Luke records in the Acts of the Apostles that Jesus ascended into Heaven from the Mount of Olives (cf. Acts 1:9-12), which was located to the east of Jerusalem. The Roman liturgy associates Psalm 67:33-34 with the Solemnity of the Ascension; the Latin Vulgate reads "*psallite Deo qui ascendit super caelum caeli* ad orientem," which the Douay-Rheims Bible

---

[16] This hymn comes from the "O Antiphons," the antiphons for the *Magnificat* prayed during the Liturgy of the Hours on the seven evenings concluding Advent, the season in which the Church celebrates the first coming of Christ and anticipates His second coming.

renders as "Sing ye to God Who mounteth above the heaven of heavens, *to the east.*"

The Second Coming

The Church saw the *oriens* not only as a symbol of the Resurrection, but also of "a presentation of the hope of the parousia," the second coming of Christ. Indeed, "every Mass is an approach to the return of Christ." (*Feast of Faith*, pp. 140-141)

The angels at the Ascension told the Apostles that Jesus "will come in the same way as you saw him go into heaven." (Acts 1:11) Jesus prophesied His return from the east: "as the lightning comes *from the east* and shines as far as the west, so will be the coming of the Son of man." (Matt. 24:27) When Jesus returns, His appearance will probably be like that seen by St. John as recorded in the book of Revelation: "his face was like *the sun* shining in full strength." (Rev. 1:16) In the heavenly Temple, Jesus is the lamp. (cf. Rev. 21:23; 22:5)

The East and the Cross

St. John also saw "another angel ascend *from the rising of the sun*, with *the seal* of the living God." (Rev. 7:2) The seal of God is believed to be the sign of the Son of Man, which is the cross. (cf. Ezek. 9:4; Rev. 7:2-3)[17]

The early Christians marked the eastern wall of their meeting-houses with a cross first as a sign of hope for Christ's return and only later as a reminder of His Passion. (*Feast of Faith*, p. 141) This tradition was the origin of the rubric, still present in the Extraordinary Form of the Mass, which required there to be a crucifix on the altar, so that Mass would be celebrated not only facing east, but also facing the cross. In the Ordinary Form of the Mass, a crucifix is still required, but it can be *near* the altar if not *on* it. (GIRM 117)

The east, the *oriens*, signifies the whole Christian concept of time: the Lord is "the rising sun of history." (*The Spirit of the Liturgy*, p. 84) So while it is not proper to say that the Eucharist is celebrated facing the tabernacle or even facing the altar, it can be said that the Eucharist is celebrated "facing the image of the cross, which embodied in itself the whole theology the *oriens*." (*Feast of Faith*, p. 141)

---

[17] This link is described in *Praying the Mass: The Prayers of the People*, Chapter 2.

Historical Continuity

The Church, in both the east and west, has traditionally prayed facing the east.[18] If you attend a Byzantine Divine Liturgy, you will see that the priest prays the majority of the anaphora (the Eucharistic Prayer) facing the east, probably behind an iconostasis (a screen with doors decorated with icons of Jesus, the Blessed Virgin Mary, and other saints and angels). The priest will from time to time turn to speak to face the congregation to speak to them; this happens in the Extraordinary Form of the Mass as well.

Eastward posture is the traditional posture of the Latin Church as well, although changes started occurring in the middle of the twentieth century, even before the Second Vatican Council. The Constitution on the Sacred Liturgy said nothing about turning altars around. Still, the practice of priests celebrating Mass "facing the people" (*versus populum*) – standing on "the other side" of the altar – became more and more prevalent so quickly that it became the perceived norm, to the point where Mass celebrated *ad orientem* seemed to be incompatible with the Ordinary Form. However, as Pope Benedict XVI has shown by his example, the Ordinary Form of the Roman Rite can be celebrated *ad orientem*; in fact, the *Roman Missal* anticipates that the priest will be celebrating Mass in this manner because on several occasions its rubrics[19] instruct him to face the people or the altar, instructions that are redundant if those two directions are always the same.[20]

An unfortunate "Latinization" of the Eastern Rites, by which they adopted traditions and characteristics particular to the Latin Rite (often at the expense of their own), has occurred at times during the Church's history. In 1996, the Vatican Congregation for Eastern Churches put out a document on Eastern liturgical worship, *Pater Incomprehensibilis* (PI). The document praises the "the inalienable value of the particular heritage of the Eastern Churches" (PI 7) and stresses the need for preserving the

---

[18] St. Basil of Caesarea, a 4th century bishop in Asia Minor (modern-day Turkey), wrote that the custom of "turn[ing] to the East at the prayer" is not a written teaching but a practice received "in a mystery by the tradition of the apostles." (*On the Holy Spirit* 66)

[19] See the *Order of Mass* 1, 29, 127, 132, 133, 139, 141, and 144; also see GIRM 124, 146, 154, 157, 165, 181, 244, and 268.

[20] When a church's architecture does not place the sanctuary and altar in the eastern end of the building, one could treat that part of the church where the altar is located as a "liturgical east."

Eastern liturgical traditions. One such tradition, prayer facing east, was being endangered by "a new and recent Latin influence" (PI 107) that spread in the years following the Second Vatican Council. After quoting St. John of Damascus at length (who provided numerous proofs from Scripture of God's hallowing of the east[21]) and addressing that the priest is "guiding the people in pilgrimage toward the Kingdom" rather than has his "back turned to the people," the document calls for the retention and safeguarding of prayer facing east as "truly coherent with the Eastern liturgical spirituality" and having "profound value." (*Ibid.*)

The Cross as East

Pope Benedict XVI, both before his election to the papacy and after, has suggested an alternative approach to facing east: "the cross can serve as the interior 'east' of faith." (*The Spirit of the Liturgy*, p. 83)

Because the Liturgy of the Eucharist is not about a dialogue between the priest and the congregation, but between the whole church and God, the cross can serve as a focal point when the priest and the congregation face each other: because the cross can be placed on the altar, rather than just near it, it serves to distinguish the Liturgy of the Word from the Liturgy of the Eucharist. (*Feast of Faith*, p. 145) This arrangement of the altar is used at most of Pope Benedict's Masses.

An objection to this is that the cross can be regarded as a "barrier" or "obstruction" to the act taking place on the altar. Cardinal Ratzinger asks in reply, "Is the cross disruptive during Mass? Is the priest more important than the Lord?" (*The Spirit of the Liturgy*, p. 84) His response to this objection is that "the cross on the altar is not obstructing the view" and is "an open 'iconostasis.'" (*Feast of Faith*, p. 145)

Liturgical Significance

So what value is there in celebrating the Eucharist facing the east?

First, as these opening two chapters have sought to show, we can express our spiritual worship through our bodies. When the priest says "Lift up your hearts" before the Eucharistic Prayer, and the congregation

---

[21] Among these are: God is light (cf. 1 John 1:5), Christ is the "sun of righteousness" (Mal. 4:2), Christ as "the East" (Zech. 3:8, Septuagint), the location of Eden "in the east" (Gen. 2:8), the east-facing gate of the Temple (cf. Ezek. 44:1), Christ ascending toward the east (cf. Acts 1:11), and His statement about His return "from the east." (Matt. 24:27)

responds "We lift them up to the Lord," there is an internal orientation toward the Lord being spoken of. This internal reality should also be expressed by external signs if possible. Celebrating the Eucharist facing the east is an external manifestation of being directed to the Lord, of our hope for His return, for the new dawn and the endless day of Heaven.

Second, this posture should not be misconstrued as the priest having his back to the people, but as the priest and the people facing the same direction together. At the end of his sermons, St. Augustine would often say *"conversi ad Dominum"* ("let us turn toward the Lord"), which had both a spiritual (conversion) and a literal (orientation) meaning in the liturgy, as priest and people would face the east together for the Eucharistic portion of the liturgy. In this way, we resume the shared posture of the entrance procession by which we express our pilgrim state on earth, on a journey to the Lord. (*The Spirit of the Liturgy*, p. 80)

Third, churches were traditionally built facing the east, that is, with the altar at the eastern end, so that the Eucharist could be celebrated in that direction. Cardinal Ratzinger refers to this as being mindful of the "cosmic dimension" or "orientation" of the liturgy (*Feast of Faith*, p. 140) by which the whole of creation can be included in worship of God. This architecture "stand[s] in the cosmos, inviting the sun to be a sign of the praise of God and a sign of the mystery of Christ." (*Feast of Faith*, p. 143) Cardinal Ratzinger suggests that if our buildings were oriented this way, it would facilitate the recovery of a spirituality that embraces creation in a traditional manner.

Fourth, while it is reasonable for the Liturgy of the Word to be celebrated face-to-face as an exchange between the one proclaiming the word and those hearing it, this orientation is not as suited to the Liturgy of the Eucharist. The communal character of the liturgy is a positive and necessary one, but it should not be emphasized to the point that the Eucharist is regarded merely a communal meal. The Eucharist is offered first *to God* as a sacrifice, from Whom it is received as spiritual food.

Fifth, there is sometimes confusion about the various ways in which Christ is present in the liturgy. He is present in the priest in a particular way, and He is also present in the congregation, for where two or three are gathered in His name, He is present in their midst. (cf. Matt. 10:10)

But the congregation does not pray to Christ-in-the-priest, nor does the priest pray to Christ-in-the-people. God is present in nature, but we do not worship a rock or a river as God; likewise, we do not worship one another as Christ. The *manner* of God's presence is not the same in all things. The Church is not a community closed in on itself, but is open to "what lies ahead and above," to God. (*The Spirit of the Liturgy*, p. 80) The Eucharist is not a dialogue between the priest and the congregation but between the Church and the Lord.

If these first two chapters have seemed unexpectedly lengthy and dense, it is because I wish to demonstrate the sacrality of the Mass: it is not something to be entered into lightly! It requires great preparation and concentration from everyone who participates in it. It is celebrated in "the house of God," so we should all come to Mass aware of the mystery taking place, ready to enter into it: Heaven and earth will mystically meet as the songs of angels are sung, God's inspired word is proclaimed, and Christ offers Himself to the Father in the Eucharist.

"In the earthly liturgy we take part in a foretaste of that heavenly liturgy." (CS 8) The priest reflects that heavenly liturgy with his body. In the remainder of this book we will examine the prayer texts of the Mass to see how the priest's *words* reflect the heavenly liturgy as well.

Questions for Reflection: Priests

1) **Interpret:** What gestures, postures, and actions in the liturgy has Jesus given significance to by His use of them?

2) **Interpret:** How is the use of incense by the Church different from its use by ancient Israel? How is its use similar?

3) **Explain:** How can walking reflect a reverent liturgical attitude? What spiritual significance can you attach to your steps as you walk to the altar, the ambo, the tabernacle, and the people?

4) **Explain:** What pastoral issues do you see presented by worship facing east, and how might you be able to resolve them if you were to introduce it in your parish?

5) **Explain:** The prophet Elijah encountered God in Mount Horeb in a quiet whisper. (cf. 1 Kgs. 19:8-12) What value can you find in speaking to God in a "low voice"?

6) **Relate:** How do the gestures and postures of the liturgy direct your thoughts and emotions to the mysteries being celebrated?

7) **Relate:** How does the Church's mission draw you as a priest into close contact with others? Do you bear Christ's presence to others by your voice and posture?

8) **Relate:** What impact can your own body language at Mass have on the faithful?

Questions for Reflection: Laity

1) **Interpret:** Why is God spoken of in anthropological terms in the Bible? How is this a preparation for the Incarnation?

2) **Interpret:** What are some postures or gestures used in the Mass that were also made by Jesus in the Gospels? How does His use of them provide context for their liturgical use?

3) **Explain:** For what reason does the liturgy engage our bodies and our senses, and not just our minds and spirits?

4) **Explain:** Why are some gestures reserved to the priest? Why is the posture of the priest different from the posture of the laity at times?

5) **Explain:** Why does the liturgy prescribes so many gestures and postures?

6) **Relate:** What are some liturgical postures and gestures which are used in secular affairs? Is their meaning the same? What are some secular postures and gestures that are inappropriate for use liturgically?

7) **Relate:** What Christian attitudes does the liturgy seek to instill through its gestures and postures?

8) **Relate:** What gestures or postures do you incorporate into your personal prayer? Why do you use them, and what do they mean to you?

I will go in to the altar of God:
to God who giveth joy to my youth.
(Psalm 42:4, Douay-Rheims)

We have confidence to enter the sanctuary by the blood of Jesus,
by the new and living way which he opened for us...
(Hebrews 10:19-20)

3

Introductory Rites

THERE ARE FOUR PRINCIPAL parts of the Mass, known as the Introductory Rites, the Liturgy of the Word, the Liturgy of the Eucharist, and the Concluding Rites. In the Introductory Rites, the priest, his ministers, and the congregation are prepared to enter into the sacred mysteries being celebrated. This preparation is not the sacred counterpart to the social niceties that precede board meetings or secular community gatherings: if everyone at a board meeting knows one another, the chairman might suggest they all skip the formalities and get right to business. This is not the case with the Mass.

Eucharistic Prayer III reminds us that God never ceases to gather a people to Himself. (cf. Deut. 7:6; Acts 15:14) The Introductory Rites are a ceremonial reminder that we have been gathered as a people by God; as Jesus chose His disciples, now He also chooses us. These rites involve a procession to the sanctuary, the Sign of the Cross, a sacred greeting taken directly out of Scripture, an act of penitence, a song of glory to God, and finally a prayer that expresses the spiritual "intention" of the Mass. Their purpose is to ensure that the faithful "establish communion and dispose themselves to listen properly to God's word and to celebrate the Eucharist worthily." (GIRM 46)

Entrance Procession

Before the first words of the Mass are spoken, the faithful must come together, and the priest and his ministers must make their way into the sanctuary, the part of the church where the altar, the ambo, and the celebrant's chair are located.[1] Why is this procession part of Mass? Why doesn't the Mass start with everyone already in their places? Because the very act of processing to the sanctuary has spiritual significance. It is evocative first of all of Jesus' jubilant entry into Jerusalem on the day we celebrate as Palm Sunday. (cf. Matt. 21:8-11) But it also evokes a present reality: the Church on earth is a pilgrim (Vatican II, *Dei Verbum* 7), on the way to God – for "our commonwealth is in heaven" (Phil. 3:20) – but we are also accompanied by God as we go.

This is represented in the procession by three signs. First, the priest approaches the **altar**, signifying Christ our goal. Second, at the head of the procession is the **crucifix**, which is a sign of Christ leading us on the way of salvation: our pilgrimage "in this life is nothing but a following of Christ crucified" (*Douay Catechism* 149), and Jesus Christ is "the pioneer and perfecter of our faith." (Heb. 12:2) Third, the presence of the **priest** at the back of the procession is a sign of Christ as "the good Shepherd" Who looks after His sheep and guides them home in safety. (John 10:14; cf. Heb. 13:20; *Catechism* 1348)

Reverencing the Altar

When the priest and his ministers reach the entrance to the sanctuary, they make a sign of reverence, a bow of the body to the altar. (If the tabernacle with the Blessed Sacrament is in the sanctuary, then instead of bowing to the altar, they should genuflect to the Blessed Sacrament.) Then the priest ascends to the altar and kisses it before going to his chair; the deacon kisses the altar as well. On particularly solemn occasions, the priest may even bless the altar with incense. Why is all this attention paid to the altar? Because the altar is a sign of Christ; according to one of the Prefaces for the Eucharistic Prayer during the Easter season, Christ is the "*sacerdos, altare et agnus*" ("priest, altar, and lamb") of His sacrifice.[2]

---

[1] The sanctuary is separated from the rest of the church by a few steps, a gate, and/or an altar rail.
[2] According to Rev. Jean Danielou, S.J., this expression can be traced to St. Cyril of Alexandria and Origen. (cf. *The Bible and the Liturgy*, p. 130)

It is easy to recognize Christ as the priest and the lamb (that is, the victim); why He is the Altar deserves some explanation to our modern minds. St. Ambrose, bishop of Milan in the fourth century and spiritual father of St. Augustine, took the image of Christ-as-altar for granted in his treatise *De Sacramentis*, where he writes (without much explanation) that "the altar is a type [i.e. sign] of the body [of Christ]" (Book IV, 7) and then again almost as an aside, "for what is the altar but the type of the body of Christ?" (Book V, 7)

Consider first the composition of the altar. Traditionally, the altar is made of stone and is immovable – although some countries, such as the United States, may use wood for the altar, provided it is "worthy, solid, and well-crafted." (GIRM 301) Why stone for the altar? St. Paul speaks of Christ as "the supernatural Rock" that accompanied the Israelites in the desert during their exodus from Egypt, the Rock from which flowed water for their sustenance. (1 Cor. 10:4; cf. Ex. 17:6) Sts. Paul and Peter identified Christ as the "cornerstone" (Eph. 2:20; 1 Pet. 2:6), and Jesus used this language referring to Himself. (cf. Luke 20:17-18) The concept is found in Psalm 118:22-26, the very same psalm that the inhabitants of Jerusalem sang as Jesus entered their city.

Not only is Christ "that living stone" (1 Pet. 2:4), but we too are called to be "living stones." (1 Pet. 2:5) This means the altar is also a sign of the Church, made up of diverse people, living stones, gathered and built into one, in peace and unity. St. Paul described the Church as being made up of those Jews and Gentiles who accepted Christ, and that Christ "is our peace, who has made us both [Jew and Gentile] one." (Eph. 2:14) Jesus "kissed [this altar, the Church] in the middle" with the "holy kiss of peace and unity" (*Douay Catechism* 125), so the priest imitates Christ in kissing the altar and in doing so, shows "a sign of his affection and close adherence to Christ." (*The Glories of the Catholic Church*, p. 222)

Now consider what takes place on the altar. An altar is a place of sacrifice, a place of offering something to God, a place of encountering God. Jesus offered Himself on earth on the "altar of the cross," and that offering is now made present on the Church's altar. The altar is related to our Lord's Passion and represents the cross, so the priest bowing before the altar "signifies the prostrating of Christ in the garden, when he began his passion." (*Douay Catechism* 125; cf. Matt. 26:39) Jesus went so far as to identify the Temple (and its altar) with Himself:

> Jesus [said], "Destroy *this temple*, and in three days I will raise it up." The Jews then said, "It has taken forty-six years to build this temple, and will you raise it up in three days?" But he spoke of *the temple of his body.* (John 2:19-21)

> "For which is greater, *the gold or the temple* that has made the gold sacred? ... For which is greater, *the gift or the altar* that makes the gift sacred?" (Matt. 23:17-19)

Jesus is the "gift" being offered on the altar, but He makes it clear that the altar makes the gift sacred; you certainly would not offer a sacrifice on an altar less dignified than the sacrifice itself. That makes Jesus (Who sanctifies) both the gift *and* the altar.

Rev. Maurice de la Taille, SJ, meditating upon Christ as altar in his 1915 book *The Mystery of Faith*, illuminates further:

> Those who desired to offer sacrifices to God, had to do so necessarily through an altar. But Christ, the Victim of salvation, approached to God *through Himself.* Hence He was also the altar of His own sacrifice. *For us too* in like manner, He is the altar of every one of our sacrifices, for we can bring no offering to God except through Christ. (Chapter 5, Section 2)

Not only did Christ approach the Father through Himself as an altar, but now Christ is our altar through Whom we approach the Father. St. Paul exhorted the Romans, "present your bodies as a living sacrifice, holy and acceptable to God, which is your *spiritual worship.*" (Rom. 12:1) This thought was taken up by St. Peter who completed it when he wrote that we are "to offer spiritual sacrifices acceptable to God *through Jesus Christ.*" (1 Pet. 2:5) It is no accident that we offer our prayers to God "through Christ our Lord."

In the Extraordinary Form of the Mass, two prayers accompany the approaching and kissing of the altar. As he ascends the steps to the altar, the priest prays that the Lord remove our iniquity so that we might enter the *Sancta Sanctorum* ("Holy of Holies") worthily, with pure minds. This prayer is not present in the Ordinary Form,[3] but the priest should still be aware of its sentiment as he approaches the altar of sacrifice. In the

---

[3] In the Extraordinary Form, the Penitential Act happens *before* the priest goes to the altar, while in the Ordinary Form, the Penitential Act happens *after* he has gone to the altar. This may explain this prayer's omission from the Ordinary Form.

prayer that accompanies the kissing of the altar, the priest asks God pardon for his sins, by the merits of His "saints whose *relics* are here" and of all the saints. While this prayer is not found in the Ordinary Form, the Church has retained the ancient tradition of placing relics of saints within the altar stone. (GIRM 302) This practice calls to mind the early history of the Church, when persecuted Christians used martyrs' tombs for altars. (*Baltimore Catechism III* 937) By kissing the altar above the place where the relics are reserved, the priest silently declares his union with and affection for the saints who have gone before him. This kiss is a "holy kiss" (Rom. 16:16), a "kiss of love" (1 Pet. 5:14), for Christ and for His Church and her members. It is a kiss by which we begin to learn that the liturgy is "the purest and most sublime school of love." (*The Splendour of the Liturgy*, p. 38)

This all takes place before the priest has even spoken a word. If this seems like a lot to be paying attention to or concentrating on… relax. The signs and symbols of the liturgy are rich in content, and you are not expected to grasp their many-layered meanings immediately, nor all at once: they are there to lead you into the mystery of the liturgy, not to confuse you.

Entrance Chant

Accompanying the entrance procession is a chant or hymn. Its purpose is not to greet the priest, but rather "to open the celebration, foster the unity of those who have been gathered, [and] introduce their thoughts to the mystery of the liturgical season or festivity." (GIRM 47) The congregation is not singing to the priest nor to one another, but to the Lord, again evoking that triumphal entry of Jesus into Jerusalem amid shouts of "Hosanna to the Son of David!" (Matt. 21:9; cf. Ps. 118:25-26) Several psalms contain expressions of joy at going up to the Temple in Jerusalem, to "the house of the LORD." (Ps. 122:1) Psalm 95 begins, "O come, let us sing to the LORD; let us make a joyful noise to the rock of our salvation! Let us come into his presence with thanksgiving; let us make a joyful noise to him with songs of praise!"

While most of us are used to opening our hymnals and singing a "gathering song," the Church has already provided words and music for this part of the Mass, even for the particular Mass being celebrated. This chant is part of the "propers" of the Mass (parts that are particular to a given liturgical day); it is called the *introit* (Latin for "he enters") or the "entrance antiphon," and it is usually a selection of verses from a Psalm, although occasionally it comes from other books of the Bible. The introit is thematically related to the Mass, either in the Scriptures to be read or the particular mystery or feast being celebrated.

The introit is not part of the common liturgical experience of many Catholics today (despite being the first option for the entrance chant), but it still makes its presence known in the naming of certain Masses throughout the year. Perhaps you have heard that the Third Sunday of Advent is called *Gaudete* Sunday, or that the Fourth Sunday of Lent is called *Laetare* Sunday. These are the first words in Latin of the entrance antiphons for those two days of the liturgical year: *Gaudete in Domino semper* ("Rejoice in the Lord always...", Phil. 4:4-5) for Advent III, and *Laetare Ierusalem* ("Rejoice, O Jerusalem...", cf. Isa. 66:10-11) for Lent IV. This naming convention has even worked its way into popular culture, for example, in Victor Hugo's *The Hunchback of Notre Dame*. The title character is left, as an infant, on the doorstep of the church on the octave of Easter; the priest who finds him names him Quasimodo, which was the opening of the introit that day: *Quasi modo geniti infantes...* ("Like newborn infants...", 1 Peter 2:2).

Greeting

Unless he was singing the entrance chant or hymn, the priest still has not said anything yet, but everything he has done has been part of his prayer: his deliberate steps to the sanctuary, his reverence to the altar, even his standing at his chair. From his chair, once the chant has concluded, the priest says those familiar words that should begin and end *every* prayer we offer:

Sign of the Cross

In nómine Patris, et Fílii, et Spíritus Sancti.

In the name of the Father, and of the Son,   *Matt. 28:19*
and of the Holy Spirit.

As he says these words, he bows his head as a sign of reverence at the invocation of the Trinity (GIRM 275a), and he traces the Sign of the Cross from his head to his torso, and from his left shoulder to his right; the congregation does the same, and replies with "Amen."

The Sign of the Cross was described in Chapter 2 of this book, and the words that accompany it are explained in great detail in *Praying the Mass: The Prayers of the People*, Chapter 2. It will suffice to make a few brief observations.

We believe that God is a Holy Trinity, three Divine Persons existing for all eternity in one God: Father, Son, and Holy Spirit. The priest does not say "In the name of the Creator, the Redeemer, and the Sanctifier." Although God is Creator, Redeemer, and Sanctifier, those describe what God does for us in time, not Who God is of Himself for all eternity.

When we pray the Sign of the Cross, we confess that God has one name: "In *the* name of the Father, *and* of the Son, *and* of the Holy Spirit." Not "names" but "name." God revealed His name to Moses when He commissioned him to go to Egypt and be His instrument of liberation for His people Israel. God tells Moses that he is to "say this to the sons of Israel, 'I AM has sent me to you.'" (Ex. 3:14) The revealed covenant name of God is *Yahweh*[4] (often represented by the letters *YHWH*) which means "I AM WHO AM."

When Mary and Joseph were told of the impending birth of the Son of God, they were told that the name the child was to be given was already decided for them from before the foundation of the world: "You shall call his name Jesus, for he will save his people from their sins." (Matt. 1:21; cf. Luke 1:31) The English spelling "Jesus" comes from the Latin *Iesus*, which came from the Greek *Iesous*, which came from the Hebrew *Yehoshua* (or the Aramaic *Yeshua*). This name means "*Yah*[weh] saves" (*Yᵉhoshua*). The very name that the Son of God is given at His Incarnation is "God saves," and the angel tells Joseph that this child will grow up to "save *his* people from their sins." The angel is affirming the

---

[4] The use of the Divine Name *Yahweh* is not permitted during the liturgy; the word *Lord* should be used instead. The Divine Name was not spoken aloud in Israel's worship (substituting *Adonai* instead), and the first Christians (Jews and Greeks alike) used the Greek word *Kyrios* instead of the Divine Name. The tradition of the Church has been to avoid speaking the Divine Name aloud. (cf. *Letter to the Bishops' Conferences on "The Name of God"*, dated 29 June 2008, Prot. N. 213/08/L)

age-old Christian truth: Jesus is God! While the name Jesus is proper to the Son alone, it is truly the name of God, because it reveals not only Who God is – "I AM WHO AM" – but also what God does: "God saves."

The Mass begins with the Sign of the Cross to fulfill what St. Paul wrote to the Corinthians: "We preach *Christ crucified...* Christ the power of God and the wisdom of God." (1 Cor. 1:23-24) It is Christ Who has called together the congregation: in His name, and under His sign.

Greeting

The priest, facing the congregation, then greets them with one of three salutations found in the letters of St. Paul. As he does so, he extends and joins his hands in a gesture of genuine Christian welcome, "an expression of peace and an invitation to prayer and recollection." (CMRR 188) The priest gives this greeting only after he has kissed Christ in the altar, as if his lips have thereby been imbued with His presence, which he then imparts to the congregation. (*The Splendour of the Liturgy*, p. 38)

The first option for the priest's greeting is distinctly Trinitarian:

**Grátia Dómini nostri Iesu Christi, et cáritas Dei,
et communicátio Sancti Spíritus sit cum ómnibus vobis.**

The grace of our Lord Jesus Christ, and the love of God,   *2 Cor. 13:14*
and the communion of the Holy Spirit be with you all.

The three Persons of the Trinity work together, so it is not correct to say that grace only comes from the Son, or that love only comes from the Father, or that communion only comes from the Holy Spirit. And yet, this greeting highlights these three gifts – grace, love, and communion – and associates each with a different Person of the Trinity. Let us look at these three pairings more closely.

"The grace of our Lord Jesus Christ." It might surprise you to learn that the word "grace," so fundamental in the preaching of the Apostles after Pentecost, occurs only eight times in the Gospels: four times in Luke 1–2 (sometimes translated as "favor"), and four times in the introduction to St. John's Gospel:

And the Word became flesh and dwelt among us, *full of grace and truth....* And from his fulness have we all received, grace upon grace. For the law was given through Moses; *grace and truth came through Jesus Christ.* (John 1:14-17)

As brief as that may seem, it is an excellent introduction to the concept of grace in the divine economy: grace comes to us through Jesus Christ. The doctrine of grace is fundamental to genuine Christianity: "Grace is favor, the free and undeserved help that God gives us to respond to his call to become children of God, adoptive sons, partakers of the divine nature and of eternal life." (*Catechism* 1996) Grace is so important in the Christian life that St. Paul mentioned it in every single one of his letters, often in a formula like "grace in [*or* through *or* from] Christ."

"The love of God." St. John could very well be called the evangelist of love. From his inspired hand we read that "God so loved the world that he gave his only-begotten Son" (John 3:16), that "love is of God" (1 John 4:7), and the profound but simple "God *is* love." (1 John 4:8) It is in St. John's Gospel that we find the "new" commandment to love one another, not merely as we would wish to be loved, but as Jesus loves us. (cf. John 13:34) And how does Jesus love us? As God the Father has loved Him. (cf. John 15:9) It is only by the love of God that we can love one another, especially those who do not love us. (cf. Matt. 5:44) Love is more than an emotion or a feeling: it is a theological virtue (along with faith and hope). If our love is to be genuine, it must not just model itself after God's love, it must be a true participation in His love, which includes obedience to Him. (cf. 1 John 5:2-3)

"The communion of the Holy Spirit." The word "fellowship" in this greeting has been changed to "communion." Although you will probably see the word "fellowship" used in your Bible in 2 Corinthians 13:14,[5] that word can have secular connotations that fall short of the theological weight that the word "communion" has amassed over nearly 2000 years of Christianity. Consider the "Fellowship of the Ring" from J.R.R. Tolkien's *The Lord of the Rings*. This fellowship of nine adventurers had unity of purpose (the destruction of the Ring), but discord as to how to achieve that end. That fellowship was fleeting and superficial at times, and did not last as it was meant to. Communion, on the other hand, is deeper and more intimate than fellowship. It means "in union with," and

---

[5] The Greek word *koinonia* is found in Acts 2:42, 1 Corinthians 1:9, 2 Corinthians 6:14 and 13:14, Galatians 2:9, and 1 John 1:3-7, and is translated in Latin as *communicatio* ("communion"), *societatem* ("fellowship"), and *participatio* ("participation").

the basis of this union is the presence of the Holy Spirit in us that makes us sons and daughters of a common Father, and sisters and brothers of a common Savior. Two people in *fellowship* may agree on some things and enjoy each other's company from time to time, but to be in *communion* with Jesus Christ in the Holy Spirit means that Jesus abides in you and you abide in Jesus. (cf. John 15:4; 1 John 4:16) God exists in an eternal communion, not just a fellowship, and the "communion of the Holy Spirit" brings us into that divine and eternal relationship: the role of the Holy Spirit is that "we know that [God] abides in us, by the Spirit which he has given us." (1 John 3:24) Finally, this communion is not only with God, but also with all who are themselves in communion with Him: we are a "community," in the truest sense possible, in God.

That is what St. Paul was writing about, and that is what the priest is saying to the congregation. This is no "Good morning" or "Thanks for coming today." This is divine communication, the work of the Holy Spirit in our lives, most especially as we begin the Eucharistic liturgy.

The second option for the greeting is:

Grátia vobis et pax a Deo Patre nostro et Dómino Iesu Christo.

Grace to you and peace	*Col. 1:2; 1 Th. 1:1; 1 Pet. 1:2; 2 Pet. 1:2; Rev. 1:4*
from God our Father	*Rom. 1:7; 1 Cor. 1:3; 2 Cor. 1:2; Gal. 1:3*
and the Lord Jesus Christ.	*Eph. 1:2; Phil. 1:2; 2 Th. 1:2; Phlm. 3*

The wording has changed slightly from the old translation, matching the greeting found in eight of St. Paul's letters. The slightly unnatural word order ("grace to you and peace" rather than "grace and peace to you") is not just some mechanical adherence to the Greek words of Scripture and their Latin translation; it matches the traditional rendering of these verses as found in most English Bibles. This wording should slow us down to consider the meaning of this greeting.

This greeting is found not only in St. Paul's letters, but also in those of St. Peter – "May grace and peace be multiplied to you" – and in the book of Revelation – "Grace to you and peace from him who is and who was and who is to come." We have already considered the grace we receive from God in and through Jesus Christ; what about His peace?

The opening chapters of the Gospel of St. Luke introduce us to the type of peace that comes from God: the *Benedictus* prayer of Zechariah thanks God for His "tender mercy" that brings about the light that shall "guide our feet into the way of peace" (Luke 1:78-79); angels sing "Glory to God in the highest, and on earth peace among men with whom he is pleased" (Luke 2:14); and Simeon, upon seeing the infant Savior in the Temple, prays to God to "let your servant depart in peace" because his eyes have "seen your salvation." (Luke 2:29-30)

Contrast these with one of Jesus' hard sayings: "Do you think that I have come to give peace on earth? No, I tell you, but rather division." (Luke 12:51) Does Jesus come to bring peace or division? The sad truth is that the peace that Jesus brings is not universally accepted, and as a result, "in one house there will be five divided, three against two and two against three." (Luke 12:52) The peace that Jesus gives to us is not a worldly peace, but an other-worldly peace. Jesus describes it at the Last Supper: "Peace I leave with you; my peace I give to you; not as the world gives do I give to you. ... I have said this to you, that in me you may have peace. In the world you have tribulation; but be of good cheer, I have overcome the world." (John 14:27; 16:33) Jesus offers us a peace that is not worldly security, but comfort in victory over the world.

We receive the peace of Christ through the Holy Spirit: peace is a fruit of the Spirit (cf. Gal. 5:22) that comes when we turn our minds from things of the flesh to things of the Spirit. (cf. Rom. 8:6) This is the peace that the priest offers the people at the beginning of Mass. In his book *The Bible and the Mass*, Rev. Peter Stravinskas links this greeting to the altar: "The priest then wishes for the people the grace and peace of God, which he has received from his kissing of the altar." (p. 14)

The third option, which is used several times in the Mass, is:

Dóminus vobíscum.

The Lord be with you. *Ruth 2:4; 1 Sam. 17:37; 2 Th. 3:16*

This is a simple greeting, but it speaks volumes. Instead of speaking of God's peace, love, grace, or communion, the priest prays for us to be in the very presence of the Lord. What does it mean when the Lord is in our midst? It means refuge from worldly strife (cf. Ps. 46:7), victory over sin (cf. Rev. 21:3-4), deliverance from our enemies (cf. 1 Sam. 17:37), and success in our godly endeavors. (cf. Josh. 1:9) Wherever the Lord is, there too are His many graces and blessings. Rev. Nicholas Gihr summarized that "the priest could not wish anything better to the faithful than what is included in the greeting *Dominus vobiscum*" (*The Holy Sacrifice of the Mass*, p. 457), for "if God is for us, who is against us?" (Rom. 8:31)

If you know any Latin, you might wonder why *Dominus vobiscum* is translated as "(may) the Lord *be* with you" (an expression of a hope or desire) rather than "the Lord *is* with you" (a statement of fact). One reason is that by saying "(may) the Lord be with you," the priest offers a prayer for the congregation, rather than simply talking to them about God. Another reason is that it avoids being presumptuous about being in favor with the Lord. Twice in Scripture, a person receives an angelic greeting of "The Lord *is* with you." (Judg. 6:12; Luke 1:28) These angels had it on the highest authority (God Himself) that the Lord was indeed with the person. But there are times in Scripture when a *man* says "The Lord is with you" and he turns out to be wrong. For example, when King David spoke to Nathan the prophet about his desire to build a dwelling for the Lord, Nathan replied, "Go, do all that is in your heart; for the LORD is with you." But he spoke too soon: that very night, the Lord corrected him and revealed what His will was concerning David and the Temple he had intended to build. (cf. 2 Sam. 7:3ff)

The words "The Lord be with you" are nearly identical in meaning to the name "Emmanuel" ("God (is) with us"), which Isaiah prophesied and St. Matthew identified with Jesus. (cf. Isa. 7:14; Matt. 1:23) Thus this greeting is a prayer of the hope for salvation, for Jesus came to "save his people from their sins." (Matt. 1:21)

Before looking at the response of the congregation, there is another greeting to consider. A bishop can say:

Pax vobis.

Peace be with you.   *Judg. 6:23; John 20:19; Eph. 6:23*

While the priest's greetings come from the words of St. Paul, the bishop's greeting comes from the lips of Jesus Himself:

> On the evening of that day, the first day of the week, the doors being shut where the disciples were, for fear of the Jews, Jesus came and stood among them and said to them, *"Peace be with you."* When he had said this, he showed them his hands and his side.

> Then the disciples were glad when they saw the Lord. Jesus said to them again, *"Peace be with you.* As the Father has sent me, even so I send you."* (John 20:19-21)

These words were spoken by the Lord to his frightened disciples on the day of the Resurrection. The peace that Jesus offers dispels fear. Consider how consoling these words are to Catholics who live in fear of daily persecution, just as the first Christians did. The words of Christ install fortitude in weak hearts and reawaken in souls the spark of the Holy Spirit of God, for Whom all things are possible.

St. Peter, the prince of the Apostles, Vicar of Christ, and first Pontiff of the Church, offered this greeting in both of his letters: "May grace and peace be multiplied to you." (1 Pet. 1:2; 2 Pet. 1:2) Every bishop, as a successor of the Apostles, is privileged to use this greeting because he is a special representative of Christ (especially in his own diocese) carrying out His three-fold office of teaching, governing, and sanctifying.

After Jesus gave His peace to the disciples, He announced that He was sending them as the Father had sent Him; then He breathed on them and they received a foretaste of the Holy Spirit Whom they would receive to a greater degree at Pentecost. We will return to this peace and this sending in later chapters.

Response

Each greeting is a prayer asking God for His saving presence among us and His assistance in all we do, especially in these mysteries into which we are entering. The congregation responds by saying "And with your spirit." (cf. Gal. 6:18; 2 Tim. 4:22)

Because the priest's greeting is not simply the religious equivalent of a secular "Good morning" or "How are you?", the response cannot be misunderstood as a "You too." The greeting and its response ground the celebration of Mass in the business of Heaven – what God is doing (the Divine Liturgy), His presence, His power – rather than the business of earth – what we are doing, our personal dispositions, or the weather. These words connect us to the sacred mysteries we are entering and draw us out of our common worldly surroundings.

The response has changed from "And also with you" to "And with your spirit," a change that brings the English text in line not only with the Latin, but also with the Spanish, French, Italian, and German texts.[6] The use of the word "spirit" may seem archaic or even dualist – don't we wish for the Lord to be with the whole priest, not only his spirit? We should look at how St. Paul used the word "spirit" to better understand what he meant.[7] For that, I turn to an explanation given by Msgr. Bruce Harbert, a British priest and participant in the translation process:

> Two descriptions of Paul's view on the spirit have helped me:
>
> One says that in the composition of the human person, the spirit is that part of us which is closest to God and most open to God's gifts, especially to the gift of God's Spirit: my spirit is the bit of me which is closest to God.
>
> The other thing that I read that I found helpful was a reminder that in Paul, "spirit" is not so much contrasted with "body" as with "flesh," and the basis of the contrast in Paul is not between *material* and *immaterial* but between *strength* and *weakness*: the flesh is weak, the spirit is strong.

So then, according to Msgr. Harbert, addressing the spirit of the priest means you are speaking of the strength of God within them.

Another explanation is that we are addressing the priest specifically in that priestly character imprinted on his soul at his ordination. The priest does not greet the people as himself, but as Christ, *in persona Christi*. In his book *What Happens at Mass*, Rev. Jeremy Driscoll, OSB, writes that the people are "addressing the 'spirit' of the priest; that is, that deepest interior part of his being where he has been ordained precisely to lead the people in this sacred action." (p. 25)

St. John Chrysostom (A.D. 347-407), bishop of Constantinople and a Church Father, spoke about the response "and with your spirit" in a sermon at a Divine Liturgy celebrated by another bishop:

> If the Holy Spirit were not in [Bishop Flavian], you would not recently, when he ascended to the holy chair and wished you all peace, have cried out with one accord, "And with your spirit." Thus you cry out to him, not only when he ascends his throne,

---

[6] "English is the only major language of the Roman Rite which did not translate the word *spiritu*. The Italian (*E con il tuo spirito*), French (*Et avec votre esprit*), Spanish (*Y con tu espíritu*) and German (*Und mit deinem Geiste*) renderings of 1970 all translated the Latin word *spiritu* precisely." (USCCB Bishops' Committee on the Liturgy Newsletter, vol. XLI) Non-Romance languages like Russian and Slovak also translate *et cum spiritu tuo* literally.

[7] St. Paul uses the expression four times: Galatians 6:18, Philippians 4:23, 2 Timothy 4:22, and Philemon 1:25.

when he speaks to you and prays for you, but also when he stands at this holy altar to offer the awesome Sacrifice. He does not touch that which lies on the altar before wishing you the grace of our Lord and before you have replied to him: "And with your spirit." By this cry you are reminded that he who stands at the altar does nothing, and that the gifts that rest thereon are not the merits of man, but that the grace of the Holy Spirit is present and, descending on all, accomplishes this mysterious Sacrifice. We see indeed a man, but God it is Who acts through him. Nothing human takes place at this holy altar. (*First Homily for the Feast of Pentecost*, 4)

According to St. John Chrysostom, the response to the bishop (or priest) emphasizes the presence and action of the Holy Spirit in him.

Having called upon the Lord and greeted one another with dignity befitting sons and daughters of God, the priest and people turn their attention inward briefly to recognize their sins and seek reconciliation.

Penitential Act

Shortly after Jesus' entry into Jerusalem on that first Palm Sunday, after the crowds had greeted Him, He made his way to the Temple. There He drove out the money changers (who exchanged foreign currency for the Temple coinage at dishonest rates). Then He healed the blind and the lame who came to Him. (cf. Matt. 21:12-14) We experience this too: after the entrance procession and the greeting, our temples get cleansed and our infirmities are healed.[8] This cleansing and healing is necessary because we are temples of the Holy Spirit. (cf. 1 Cor. 6:19; 2 Cor. 6:16)

First, the priest invites the congregation to the Penitential Act:[9]

**Fratres, agnoscámus peccáta nostra,
ut apti simus ad sacra mystéria celebránda.**

Brethren (brothers and sisters),	*Ps. 32:5; 38:18; Sir. 4:26*
let us acknowledge our sins,	*Jer. 14:20; Jas. 5:16; 1 John 1:9*
and so prepare ourselves	
to celebrate the sacred mysteries.	*1 Macc. 4:56; 1 Cor. 4:1; 5:8*

---

[8] The Penitential Act *does not* take the place of confession of mortal sins, which can only normally be absolved through the sacrament of Reconciliation.

[9] One element of the liturgical reform called for by the Second Vatican Council was the inclusion of occasional directives spoken by the priest serving as introductions to the various actions of the Mass: "Instruction which is more explicitly liturgical should also be given in a variety of ways; if necessary, short directives … should be provided within the rites themselves. But they should occur only at the more suitable moments, and be in prescribed or similar words." (SC 35)

The Penitential Act is a reminder that we who worship God belong to a community with flaws, "full of people who need to confess their sins and pray for one another." (*Beyond Smells and Bells*, p. 36) St. Paul wrote of its necessity to the Corinthians: "Let a man examine himself, and so eat of the bread and drink of the cup." (1 Cor. 11:28) By the early second century, an act of confession was part of the Eucharistic liturgy. The *Didache*, an early Christian instruction on doctrine, liturgy, and morality, exhorts the faithful to gather on the Lord's Day, "first confessing your transgressions, that your sacrifice may be pure." (*Didache* 14:1)

As the words of the priest indicate, this preparatory action requires us to "acknowledge our sins." Instead of just calling them to mind (as in the old translation), we are acknowledging them before God, the saints and angels in Heaven, and our brothers and sisters around us. We admit our sins and ask God for His mercy, so that we can be reconciled with one another before approaching the altar. (cf. Matt. 5:23-24) As the *Catechism of the Catholic Church* instructs us, "forgiveness is the prerequisite for both the Eucharistic liturgy and personal prayer." (*Catechism* 2631)

It is no accident that the priest uses the word "sins" rather than, say, "weaknesses." Jesus did not come to save us from our weaknesses, but from our sins. (cf. Matt. 1:21; Luke 1:77) In fact, St. Paul speaks rather highly of his weaknesses (not his sins) in his second letter to the Church in Corinth: "I will all the more gladly boast of my weaknesses, that the power of Christ may rest upon me. For the sake of Christ, then, I am content with weaknesses, insults, hardships, persecutions, and calamities; for when I am weak, then I am strong." (2 Cor. 12:9-10; cf. 2 Cor. 11:30) We can be content with weaknesses, but never with sin.

After this introduction to the Penitential Act, there is a moment of silence. We should use this silence properly: it is not meant for dramatic effect, but for silent reflection and examination of conscience. If you are having trouble finding any sins when you examine your conscience, you may be lacking a decent definition of "sin."

The Hebrew word for "sin" is *chet*, a term used in archery, meaning "to miss the mark," to fall short of the target. St. Paul, in a well-known verse from his letter to the Romans, defines sin in exactly this way: "all have *sinned* and *fall short* of the glory of God." (Rom. 3:23) God's glory,

His perfect goodness and love, is our target, and when we fail to hit that target, we sin. Another way to describe sin is as an act of separating God from a part of your life. For example, if you sin by mistreating your brother, not loving him as you should, you are in effect saying to God, "I am separating my relationship with my brother from You; *my* rules, not Yours, govern this part of my life."

The *Catechism* provides a very succinct definition of sin: "an *abuse of the freedom* that God gives to created persons so that they are capable of loving him and loving one another." (*Catechism* 387) Sin is a corruption of our freedom: God gives us the freedom to choose the good, but we misuse that freedom to choose evil. It may sound silly at first that God gives us freedom so that we can choose to do good, but if you have ever been pressured into doing wrong, it should be clear to you how hard it can be sometimes to do the right thing. Sin is slavery; virtue is freedom.

Sins do not "hurt" God in the same way that sticks and stones can break our bones, but they do offend Him and dishonor Him. Sin is an insult to God, a refusal to show Him the love and respect and obedience that are due to Him. Yet there is a way that sin *can* be said to hurt God: the Son of God accepted the ability to suffer when He assumed a human body, and He did indeed suffer hunger, thirst, and exhaustion, as well as most terrible pains in His Passion. In His glorified Body, He can no longer suffer pain, but in His Mystical Body – that is, the Church – He can and does suffer. St. Paul, in a mystical and admittedly confusing verse of his letter to the Church in Colossae, wrote: "I rejoice in my sufferings for your sake, and in my flesh *I complete what is lacking in Christ's afflictions* for the sake of his body, that is, the Church." (Col. 1:24) He came to this wondrous knowledge from the very first words our Lord ever spoke to him: "Saul, Saul, why do you persecute *me*?" (Acts 9:4) When Saul was persecuting the Church, he was actually persecuting Jesus Christ Himself. What does this all mean regarding sin? Our sins hurt the Mystical Body of Christ, the Church: no sin is strictly private (between you and God); all sin has a social consequence, though we may not see it in this life: "If one member suffers, all suffer together." (1 Cor. 12:26) This personal act of penitence at the beginning of Mass reminds us that in order to correct the "structures of sin" (Ven. Pope John Paul II,

Sollicitudo Rei Socialis 36) that plague our society, we must first look into our *own* souls: "the only adequate cure for sin must begin at the centre of the soul." (*The Splendour of the Liturgy*, p. 27)

With all that in mind, we can participate in the Penitential Act with a contrite heart, striving "for the holiness without which no one will see the Lord." (Heb. 12:14) In the Extraordinary Form of the Mass, there is only one form of the Penitential Act, but in the Ordinary Form there are three forms, and on Sundays (especially during the Easter season) this can be replaced by a rite of the blessing and sprinkling of water, a reminder of our Baptism in which we received forgiveness from sin and "appeal[ed] to God for a clear conscience." (1 Pet. 3:21)

Form A (*Confiteor*)

The first form is known as the *Confiteor* (the first word of the prayer in Latin, meaning "I confess"). In this prayer, we confess our sins to God and to one another and invoke the communion of saints, asking all the angels and saints, as well as one another, to pray for us to God.[10]

In the Extraordinary Form the *Confiteor* is prayed first by the priest and then by the servers and the rest of the congregation; in the Ordinary Form it is prayed by the priest and congregation together. We must all remember that every priest, just as much as every layman, is in need of forgiveness for his sins: "the holiness of [the priest's] priesthood which he owes to Christ does not exempt him from the common weakness of men which he owes to his humanity." (*The Splendour of the Liturgy*, p. 29)

It is worth pointing out that the *Confiteor* in the Extraordinary Form, as prayed by the congregation, does not consider sins of omission, nor does it mention "my brothers and sisters," while the version prayed in the Ordinary Form does. Remember that just as you are asking your brothers and sisters in the congregation to pray for you, *they* are asking *you* to do the same. Do not neglect so great a responsibility!

Form B

The second form is a dialogue between the priest and the congregation; the priest begins a verse of Scripture, and the congregation completes it.[11]

---

[10] The *Confiteor* in the Ordinary Form invokes the Blessed Virgin Mary. The Extraordinary Form invokes additional saints by name: Michael the Archangel, John the Baptist, and Peter and Paul.
[11] Form B is based on the concluding dialogue of the Penitential Act in the Extraordinary Form.

This style of praying is called *antiphonal*; it is often used when the psalms are prayed by a monastic community: one half of the group would chant the first half of a verse, and the other half of the group would chant the second half.

The priest begins with Baruch 3:2, saying:

Miserére nostri, Dómine.

Have mercy on us, O Lord.   *Bar. 3:2*

and the congregation replies, "For we have sinned against you."[12]   Then the priest prays the first half of Psalm 85:7.

Osténde nobis, Dómine, misericórdiam tuam.

Show us, O Lord, your mercy.   *Ps. 85:7*

which the congregation completes: "And grant us your salvation."

Dom Prosper Guéranger, a nineteenth century Benedictine priest and liturgical scholar, explained why this verse from Psalm 85 is used:

> [These are] the words of David, who … is praying for the coming of the Messias. In the Mass, before the Consecration, we await the coming of our Lord, as they, who lived before the Incarnation, awaited the promised Messias. By that word *mercy*, which is here used by the Prophet, we are not to understand the goodness of God; but, we ask of God, that he will [send us] the Saviour, by whom salvation is to come upon us. These few words of the Psalm take us back in spirit, to the season of Advent, when we are unceasingly asking for him who is to come. (*Explanation of the Prayers and Ceremonies of Holy Mass*, p. 7)

Dom Guéranger's point should remind us, as we look at the rest of the prayers of the Mass, that to understand the words of the prayers that come from Scripture, we need to look at their context in Scripture.

So where do the words from Baruch fit in? Baruch 1:15–3:8 is one long prayer of contrition to the Lord: it expresses the righteousness of the Lord in contrast to the unfaithfulness of Israel to their covenant with God, which led to their exile. Much like the *Confiteor* includes a threefold admission of guilt – "through my fault, through my fault, through my most grievous fault" – so in the prayer of Baruch we read "we have *sinned*, we have *been ungodly*, we have *done wrong*, O Lord our God, against

---

[12] This verse is the antiphon of the Lenten hymn *Attende Domine* ("Hear us, O Lord").

all your ordinances." (Bar. 2:12) The prayer goes on to recognize that the Israelites were moved to contrition by God Who, in His compassion, gave them "a heart that obeys and ears that hear." (Bar. 2:31)

As these words from Baruch are spoken at Mass, let us remember that we who belong to God because of the New Covenant that He established with us in the Blood of His Son are still sinners and are still in need of forgiveness every day. We must live "worthy of the calling to which [we] have been called" (Eph. 4:1), and when we fail to do so, we must turn to the Lord with contrite hearts and seek His mercy. His mercy has been manifested in the flesh: His Son, Jesus Christ, Who is our salvation. It is so easy for us to say these words, but so difficult to keep their promise. (*The Splendour of the Liturgy*, p. 24)

Form C

The third form integrates three petitions to the Lord Jesus Christ with the *Kyrie* to form a litany. The petitions made by the priest, deacon, or cantor can vary, but the responses ("Lord, have mercy" and "Christ, have mercy") are always the same. One common set of petitions follows:

Qui missus es sanáre contrítos corde:
Kyrie, eléison.

You were sent to heal the contrite of heart:	*Ps. 147:3; Isa. 57:15; 61:1*
Lord, have mercy. (*Kyrie, eleison.*)	*Ps. 123:3; Matt. 20:31; Luke 17:13*

Qui peccatóres vocáre venísti:
Christe, eléison.

You came to call sinners:	*Matt. 9:13; 1 Tim. 1:15*
Christ, have mercy. (*Christe, eleison.*)	*1 Tim. 1:2; Jude 21*

Qui ad déxteram Patris sedes, ad interpellándum pro nobis:
Kyrie, eléison.

You are seated at the right hand of the Father	*Eph. 1:20; Col. 3:1; Heb. 1:3*
to intercede for us:	*Rom. 8:34; Heb. 7:25*
Lord, have mercy. (*Kyrie, eleison.*)	

These petitions originated as "tropes," embellishments to the *Kyrie* in its various musical settings.

All three petitions are specifically related to sin and forgiveness. The first evokes Isaiah 61:1, some of which Jesus read in the synagogue at His hometown of Nazareth: "The Spirit of the Lord GOD is upon me … to bind up the brokenhearted." The second comes from St. Matthew's Gospel where he records the Lord's call to him, a tax collector: "I came not to call the righteous, but sinners." (Matt. 9:13) The third comes from St. Paul's letter to the Romans where he says that Christ "is at the right hand of God, [where he] indeed intercedes for us." (Rom. 8:34)

The petitions in general describe what our Lord has done, is doing, or will do, as if the priest were saying, "Lord, sent to heal the contrite of heart, have mercy." Christ came for us sinners, but forgiveness requires contrition on our part, and His work on our behalf continues in Heaven, "since he always lives to make intercession for [us]." (Heb. 7:25) This is why, even after being baptized into Christ, we still require forgiveness of our sins and confess them. The concept of "once saved, always saved" popular with some Protestants is not compatible with Catholic doctrine, which takes into account the numerous exhortations found in the New Testament to persevere in faith (cf. Matt. 24:13; 2 Tim. 2:12; Heb. 12:1) and not to be presumptuous. (cf. 1 Cor. 9:27; 10:12; Heb. 2:1; 3:12) Our Catholic identity calls us to continual conversion and contrition for our sins, lest we harden our hearts and lose our salvation through mortal sin.

Absolution after the Penitential Act

Following all three forms of the Penitential Act is an "absolution" by the priest, not to be confused with the absolution received in the sacrament of Confession; in the Mass, this prayer of absolution is not a declaration but a petition.[13]

Misereátur nostri omnípotens Deus et, dimíssis peccátis nostris, perdúcat nos ad vitam ætérnam.

May almighty God have mercy on us, *Ps. 123:2-3*
forgive us our sins, and bring us to everlasting life. *Matt. 25:46; Jude 21*

The three things this prayer mentions – mercy, forgiveness, and being brought to everlasting life – are not just items on a checklist. Rather, the prayer is showing that it is by God's mercy that our sins are forgiven, and

---

[13] This is supported by the fact that in the Extraordinary Form the congregation (or altar server) prays such an absolution for the priest after he has prayed his *Confiteor*. In addition, there is no Sign of the Cross directed to be made in the Ordinary Form as the priest says this prayer.

it is with our sins forgiven (as the Latin text literally states[14]) that God brings us to everlasting life.

Consider this analogy: a ten-year-old boy is playing outside at home, and his mother comes out and tells him, "put away your toys, wash your hands, and get into the car so we can go to grandma's house." The boy puts away his toys and washes his hands, but on the way to the car he manages (as only boys his age can) to get his hands dirty again. The boy did as he was told, did he not? But that is not what his mother meant: she expected his hands to be clean *when* he entered the car. That is what this prayer means as well. Being forgiven of our sins is a necessity for being brought to everlasting life, just as having clean hands was a necessity for getting into the car, for "nothing unclean shall enter" the Temple of God in Heaven. (Rev. 21:27)

The prayer asks God to "bring us" to everlasting life, and we should have the image of Jesus as the Good Shepherd in our heads. The word "bring" can sound completely passive, but the Latin word *perducere* means "to bring" and "to lead." God brings us, He leads us, to His divine life, as if holding us by the hand. Jesus the Good Shepherd, "calls his own sheep by name and *leads* them out" to pasture. (John 10:3) Jesus leads us, and we follow Him willingly; He brings us through the trials of this life, not without our cooperation, but with our assent, our "Amen."

Kyrie

If Form A or B of the Penitential Act is used, the *Kyrie* follows. (It is omitted if Form C is used, which includes the *Kyrie*.) The acclamations "*Kyrie, eleison*" and "*Christe, eleison*" are Greek for "Lord, have mercy" and "Christ, have mercy." Even when Mass is celebrated entirely in Latin, these words are never translated from Greek to Latin.

Kýrie, eléison.
Christe, eléison.
Kýrie, eléison.

Lord, have mercy.   *Ps. 123:3; Matt. 20:31; Luke 17:13*
Christ, have mercy.   *1 Tim. 1:2; Jude 21*
Lord, have mercy.

---

[14] The phrase "*et, dimíssis peccátis nostris, perdúcat nos*" literally means "and, with our sins forgiven, bring us."

These acclamations are said two or three times, alternating between the priest (or choir) and the congregation. The repetition of these prayers is a sign of their urgency and fervency: we are always in need of God's mercy, and there is never a reason to delay seeking it.

Following the *Kyrie*, the *Gloria* is sung (or said) on Sundays outside of Advent and Lent and on other solemnities and feasts.

Collect

The Introductory Rites conclude with the *Collect* (emphasis on the first syllable), which is the first of three "proper" prayers in the Mass, the other two being the Prayer over the Offerings and the Post-Communion Prayer. The propers vary from day to day, and relate to the current liturgical season or the particular mystery of the faith being celebrated.[15] Because these prayers vary, their content is not within the scope of this book; however, we can still reflect on their purpose so as to be able to understand them more deeply when they are prayed.

Before the priest prays the Collect, he joins his hands and invites the people to pray:

Orémus.

Let us pray.

After this, everyone observes a brief silence, and then the priest opens his arms and prays the Collect, closing them once again as he reaches the conclusion. Let us consider the words and the silence.

There is a great deal packed into that one Latin word, these three short English words. As Rev. Turner points out in his essay on liturgical texts, one could argue that the priest and people have already *been* praying, so saying "Let us pray" seems redundant. Shouldn't he say "Let us *continue to* pray"? Rev. Turner answers that question:

> It is true that everyone has addressed God already at least in the act of penitence and the Glory to God. But the priest and people have also been addressing each other in texts like the greeting and introductions. The purpose of the *Oremus* is to focus our attention

---

[15] Each of these proper prayers follows a procession: the Collect after the Entrance procession, the Prayer over the Offerings after the Offertory procession, and the Post-Communion Prayer after the Communion procession.

on what we are about to do; it need not refer back to a part of what we have just done. (*Pastoral Ramifications of Liturgical Texts*)

There are no wasted words in the liturgy; Rev. Turner goes on to say that "When the priest says, 'Let us pray,' his words should genuinely prompt prayer." Cardinal Ratzinger has the same idea: "spoken words also have a meaning. ... 'Let us pray' [is] an invitation to share in a movement which reaches down into our inner depths." (*Feast of Faith*, p. 89)

The priest does not say, "Let *me* pray," as if the congregation has nothing to do with the Collect; he says "Let *us* pray." The priest invites the whole congregation to pray with him. The Collect orients all our prayers, binding them into one and presenting them, in the words of the Church, to God. Although the Collect is a "presidential" prayer (proper to the celebrant of the Mass), everyone at Mass assents to it by saying "Amen" at its conclusion. While the priest is praying the Collect, the congregation should be participating through attentive listening, so that they can be praying it silently in their hearts.

The silence that follows the invitation to prayer is not there simply to cover the time it takes for an altar server to bring the *Roman Missal* up to the priest. Between the words "Let us pray" and the Collect, everyone should "be conscious of the fact that they are in God's presence and ... formulate their petitions mentally." (GIRM 54) Liturgical silence is never supposed to be uncomfortable or awkward; it should be reverent, powerful, and prayerful. "Silence speaks profoundly to the inner being," writes Rev. Gunter, and it "needs to be fostered in the Ordinary Form as a normal and humble response to mystery."

The priest then prays the Collect. The Church calls this prayer the Collect (not simply the "opening prayer") because "it collects and gathers together the supplications of the multitude, speaking them all with one voice." (*Douay Catechism* 126) The "opening prayer" of the Mass, as we have seen, is the Sign of the Cross, if not the entrance antiphon.

The Collects in the Roman tradition are often marked by use of antithesis, that is, the juxtaposition of two ideas or concepts, one earthly and the other heavenly. Msgr. Charles Pope, in a series called "Mass in Slow Motion" for the web site of the Archdiocese of Washington, lists three common pairings: human struggle and divine help; temporal deeds or situations and eternal truths; earthly suffering and eternal blessedness.

Most Collects address the Father, although some address the Son. They usually adhere to the following pattern: an **invocation** of God, the **recollection** of His works or characteristics, the presentation of a **petition** and its **purpose**, and a **conclusion**.

Here is the Collect from the Fourth Sunday of Lent as an example:

Deus,
qui per Verbum tuum
humáni géneris reconciliatiónem mirabíliter operáris,
praesta, quaesumus,
ut pópulus christiánus prompta devotióne et álacri fide
ad ventúra sollémnia váleat festináre.

Per Dóminum...

O God,	*Invocation*
who through your Word	*Recollection*
reconcile the human race to yourself in a wonderful way,	
grant, we pray,	
that with prompt devotion and eager faith	*Petition*
the Christian people may hasten	*Purpose*
toward the solemn celebrations to come.	
Through our Lord, Jesus Christ, your Son,	*Conclusion*
who lives and reigns with you in the unity of the Holy Spirit,	
one God, for ever and ever.	

God is invoked as the One Who reconciles (in the *present* tense) humanity to Himself through His Word, the mystery that is at the core of the season of Lent; He is petitioned as the One Who can give strength to the Christian people especially during this penitential season, so that we can come to the solemnities of Holy Week and the Paschal Triduum with devotion and eager faith. This prayer is made, as all our prayers, through our Lord Jesus Christ who lives and reigns with the Father in the unity of the Holy Spirit.

The prayers of the Introductory Rites are "a unity, leading us in a kind of crescendo, whereby we are brought from a sinful world into the presence of God and made worthy to approach Him, so as to hear His word and to participate in the offering of the Eucharistic Sacrifice and in the reception of the fruits of that sacrifice." (*The Bible and the Mass*, pp. 19-20)

These rites begin with a procession to the altar and end with a prayer that seeks the assistance of God in our procession toward Heaven. Every element, from the Sign of the Cross to the Collect, unites us as one in worshiping God: one Body in His name, in His presence, in need of His mercy, praising His goodness, and presenting our common needs. The congregation has approached God under the leadership of the priest, and now He approaches in the Liturgy of the Word.

Questions for Reflection: Priests

1) **Interpret:** How does the reverence that Moses showed to the "holy ground" (Ex. 3:5) and that Israel showed to the Temple translate into the Church's reverence for her own sacred spaces?

2) **Interpret:** How is water used in the Old Testament as a symbol of purification?

3) **Interpret:** How does the role of the priest in the Church differ from the role of the priest in the Mosaic Covenant? How are the two similar?

4) **Explain:** Of all the possible ways to show reverence to the altar, why does the Church choose a kiss?

5) **Explain:** How can silence be used to create an atmosphere of prayer?

6) **Explain:** Why does the *Catechism* teach that prayer (including the Mass) should begin with contrition? (cf. *Catechism* 2631)

7) **Explain:** How can "let us pray" be spoken as a prayer? How can it be spoken in such a way as to elicit genuine prayer?

8) **Relate:** How can the Introductory Rites of the Mass remind us of the beginning of our Christian life?

9) **Relate:** How does the *Confiteor* remind us of our duty of prayer for one another?

10) **Relate:** What can you do to help your congregation pay closer attention to the Collect and the other proper prayers of the Mass?

Questions for Reflection: Laity

1) **Interpret:** The Israelites were commanded by God to treat with kindness all strangers and sojourners, because they were strangers in Egypt. (cf. Lev. 19:33-34) How are visitors (Catholic and non-Catholic) treated in your parish?

2) **Interpret:** Read some of the Songs of Ascent (Psalms 120-134), which were sung by pilgrim Jews on their way up to Jerusalem. What do these psalms teach you about what Jews thought of their holy city and Temple? How can these psalms shape your attitude toward going to Mass?

3) **Interpret:** Jesus encourages His disciples both to spend time in private prayer (Matt. 6:6) and communal prayer. (cf. Matt. 18:20) What are the advantages of each? Which is more predominant in the Mass, and why?

4) **Explain:** Which greeting speaks most to you? What about it is inviting, challenging, or consoling?

5) **Explain:** Why do we ask God for forgiveness at the *beginning* of the Mass?

6) **Explain:** How do you respond to "Let us pray"? Do you treat these words as just some ritual expression, or as an authentic invitation to prayer?

7) **Relate:** Do you listen to the invocations during Form C of the Penitential Act? What do they tell you about Who Jesus is?

8) **Relate:** How can you use the Introductory Rites as a model or example for starting your day in prayer?

9) **Relate:** Do the Introductory Rites remind you of your baptism? What do the two have in common?

10) **Relate:** Do you pay attention to the Collect? How can it direct your thoughts throughout the Mass?

Joshua said to the sons of Israel,
"Come here, and hear the words of the LORD your God."
(Joshua 3:9)

Blessed is he who reads aloud the words of the prophecy,
and blessed are those who hear, and who keep what is written therein.
(Revelation 1:3)

4

Liturgy of the Word

WHEN YOU READ the phrase "the word of the Lord" in Scripture, it generally means "a revelation from God." By His word, God reveals Himself to man. That self-revelation reached its summit in the Incarnation of the Word, Jesus Christ, the Son of the living God.

God reveals Himself to us – that is, we encounter Him – in many ways at Mass. The Constitution on the Sacred Liturgy lists these ways:

> Christ is always present in His Church, especially in her liturgical celebrations. He is present in the sacrifice of the Mass, not only **(1)** in the person of His minister, "the same now offering, through the ministry of priests, who formerly offered himself on the cross," but **(2)** especially under the Eucharistic species. By His power He is present **(3)** in the sacraments, so that when a man baptizes it is really Christ Himself who baptizes. He is present **(4)** *in His word*, since it is He Himself who speaks when the holy scriptures are read in the Church. He is present, lastly, **(5)** when the Church prays and sings, for He promised: "Where two or three are gathered together in my name, there am I in the midst of them." (SC 7)

While the Second Vatican Council reaffirmed the Church's belief that Christ is present in a most excellent and substantial way in the Eucharist, it also recognized that the Scriptures are another genuine point of contact with the Lord, because Scripture *is* the word of the Lord: the books of the Bible were written under the inspiration of the Holy Spirit and have God as their primary author. (cf. *Catechism* 105) Although the words are human words, they are the words of God. God took on human *nature* in the Incarnation; He took on human *expression* in Scripture.

In the readings from Scripture, "God speaks to his people, opening up to them the mystery of redemption and salvation and offering them spiritual nourishment." (GIRM 55) This communication between God and man is explained by the homily given after the Gospel. All should be listening attentively in silence as the readings are proclaimed, and there is no need to rush from reading to reading: the Liturgy of the Word should "promote meditation, and so any sort of haste that hinders recollection must clearly be avoided." (GIRM 56) It is permitted for the celebrant to "give the faithful a *very brief* introduction ... to the Liturgy of the Word (before the readings)" (GIRM 31), but that introduction should not take the form of a miniature homily – it is important not to disrupt the natural flow of the liturgy with copious instructions and commentaries that are more appropriate outside of Mass (or possibly in the homily).

Origen, a third century theologian, drew a poignant parallel between the Eucharist and the Scriptures:

> When you receive the body of the Lord ... you protect it with caution and veneration lest any small part fall from it, lest anything of the consecrated gift be lost. For you believe, and correctly, that you are answerable if anything falls from there by neglect. But if you are so careful to preserve his body, and rightly so, how do you think that there is less guilt to have neglected God's word than to have neglected His Body? (*On Exodus*, 13, 3)

In this chapter you will see how highly the Church regards and venerates the Holy Scriptures.

"The word of the Lord."

In his book of Revelation, St. John writes the following words: "Blessed is he who *reads aloud* the words of the prophecy, and blessed are those who *hear*." (Rev. 1:3) This applies not only to that particular book, but to all of Scripture, and especially to its proclamation in the liturgy. Private reading of the Bible is great, but the Church compiled the books of the

Bible to be read communally and liturgically.[1] The blessing announced in the book of Revelation is realized at every Mass when someone "reads aloud the words of the prophecy" and when the rest of us "hear."

Traditionally, the liturgical reading of Scripture is a ministerial duty (not a presidential one) meaning that it is proper for a lector to read the First and Second Readings, and a deacon (or even a priest other than the celebrant) to read the Gospel. The lector makes a profound bow to the altar before entering the sanctuary (*Ceremonial of Bishops* 72), and then stands at the ambo to proclaim the reading. At the end of the First and Second Readings, the lector says:

Verbum Dómini.

The word of the Lord.   *Gen. 15:1; Jer. 1:4; Acts 8:25; 13:49*

This is a statement of fact – we have just heard the word of the Lord proclaimed in our midst – but it is also a prayer in its own way. It is as if the lector has said to us the words of the psalmist: "Today, when you hear his voice, do not harden your hearts." (Heb. 4:7; cf. Ps. 95:8) The lector is a prophet of sorts, speaking God's revelation to His people; he wants you to know and to believe that what he has proclaimed and what you have heard is truly from God.

The lector echoes the prayer of thanksgiving from St. Paul's first letter to the Thessalonians: "we also thank God constantly for this, that when you received the word of God which you heard from us, you accepted it not as the word of men but as what it really is, the word of God, which is at work in you believers." (1 Th. 2:13) Some previous English translations rendered this acclamation by the lector as "*This is* the word of the Lord," perhaps for this very reason.

What do we *do* with the word of the Lord? First and foremost, we hear it. In this regard, the participation of the priest is the same as that of the congregation: during the readings, all sit in reverent silence, listening intently to the proclamation of God's word. Second, we follow the example set for us by the Blessed Mother, who "kept all these things" she had seen and heard, "pondering them in her heart." (Luke 2:19) That

---

[1] In fact, the Church grants an indulgence to those faithful who, with that veneration due to the divine word, read the Scriptures in a spirit of prayer. (cf. *Enchiridion Indulgentiarum* 30)

sentence could also be translated as *"treasured* all these things, *encountering* them in her heart." We should do likewise, treating the word we hear as a treasure, storing it in our minds and hearts, and returning to it to encounter it as "living and active." (Heb. 4:12) And third, because it is "living and active," it should move us to go out and live according to the word we have received, sharing it with the world. We must not be hearers of the word only, but doers of the word as well. (cf. Jas. 1:22)

What happens when the living and active word of God is lived in and shared with a world that is, in comparison, lifeless and stagnant? We can find an answer in a vision received by the prophet Ezekiel that shows just how powerful the word of the Lord is:

> The Spirit of the LORD ... said to me, "Prophesy to these bones, and say to them, O dry bones, *hear the word of the LORD.* Thus says the Lord GOD to these bones: Behold, I will cause breath to enter you, and *you shall live."* (Ezek. 37:1-5)

The Sequence

A few times throughout the year, there is an additional chant sung during the Liturgy of the Word before the Gospel. This chant is called a *Sequence* and is a "proper" liturgical hymn of the Mass. (The hymns that we are familiar with singing at Mass are not actually part of the Roman Rite, but the Sequence hymns *are* part of the Roman Rite. Another example of a proper hymn is *Gloria, laus, et honor* sung during the procession on Palm Sunday; you probably know this hymn by its rather accurate English translation, "All Glory, Laud, and Honor.") Because the Sequences are so rare – there are only four of them, and two are optional – when they are sung they should command our full attention, as they proclaim in song the mystery being celebrated that day.

There are four sequences, written between the eleventh to thirteenth centuries, designated for particular feasts of the year: *Victimae paschali laudes* ("Praise the Paschal Victim") on Easter Sunday, *Veni Sancte Spiritus* ("Come, Holy Spirit") on Pentecost Sunday, *Lauda Sion Salvatorem* ("Zion, Praise the Savior") on the Solemnity of the Most Holy Body and Blood of the Lord (also known as *Corpus Christi*), and *Stabat Mater* ("The Mother, Standing") on the feast of Our Lady of Sorrows.[2]

---

[2] The Sequence is optional, except on Easter Sunday and Pentecost Sunday. (cf. GIRM 64)

Blessing for the Gospel

After the readings, the congregation sings the Alleluia (or its replacement during Lent). As this is being sung, the deacon or priest who will read the Gospel prepares himself for this most important ministry of the word. This is the first prayer of the Mass prayed in a "low voice," that is, quietly. There are two prayers, and the one used depends on who will be proclaiming the Gospel.[3]

If a priest proclaims the Gospel, he stands before the altar and, making a profound bow, prays in a low voice:

Munda cor meum ac lábia mea, omnípotens Deus,
ut sanctum Evangélium tuum digne váleam nuntiáre.

Cleanse my heart and my lips, almighty God,	*Isa. 6:5-7*
that I may worthily proclaim your holy Gospel.	*Eph. 6:19*

This prayer's word order has changed slightly to better match the Latin, and the priest says "your holy Gospel" instead of just "your Gospel."

If, however, a deacon is proclaiming the Gospel, he stands before the celebrant, and making a profound bow, says:

Iube, domne,[4] benedícere.

Your blessing, Father.

In the old translation, the deacon said, "Father, *give me* your blessing." The quality of that language calls to mind for me the Prodigal Son in the parable: "Father, *give me* the share of property…" (Luke 15:12) Now the words sound less like a demand and more like a polite, yet confident, request: "Your blessing, Father."

The priest replies with the following prayer, also said in a low voice:

Dóminus sit in corde tuo et in lábiis tuis:
ut digne et competénter annúnties Evangélium suum:
in nómine Patris, et Fílii, et Spíritus Sancti.

May the Lord be in your heart and on your lips,	*Ps. 19:14*
that you may proclaim his Gospel worthily and well,	*Eph. 6:19*
in the name of the Father and of the Son + and of the Holy Spirit.	

---

[3] Both prayers are used, one after the other, in the Extraordinary Form.
[4] The word *domne* in the Latin text is not a typo for *Domine* ("Lord"), but an abbreviation of that word to distinguish the Lord from the priest who acts in His person.

As the priest invokes the Holy Trinity, he makes the Sign of the Cross over the deacon, who also makes the Sign of the Cross and says "Amen."

These two prayers look similar, and you might wonder why both of them are used in the Extraordinary Form if one is simply a repetition of the other. However, the prayer that the priest prays for himself is for *purification* (cleansing), while the prayer that is prayed over the deacon is for *benediction* (blessing). In the Extraordinary Form, then, the first prayer prepares the priest for the second prayer.

God's call to Isaiah provides the reason for these prayers. As he had a vision of the Lord seated upon His throne in the heavenly Temple, he cried out, "I am a man of unclean lips, and I dwell in the midst of a people of unclean lips." (Isa. 6:5) But then one of the angels he saw in his vision came to him,

> having in his hand a burning coal which he had taken with tongs from the altar. And he touched my mouth, and said: "Behold, this has touched your lips; your guilt is taken away, and your sin forgiven." And I heard the voice of the Lord saying, "Whom shall I send, and who will go for us?" Then I said, "Here am I! Send me." And he said, "Go, and say to this people..." (Isa. 6:5-9)

First Isaiah is purified by the burning coal taken from the altar of incense. In like manner, the priest asks that his lips and heart might be purified through the gracious mercy of God, so that he may worthily proclaim the Gospel.[5] The need for this prayer for purification of the lips (and by association, the tongue) is affirmed by St. James: the tongue is "a restless evil, full of deadly poison. With it we bless the Lord and Father, and with it we curse men, who are made in the likeness of God. From the *same mouth* come blessing and cursing. My brethren, this ought not to be so." (Jas. 3:8-10) This purification of the lips should also be a reminder to the priest of when his lips touched the altar at the beginning of Mass: may he not let those lips that "retain the print of the altar ... profane the language of love." (*The Splendour of the Liturgy*, p. 37)

Isaiah, having been purified, is sent to speak prophetic words; that is, he has God's blessing to preach: "Go, and say..." Thus the deacon asks the priest for a blessing from God, and the priest prays that God would

---

[5] The prayer for purification in the Extraordinary Form explicitly mentions the cleansing of the lips of Isaiah and the "gracious mercy" of God; this is not present in the Ordinary Form.

be in the heart and on the lips of the deacon: in his heart, that he will worthily (*digne*) announce the good news "with recollection and attention, with a holy joy and zeal, with profound humility and reverence," and on his lips, that he will announce it well (*competenter*) "in a proper manner, clearly and distinctly, with power and energy, so that all may be edified." (*The Holy Sacrifice of the Mass*, p. 514)

As ministers of the Gospel and stewards of the mysteries of God, priests and deacons must be worthy of the great treasure entrusted to them. (cf. 1 Cor. 4:1-2; Eph. 3:7; 1 Th. 2:4) These prayers of preparation enable them to make their own the prayer of the psalmist: "Let the words of my mouth and the meditation of my heart be acceptable in your sight, O LORD." (Ps. 19:14) We should join our prayers to those of our priests or deacon "that utterance may be given [him] in opening [his] mouth boldly to proclaim the mystery of the gospel." (Eph. 6:19)

For the priest or deacon, these preparatory prayers serve to remind him of the grandeur of his mission and his need for God's grace to carry it out well. The congregation, for their part, should consider their own need to be well-prepared to receive the words of the Gospel, take them to heart, and put them into practice.

Cardinal Ratzinger advises priests to speak the words of the prayer of preparation "with real recollection and devotion," conscious of what proclamation of the Gospel requires of them.

> When the priest does this, he shows the congregation the dignity and grandeur of the Gospel and helps them understand how tremendous it is that God's Word should come into our midst. The priest's prayer creates reverence and a space for hearing the Word. Again, liturgical education is necessary if the priest's prayer is to be understood and the people are not only to stand up physically but also to rise up spiritually and open the ears of their hearts to the Gospel. (*The Spirit of the Liturgy*, p. 213)

His last sentence leads us into the next dialogue of the Mass and the gesture that accompanies it.

"A reading from…"

The priest or deacon greets the congregation, saying "The Lord be with you," and the congregation responds "And with your spirit." It can be easy to pass by these words as a mere repetition of the greeting at the beginning of Mass, but we should consider why they are spoken again before the Gospel is read. The priest (or deacon) and the congregation are mutually wishing for one another that the Lord would be present with them in the proclamation of His Gospel. We want not only to hear the words of the Gospel, but to have the seed of the word sown in our hearts and take root, by the grace of God. (cf. Matt. 13:18-23) For God's word shall not return to Him void, but it shall accomplish the purpose for which He sends it. (cf. Isa. 55:10-11)

Then the priest or deacon introduces the reading:

Léctio sancti Evangélii secúndum _N._

A reading from the holy Gospel according to _N._

While the authors of the letters read in the Second Reading are preceded by the title "Saint," this practice is not used for the evangelists when the Gospel is introduced, so as not to divert attention away from the divine Gospel to its human author.

This is just one of the ways in which the Church expresses through her liturgy the special pre-eminence that the Gospels have among all the Scriptures, because, as stated in the Second Vatican Council's Dogmatic Constitution on Divine Revelation, "they [the Gospels] are the principal witness for the life and teaching of the incarnate Word." (_Dei Verbum_ 18) In the other readings God speaks to us "by prophets" and Apostles, but in the Gospels He "has spoken to us by a Son." (Heb. 1:1-2) Other special attention is given to this part of the Liturgy of the Word: a special Book of the Gospels (_Evangeliarium_) can be used, distinct from the Lectionary for the other readings; the procession to the ambo with this book can be accompanied by incense and candles; everyone stands when the Gospel is read; and there are prayers and gestures associated with its reading. (GIRM 60)

Before we continue, we should examine the name and content of the Gospel. The name comes from Old English word "godspel" meaning "glad tidings" or "good news." (cf. Luke 1:19; 2:10; 3:18; 4:18; 8:1) In its original context, such good news would be of a military or royal victory, like that of the Philistines over Saul and his army (cf. 1 Sam. 31:9), or of the crowning of a king. (cf. 1 Kgs. 1:42) Why is the Gospel good news?

Because it too has a military and royal character: it is the message of the *victory* over sin and death through Jesus (cf. 1 Cor. 15:57), and Christ's preaching is specifically called "the gospel of the *kingdom*." (Matt. 4:23)

Such good news ennobles even its messenger, as the prophet Isaiah said: "How beautiful upon the mountains are the feet of him who brings good tidings, who publishes *peace*, ... who publishes *salvation*, who says to Zion, 'Your God *reigns*.'" (Isa. 52:7) The Gospel is an announcement of peace (cf. Luke 2:14), salvation (cf. Matt. 1:21; Rom. 1:16; Eph. 1:13), and the reign of God. (cf. Luke 1:33; Rev. 19:6) Like the other readings, the Gospel is not pronounced simply for our instruction and edification, but also as an act of worship "by which religious veneration and homage are paid to the word and truth of God, hence to God Himself, who is present in His word as our teacher." (*The Holy Sacrifice of the Mass*, p. 511)

Tracing the Sign of the Cross

After the Gospel is introduced, the congregation responds "Glory to you, O Lord." As they say this, the priest or deacon traces the cross on the page of the book (traditionally over the opening words of the reading). Why a cross?

First of all, because the cross is the symbol of the Passion and Crucifixion of our Lord, which the four Gospels narrate to us. Second, because even when we do not hear those passages of the Gospel in which the Passion is related, the cross is still the lens through which the whole teaching of Christ must be viewed: "the whole Gospel, the whole doctrine and work of salvation is comprised and contained in the one mystery of the Cross." (*The Holy Sacrifice of the Mass*, p. 516) Thus St. Paul calls the Gospel "the word of the cross" (1 Cor. 1:18) and insists that he preaches nothing but "Jesus Christ and him crucified." (1 Cor. 2:2)

In that same letter to Corinth, St. Paul wrote that "Jews demand signs and Greeks seek wisdom," and that Christ crucified is "a stumbling block to Jews" – an *anti*-sign, a scandal of *weakness* in the supposed Son of God and Messiah – "and folly to Gentiles" – the opposite of wisdom. (1 Cor. 1:22-23) In contrast to this perceived weakness and folly is the objective reality of the cross: it reveals to Christians that Christ is "the *power* of God and the *wisdom* of God," for God's "weakness" is stronger than men, and His "foolishness" is wiser than men. (1 Cor. 1:24-25) The cross imparts strength to counter our weakness, and "shows forth the love, wisdom, and providence of God" to counter our folly; by His cross, Christ teaches all Christian virtues, including "renunciation of the world and of self, humility, obedience, faith, patience, hope, love of God and of neighbor." (*The Holy Sacrifice of the Mass*, p. 516)

After the cross has been traced on the book – essentially a silent prayer of veneration – the priest or deacon traces it on his own forehead, lips, and heart; the congregation does the same.[6] This gesture is a prayer of supplication rather than of veneration; it is made *after* the signing of the Book of the Gospels, as if drawing its efficacy from the first gesture, as if the first cross *receives* something from the Gospel itself, while the second cross *deposits* it on the forehead, lips, and heart. Accompanying this gesture is a silent prayer (not found in the *Roman Missal*, but received through tradition):

May the word of the Lord be in my mind,	*Phil. 4:7; Heb. 10:16*
on my lips,	*Deut. 30:14; Rom. 10:8-10*
and in my heart.	*Ps. 119:11; Ezek. 3:10; Luke 2:19*

This gesture is commonly interpreted by liturgical commentators as a sealing of the mind, mouth, and heart with the power of the Gospel: the one so doing prays that he would not be ashamed of the Gospel (in his mind), would preach it faithfully (by his mouth), and would believe it wholly (in his heart). (*Douay Catechism* 128)[7]

That interpretation applies equally to all the faithful, but what can be said specifically about the priest or deacon? As prayers of preparation for proclaiming the Gospel (rather than hearing it), these crosses have an even more immediate application. The cross on the forehead is a prayer against embarrassment or shame in proclaiming the "hard sayings" of Christ (John 6:60); the cross on the lips is a prayer that he might speak the words of the Gospel with clarity and power (cf. 1 Th. 1:5); and the cross over the heart is a prayer that he might be intimately familiar with the words, so that they are coming not only from the page, or from his lips, but truly from the depths of his heart. These prayers reiterate the

---

[6] This gesture is explained in greater detail in *Praying the Mass: The Prayers of the People*, Chapter 6.
[7] One variant of the prayer is: "May the Gospel guard my mind, bless my lips, and stay in my heart." The intent is similar.

prayer of purification or benediction said a moment earlier, and they will come into play again *after* the Gospel is proclaimed, when it comes time for him to preach *on* the Gospel.

Before reading the Gospel, the priest or deacon may also bless the Book of the Gospels with incense.

"The Gospel of the Lord."

At the conclusion of the Gospel, the priest or deacon says:

Verbum Dómini.

The Gospel of the Lord.   *Mark 1:1; Rom. 1:1-6; 15:16*

If you have been paying attention to the Latin words of the Mass, you should have noticed that the same phrase, "*Verbum Domini*," is translated as "The *word* of the Lord" after the First and Second Readings, but as "The *Gospel* of the Lord" after the Gospel. This distinction is not present in the Latin, but it is made in the English translation to draw attention to that "special pre-eminence" of the Gospel noted earlier. The response to this acclamation is different after the Gospel: whereas the congregation says "Thanks be to God" after the earlier readings, they say "Praise to you, Lord Jesus Christ" after the conclusion to the Gospel.

The acclamation "The Gospel of the Lord" is very similar to "The word of the Lord," as a prayer of hope that those who hear Scripture proclaimed would recognize it for what it is. Sometimes this is not easy, especially when the Gospel contains a "hard saying" of Jesus, such as one of judgment or punishment. Such passages remind us that God is both merciful and just. But the Gospel that might sometimes unsettle us is the same Gospel that sets us free from fear. It is the good news of the grace of God through His Son. (cf. Acts 20:24) Whenever the Gospel reminds us of God's just judgment, we should immediately be moved to repentance and thereby seek out His mercy and rejoice in it.

Furthermore the Gospels, which "are the principal witness for the life and teaching" of Christ, are meant to be heard so as to be put into action, or as St. Paul said, to be "at work in you believers." (1 Th. 2:13) While the New Testament letters contain much in the way of moral exhortation, the source of their message is found in the Gospels. There we find the font of Christian life, there we are taught that man must live "by every word that proceeds from the mouth of God." (Matt. 4:4) That mouth took form in Jesus Christ, the Word-made-flesh, and the words that He speaks are the words of God. (cf. John 3:34; 14:10)

"Through the words..."

After the acclamation "The Gospel of the Lord," the priest or deacon lifts the open Book of the Gospels to his mouth and kisses it. At Masses celebrated by a bishop (where the Gospel is traditionally proclaimed by a deacon), the deacon might bring the Book of the Gospels to the bishop for him to kiss it, and on particularly solemn occasions, the bishop might bless the congregation by making the Sign of the Cross over them with the Book.

Venerating the Book of the Gospels with a kiss is a very ancient tradition, done first of all because of the special status that the Gospels have among all the Scriptures. The Gospel is a special "point of contact" with the Lord (like the altar, which is also kissed), so whatever reverence is shown to the Book is directed to Jesus Christ Himself. An example of this in the secular world is the kissing of a picture of a loved one in his or her absence: you are not worshiping the picture, and you know that the picture is not the person, but the care that you show to the picture is meant for the person.

The priest or deacon, having tasted and seen the goodness of the Lord (cf. Ps. 34:8), Whose words are "sweeter than honey" (Ps. 119:103), kisses the Book of the Gospels that holds that sweetness. This kiss, just like that given to the altar, should also be a genuine sign of personal affection, a "token of his love and veneration for the blessed gift of the Gospel." (*The Glories of the Catholic Church*, p. 230) After having venerating the Gospel in this way, the priest or deacon prays quietly:

Per evangélica dicta deleántur nostra delícta.

Through the words of the Gospel	*Rom. 1:16; Eph. 1:13*
may our sins be wiped away.	*Acts 3:19*

The wording of this prayer has changed slightly, from "May the words of the gospel wipe away our sins" to "*Through* the words of the Gospel may our sins be wiped away." The new translation more closely corresponds to the Latin, but that is not the only difference.

It is not the words of the Gospel themselves that wipe away sin; rather, our sins are blotted out when we take to heart the saving message of the Gospel. (cf. Rom. 1:16; Eph. 1:13) The words of the Gospel are not a sacrament, as are Baptism and Confession which *do* blot out our sins. However, the words of the Gospel can be regarded as a sort of sacramental, in the sense that they have "a great power of awakening and promoting that disposition of the soul" by which we are moved to repentance and are prepared to receive the sacraments worthily:

> The word of God, which is accompanied by the interior working of grace, exercises a redeeming, healing, and sanctifying influence on man when he is properly disposed, by exciting faith, hope and charity, fear and contrition, conversion and amendment of life. (*The Holy Sacrifice of the Mass*, p. 523)

The prayer evokes the words of St. Peter on the second occasion of his preaching to Jews after having received the Holy Spirit on Pentecost. Sts. Peter and John cured a man just outside the Temple who had been born crippled. This attracted the attention of many Jews who were there to pray, and as a crowd formed, St. Peter preached to them about Jesus Christ. In the middle of his sermon, which served as a summary of the Gospel, he exhorted them, "Repent therefore, and turn again, that your sins may be blotted out." (Acts 3:19) Thus, the preaching of the Gospel and the forgiveness of sins are directly linked, as Jesus Himself said: "Repent, and believe in the gospel." (Mark 1:15)

The Homily

After the Gospel comes the homily,[8] which is required on Sundays and other holy days of obligation, and is strongly encouraged on weekdays during Advent, Lent, and Easter. Like the reading of the Gospel, the preaching of the homily is reserved to an ordained minister: a bishop, a priest, or a deacon. (GIRM 66) The homily is an exercise of the teaching office of Christ (Who is priest, prophet, and king); prophets, regardless of their message, were commissioned to teach the People of God. The

---

[8] The Second Vatican Council called the homily a "highly esteemed as part of the liturgy" (SC 52), not an interruption of it. In the Extraordinary Form, the sermon or homily is sometimes regarded as an interruption (but not an unwelcome or unwarranted one) in the celebration of the Mass, which is why some priests will remove their maniple (and even chasuble) before preaching in the Extraordinary Form.

rite of priestly ordination mentions, among the duties of a priest, the preaching of the Gospel and the teaching of the faith.

Although the homily is not a prayer, some priests like to begin and end their homilies with the Sign of the Cross. Perhaps they are praying that the congregation is paying attention and will be edified by it… but it is more likely they do so because they want their homilies to be guided by and oriented toward the cross, which so perfectly contains the whole message of the Gospel; and if the homily has the cross as its guide and goal, it will be guided by and oriented toward the Lord Himself. An excellent homily will lead to prayer.

What *is* a homily? And is there a difference between a "homily" and a "sermon"? Msgr. Pope, in his "Mass in Slow Motion" series, provides the following background:

> *Homily* comes from the Middle English *omelie*, from Anglo-French, from Late Latin *homilia*, from Late Greek *homilein*, and emphasizes a more interpersonal "conversation" or "discourse." The Greek word *homilein* means "to consort with" or "to address a kindred or related people." The root word *homos* meaning "same" is included in the word *homily*.
>
> Hence, this is more than an impersonal address to a crowd of people only vaguely known (i.e. a sermon or lecture). Rather, this is a family conversation, a conversation or address to kindred spirits who share much in common (at least we hope!).

There seems to be a common misconception that a homily is simply an explanation of the Scriptures that were read (maybe just the Gospel) and an application of them to our lives. But a homily is meant to be more than that.

The Purpose of the Homily

The homily does not just open up the Scriptures; it teaches the faithful about the truths and mysteries of the faith, about proper Christian behavior, and about the liturgy itself. The Council of Trent urged priests to "explain frequently during the celebration of the Mass" its readings and prayers, as well as something about the "mystery of this most Holy Sacrifice," at least on Sundays and solemnities. (Session 22) It also instructed bishops to preach not only on Sundays and solemnities, but even daily during Lent and Advent if possible. (Session 24) Early in his pontificate, Ven. Pope John Paul II wrote about the importance of catechesis, saying that preaching must make the faithful familiar with "the whole of the mysteries of the faith and with the norms of Christian living." Addressing the homily in particular, he said that "it should be neither too long nor too short; it should always be carefully prepared, rich in substance and adapted to the hearers, and reserved to ordained ministers." (*Catechesi Tradendae* 48) The general purpose of a homily, then, is to be "an exposition of some aspect of the readings from Sacred Scripture or of another text from the Ordinary or from the Proper of the Mass of the day" that should "take into account both the mystery being celebrated and the particular needs of the listeners." (GIRM 65)[9]

Particularly gifted preachers have existed in every age of the Church. St. Paul sent "the brother who is famous among all the churches for his preaching of the gospel" to the Corinthians. (2 Cor. 8:18) We have many homilies from several of the bishops and priests of the first few centuries of the Church. Their homilies dove deeply into the Scriptures and drew upon their inexhaustible riches, instructing the faithful doctrinally and morally. Ven. Pope John Paul II, addressing certain bishops from the United States in 1998, spoke of the importance of priests and deacons to not only be "trained to make good use of the Bible" but also to have familiarity with the preaching of the Church Fathers, as well as the whole "theological and moral tradition" of the Church.

Pope Benedict XVI wrote about the importance of the homily in his 2007 Apostolic Exhortation. After stating rather bluntly that "the quality of homilies needs to be improved," he goes on to say that the purpose of the homily is "to foster a deeper understanding of the word of God, so that it can bear fruit in the lives of the faithful." (*Sacramentum Caritatis* 46) The homily is a time for teaching and exhortation, for doctrine and morals, for the head and the heart. As for their content, he wrote:

> Generic and abstract homilies should be avoided. … During the course of the liturgical year it is appropriate to offer the faithful, prudently and on the basis of the three-year lectionary, "thematic" homilies treating the great themes of the Christian faith, on the basis of what has been authoritatively proposed by the Magisterium in the four "pillars" of the Catechism of the Catholic

---

[9] Canon Law also addresses the importance of the homily as well. (cf. Can. 528 §1 and 767 §1 in the Western Code; Can. 614 §1 in the Eastern Code)

Church and the recent Compendium, namely: the profession of faith, the celebration of the Christian mystery, life in Christ and Christian prayer. (*Sacramentum Caritatis* 46)

The History of the Homily

The practice of giving instruction on the Scriptures during worship originated (at the latest) in Israel's post-exile liturgy. After returning from their captivity in Babylon, the Jewish people needed to be reintroduced to the Law, and they needed it explained to them as it was read:

> Ezra the scribe [brought] the law before the assembly, both men and women and all who could hear with understanding ... [And the Levites] helped the people to understand the law, while the people remained in their places. And they read from the book, from the law of God, clearly; and they gave the sense, so that the people understood the reading. (Neh. 8:1, 7-8)

There is evidence of instruction given by the celebrant during the liturgy as far back as the middle of the second century. St. Justin Martyr wrote to the Roman emperor in defense of the Church and the Christian faith, and included a summary of their order of worship. He wrote that on the first day of the week

> all who live in cities or in the country gather together to one place, and the memoirs of the apostles or the writings of the prophets are read, as long as time permits; then, when the reader has ceased, the president verbally instructs, and exhorts to the imitation of these good things. (*First Apology* 67)

St. Luke records two instances of Scriptural instruction outside of a liturgical setting. In the last chapter of the Gospel, he wrote about how Jesus interpreted all the Scriptures to His disciples showing them how they all pointed to Him. (cf. Luke 24:25-27, 44-45) In the book of Acts, he wrote about how St. Philip instructed an Ethiopian eunuch who was reading from Isaiah 53:7-8.

> Philip ... asked, "Do you understand what you are reading?" And [the Ethiopian] said, "How can I, unless some one guides me?" And he ... said to Philip, "Please, about whom does the prophet say this, about himself or about some one else?" Then Philip opened his mouth, and beginning with this Scripture he told him the good news of Jesus. (Acts 8:30-35)

These two examples show that early Scriptural instruction was centered on pointing the way to Jesus Christ: it was *Christocentric*. Homilies today should be Christocentric as well, drawing out of the sacred texts Christ's doctrine and moral instruction for us. Every homily should help us to believe what we have heard and put it into practice, so that the Scriptures read at Mass may be "fulfilled in your hearing." (Luke 4:21)

The Homily in the Mass

With that brief history and explanation of the homily behind us, let us consider how the homily fits into the prayer of the Mass. Remember the three crosses that the priest or deacon traced on his forehead, lips, and heart? The priest or deacon who has this weighty task of preaching the Gospel must be fortified by God's grace to preach well. He must believe the Gospel and not be ashamed of it if he is to preach it sincerely. He must preach confidently and eloquently, yet not beyond the power of the congregation to understand. And he must take the Gospel message into his own heart before he can sincerely exhort others to do the same; he must preach with confidence and conviction, with pastoral care and evangelical zeal. Moses, instructing the Israelites in how to follow God's commandments, told them that "the word [of God] is very near you; it is in your *mouth* and in your *heart*, so that you can do it." (Deut. 30:14) So it should be for those who preach... and for those who hear.

Prayer of the Faithful

After the homily, there is a period of silent reflection (for the priest as well as the congregation). Then follows the Creed, which is prayed by all.

At this point in the liturgy, the Ordinary Form has restored what the Second Vatican Council called the "the prayer of the faithful."

> By this prayer, in which the people are to take part, intercession will be made for holy Church, for the civil authorities, for those oppressed by various needs, for all mankind, and for the salvation of the entire world. (SC 53; cf. 1 Tim. 2:1-2)

These general intercessions were probably suppressed sometime between the fourth and sixth centuries; accordingly, they are not present in the Extraordinary Form of the Mass. It has been surmised that their absence is due to the presence of the intercessory prayers found in the Roman Canon which for centuries was the one Eucharistic Prayer of the Roman Rite. This notion is supported by the observation that the only day on which a "prayer of the faithful" is present in the Extraordinary Form is on Good Friday, the only day on which the Eucharistic Prayer is not prayed.[10]

Still, the presence of such prayers on a regular basis is an ancient tradition, liturgically fulfilling St. Paul's instructions to St. Timothy, a bishop in the early years of the Church:

> I urge that supplications, prayers, intercessions, and thanksgivings be made for *all men*, for *kings* and *all who are in high positions*, that we may lead a quiet and peaceable life, godly and respectful in every way. (1 Tim. 2:1-2)

This tradition was attested to by St. Justin Martyr in his first Apology, where he writes that after the reading of Scriptures and the exhortation by the celebrant, "we all rise together and pray, and ... when our prayer is ended, bread and wine and water are brought." (*First Apology* 67) He gives more details about those prayers earlier in the same work:

> [We] offer hearty prayers in common for ourselves and for the baptized person, and for all others in every place, that we may be counted worthy, now that we have learned the truth, by our works also to be found good citizens and keepers of the commandments, so that we may be saved with an everlasting salvation. (*Ibid.*, 65)

While in some liturgies of the Eastern Churches these petitions do not vary, in the Roman Rite, the *General Instruction* provides guidelines for the sorts of prayers to be offered, in line with what St. Paul, St. Justin, and the Council Fathers listed:

> a. For the needs of the Church; b. For public authorities and the salvation of the whole world; c. For those burdened by any kind of difficulty; d. For the local community. (GIRM 70)

By these prayers, the faithful respond "to the word of God which they have welcomed in faith and, exercising the office of their baptismal priesthood, offer prayers to God for the salvation of all." (GIRM 69) Often included are prayers for deceased members of the Church (local or world-wide), as well as a prayer for the particular intention for which the Mass is being offered.[11]

The celebrant of the Mass directs the Prayer of the Faithful from his chair. He begins with a brief introduction, inviting the congregation to prayer, and after the litany of petitions he concludes with another prayer.

---

[10] When we look at the Eucharistic Prayers, we will see that they all do include petitions of the sort recommended for inclusion in the Prayer of the Faithful.

[11] At least *one* Sunday Mass must be offered for the people of the parish. (cf. Can. 534 §1)

This ending prayer usually has the character of collecting the petitions and presenting them all to God the Father through Jesus Christ. The priest may compose the introduction and closing prayer freely, although there are models and examples provide in the Missal. If there is a deacon present, it is proper for him to read the petitions. (GIRM 71)

The *Catechism of the Catholic Church* provides this succinct summary of the Liturgy of the Word:

> The Liturgy of the Word includes "the writings of the prophets," that is, the Old Testament, and "the memoirs of the apostles" (their letters and the Gospels). After the homily, which is an exhortation to accept this Word as what it truly is, the Word of God, and to put it into practice, come the intercessions for all men, according to the Apostle's words: "I urge that supplications, prayers, intercessions, and thanksgivings be made for all men, for kings, and all who are in high positions." (*Catechism* 1349)

Comparing it with the description given by St. Justin Martyr, we can see that the basic structure of the Mass is very much the same today as it was nearly two thousand years ago. Although certain elements have appeared or disappeared (or reappeared) over time, the mystery being celebrated remains eternally one and the same.

The Liturgy of the Word leads to the Liturgy of the Eucharist. It serves to form the proper dispositions in the priest and the congregation for the celebration of that great mystery by listening to the words of Scripture: words of prophets, of Apostles, and even of Christ Himself. Then these words are explained and related through the homily. We all respond in faith by praying the Creed, and we are all moved to prayer for others in the Prayer of the Faithful. When these prayers are concluded by the priest, Mass continues with the Liturgy of the Eucharist, during which all our prayer intentions are offered to God in union with the greatest offering, the Eucharist.

Questions for Reflection: Priests

1) **Interpret:** How do those who read the Scriptures at Mass fulfill the role of the prophets in the Old Testament?

2) **Interpret:** The First Reading and the Gospel tend to be two sides of one coin, the former putting some prophecy or image in our minds, and the latter showing how Jesus fulfills that prophecy or image. How can you help your parishioners understand this in your preaching?

3) **Interpret:** How can the Levites who explained the word of God to the Jews in post-exile Jerusalem be a model for your homilies?

4) **Explain:** Why is the reading of the Gospel preceded by cries of "Alleluia"?

5) **Explain:** What do the prayers for preparation and other acts of reverence surrounding the Gospel tell you about the importance of the Gospel in the life of the Church?

6) **Relate:** How much attention do you give in your homilies to each of the four pillars of the Catechism: the Creed, the Paschal Mystery, Moral Life in Christ, and Prayer?

7) **Relate:** Do you help increase your parishioners' biblical literacy in your homilies? Do you draw from the commentaries and sermons of the Fathers and Doctors of the Church?

8) **Relate:** Do you avoid some topics simply because they are not encountered in the cycle of Sunday readings?

9) **Relate:** Does the Prayer of the Faithful call your parishioners to reflect on and put into action the word of God they have heard? Can you connect it to the propers of the day, and perhaps even to your homily?

Questions for Reflection: Laity

1) **Interpret:** How do Jesus and St. Philip demonstrate the value of the Old Testament?

2) **Interpret:** Do you listen for the connections between the First Reading and the Gospel? What does this teach you about the unity of Scripture?

3) **Explain:** Why does the Gospel reading (and the Book of the Gospels) receive such special attention?

4) **Explain:** Why is the reading (and hearing) of Scripture and the offering of prayers for the Church and for the salvation of the world a fitting preparation for the Liturgy of the Eucharist?

5) **Relate:** Have you ever felt like a "dry bone"? What word of the Lord did you hear that filled you with life again?

6) **Relate:** The priest prays that he would proclaim the word well; do you pray to *hear* and *do* the word well? If you are a lector, do you prepare to read at Mass with prayer?

7) **Relate:** What emotions and reactions do the Scriptures read at Mass elicit in you? Is there a particular passage of Scripture you have heard to which you can easily relate?

8) **Relate:** Have you heard a homily that really built up your faith or moved you to acts of Christian charity? What was it about the homily that had this effect on you?

With a contrite heart and a humble spirit may we be accepted…
Such may our sacrifice be in your sight this day.
(Daniel 3:39-40)

By the mercies of God, present your bodies as a living sacrifice,
holy and acceptable to God, which is your spiritual worship.
(Romans 12:1)

5

Offertory Prayers

THE LITURGY OF THE EUCHARIST consists of three parts: the Offertory, the Eucharistic Prayer, and the Communion Rite. (GIRM 72) The Offertory is to the Eucharistic Prayer what the Introductory Rites are to the whole Mass: a preparatory period. It might appear that bread and wine are the only things being prepared, but every external action in the liturgy corresponds to an internal one. To understand this part of the Mass, we need to know the meaning of the prayers said by the priest, but we also need to know the meaning of the physical objects and actions involved: bread, water, wine, incense (on occasion), bowing, and the washing of the priest's fingers.

The Offertory can be broken down into three parts: first the altar is prepared, then the "gifts" (or "offerings") are presented to the priest, and finally those offerings are prepared. Because of the centrality of the gifts of bread and wine to the Offertory, it is also called the "Preparation of the Gifts" (*donorum*). However, this part of the Mass ends with a prayer known as the "Prayer over the Offerings" (*oblata*). What began as *gifts* become *offerings*. What is the reason for this change of terminology?

The answer to that question is found in the overarching theme of this part of the Mass; indeed, it is one of the core themes of the Mass as a whole. In a sermon on the Passion of our Lord, St. Augustine called it a *mirum commercium*, a "wonderful exchange" in which mankind gave God a body of flesh in which He could suffer death, and God gave mankind eternal life in return. This exchange is encountered in the Eucharist: we give to God bread and wine that He changes into the Body and Blood of His Son, thus making present Christ's sacrificial death; and then God gives that Body and Blood back to us as a banquet of eternal life.

The Church in her liturgical prayer calls this the *commercia gloriosa*, the "glorious exchange." The Prayer over the Offerings for the 20th Sunday in Ordinary Time speaks of the glorious exchange in which we offer God what He has given us, and He gives us Himself in return. Not only do we receive God, we enter into a relationship with Him: the Son of God became man so that men could become sons of God.

Note what it is we offer God: what He has given us! In fact, every good thing we have in life is a gift from God. That is why we can speak of the "Preparation of the Gifts" at first, because the bread and wine are gifts *from* God. After the priest's prayers, these gifts from God have been set aside as offerings *to* Him. But before this offering can take place, the altar needs to be prepared.

Preparation of the Altar

While the preparation of the altar is not accompanied by vocal prayers, the vessels and furnishings of the altar are expressions of reverence; they are like material prayers, much like our gestures are bodily prayers.

The altar is already dressed with a cloth that covers at least its top, the "table" of the altar. On top of this cloth is placed a small linen cloth, the **corporal**. This gets its name from the Latin *corpus*, meaning "body," which points to its historical function: in the Extraordinary Form, the consecrated Host, which is the Body of Christ, would be placed directly on the corporal. While this is no longer done in the Ordinary Form, the corporal still serves a two-fold purpose: it generally denotes the "space" of the altar where the bread and wine to be consecrated are placed, but more importantly, it is there to catch any small particles of the Host or drops of the Precious Blood. At the end of the Communion Rite, the corporal is carefully folded so that no particles on it are dropped or lost.

A **chalice** (or multiple chalices) is placed on the altar. The chalice will hold the wine and water, which together become the Precious Blood of our Lord. Because of the value of what it contains, the chalice, paten, and ciborium (and other sacred vessels) should not appear to be everyday vessels, but be made of "truly noble" materials "so that honor will be given to the Lord by their use." (*Redemptionis Sacramentum* 117) For this reason, it is not permitted to use materials that can deteriorate or break easily. Because these sacred vessels are designated for carrying the Eucharist, they are set apart from all other use: a chalice is not a water goblet.[1] A **pall** (usually a stiff piece of cardboard covered in white linen) can be placed on the chalice to prevent things from falling into it. For each chalice, a **purificator** is brought to the altar as well. This is another smaller linen cloth used in the cleaning of sacred vessels.

The covering of the chalice with a **veil**, although not a requirement, is a "praiseworthy practice." (GIRM 118)[2] The chalice veil may originally have been a pouch or bag for carrying the sacred vessels, but over time it acquired a spiritual value, as did the priest's vestments. Because the chalice is a visible sign of the Eucharist, it is fitting to have the chalice veiled for the Liturgy of the Word and only uncovered as the Liturgy of the Eucharist begins, at the Offertory.

The veil is also a biblical element of worship, signifying the supreme holiness of God. When God instructed Moses in the building of the tabernacle, He prescribed the weaving of a veil to separate the Holy of Holies from the rest of the space; God instructed Solomon to do likewise for the Temple. This same Temple veil split in two from top to bottom at the moment of Jesus' death on the cross. (cf. Matt. 27:50-51) The ripping of the veil that separated the people of Israel from the presence of God in the Temple was a sign of the transition from the Old Covenant to the New Covenant.[3] In a similar way, the lifting of the veil from the chalice is a sign of the sacred mysteries about to be revealed, a transition from the Liturgy of the Word to the Liturgy of the Eucharist.

---

[1] "Do you see these holy vessels? Are they not used continually for only one purpose? Does any one ever venture to use them for any other?" (St. John Chrysostom, *Homily on Ephesians* XIV)

[2] A veil may also cover the tabernacle to signify the presence of the Blessed Sacrament in it.

[3] See St. Augustine, *De Spiritu et Littera* XV; Sermon LXXXVII, 8; *De gratia Christi* XXIX; and Pope St. Leo the Great, Sermon LXVIII, 3. Also see 2 Corinthians 3:12-16.

All the various cloths – the altar cloth, the corporal, the pall, and the purificator – allude to Christ's burial cloths, and therefore they point to the sacrificial character of the Mass. There are various interpretations of just which cloth stands for what. For some, the altar cloth is the main burial shroud in which Jesus was wrapped and the corporal is the cloth that was wrapped around His head. (cf. John 20:6-7) For others, the corporal is the burial shroud and the purificator is the head-shroud. Some see the pall as the stone that sealed the tomb, represented by the chalice. Some connect the corporal simultaneously with the "swaddling cloths" in which Jesus was wrapped as a newborn (Luke 2:7) and with His burial shroud; Ven. Pope John Paul II spoke in similar terms in a homily he gave in Bethlehem in the year 2000: "The Crib of Jesus lies always in the shadow of the Cross." This connection is a sign of the belief that the Body that Mary bore and laid in a manger, and which hung for us on the cross, is the same Body (now glorified) that we receive in Holy Communion.

The altar is a table of sacrifice, where the bread and wine will be changed into the Body, Blood, Soul, and Divinity of our Lord. But we can speak of another altar: remember what was said at the start of this chapter, that every external action corresponds to an internal one. While the physical altar is being prepared, the priest and the congregation should be preparing the altar of their hearts. These are the hearts that, in a matter of minutes, we will "lift ... up to the Lord."

The Preface dialogue will be covered in the next chapter, but it is worth pointing out here that the Latin words for "Lift up your hearts" are *Sursum corda*, which literally mean "Hearts on high!" Now, with that in mind, consider what the word "altar" means. It comes directly from the Latin *altar*, but that word is actually a contraction of two other words: *alta* ("high") and *ara* ("altar" – excuse the circular definition). So an *altar* is actually a "high altar." So our hearts, which are altars, are to be lifted up to the Lord; they are to be "high" hearts, high altars.

How are our hearts altars, and what are we offering on them? For the answer to those questions, we turn to a sermon of Pope St. Leo the Great. After saying that all Christians become kings and priests in Christ through the sacraments of initiation he asked, "What is as priestly as to dedicate a pure conscience to the Lord and to offer the spotless offerings of devotion on the altar of the heart?" (*Sermon* 4.1, quoted in *Catechism* 786)[4] The heart is an altar of prayer:

> In the sacramental liturgy of the Church, the mission of Christ and of the Holy Spirit proclaims, makes present, and communicates the mystery of salvation, which is continued in the heart that prays. The spiritual writers sometimes compare the heart to an altar. (*Catechism* 2655)

St. Augustine, for example, considered the "Our Father" – especially the petition to have our trespasses forgiven as we forgive others their – to be "the daily incense ... of the Spirit, which is offered to God on the altar of the heart, which we are bidden 'to lift up.'" (*De natura et gratia* 41)

So our hearts are altars on which we offer our devotion, our prayer, our sufferings, our sacrifices for others, and our very selves, as St. Paul wrote: "present your bodies as a living sacrifice, holy and acceptable to God, which is your spiritual worship." (Rom. 12:1) Just as Christ is the priest, victim, and altar of His own self-sacrifice, we are the priest, victim, and altar of our living self-sacrifice.

Presentation of the Gifts

Once the physical altar is prepared, the tangible gifts of bread and wine are brought forth; there is usually also a monetary collection made at this time. (cf. *Catechism* 1350-1351; GIRM 73)[5] This is called the "Offertory Procession" or "Procession of the Gifts," and it is normally accompanied by singing. There is a proper offertory chant for each day, just as there is a proper introit chant. (This offertory chant is often replaced by a hymn in typical parish experience.)

The tradition of processing the gifts to the altar (amid singing) is old, dating back almost to Apostolic times. St. Justin Martyr described it in this way, taking place after the Prayer of the Faithful:

> When our prayer is ended, bread and wine [mixed with] water are brought. ... And they who are well to do, and willing, give what each thinks fit; and what is collected is deposited with the president, who succours the orphans and widows and those who, through sickness or any other cause, are in want, and those who

---

[4] Pope Leo did, however, distinguish between this universal priesthood and "the particular service of our ministry," that is, the ordained priesthood.

[5] This monetary collection is not to remain at or near the altar. (cf. GIRM 73)

are in bonds and the strangers sojourning among us, and in a word takes care of all who are in need. (*First Apology* 67)

Financial Offerings

By the middle of the first century, this presentation of the gifts included other offerings for the Church, especially for the care of the poor. This custom "is inspired by the example of Christ who became poor to make us rich." (*Catechism* 1350; cf. 1 Cor. 16:1; 2 Cor. 8:9) The early Christians followed the example of the poor widow who gave from her livelihood, not her abundance (cf. Luke 21:1-4), as attested to by this third-century exhortation on almsgiving by St. Cyprian:

> You are wealthy and rich, and do you think that you celebrate the Lord's Supper, not at all considering the offering, who come to the Lord's Supper without a sacrifice, and yet take part of the sacrifice which the poor man has offered? Consider in the Gospel the widow that remembered the heavenly precepts, doing good even amidst the difficulties and straits of poverty... The widow, the widow needy in means, is found rich in works. (*Treatise 8*, 15)

Thus St. Cyprian shamed those wealthy Christians who partook of the Eucharist without contributing to the sacrifice, by comparing their lack of generosity to the selfless donations of the poor.

It was customary in those first few centuries for multiple groups of people – perhaps even all the faithful present – to process up with gifts, which were then sorted out by the priest and his deacons. As the number of the faithful grew, this became impractical and the rite grew more symbolic. Over time, the offering of material goods was replaced by financial donations. The collection of money to support the Church and the poor is commonly called almsgiving, and it has a strong biblical precedent, attested to by St. Paul:

> Contribute to the needs of the saints... (Rom. 12:13)
>
> I am going to Jerusalem with aid for the saints. For Macedonia and Achaia have been pleased to make some contribution for the poor among the saints at Jerusalem. (Rom. 15:25-26)
>
> Now concerning the contribution for the saints: as I directed the churches of Galatia, so you also are to do. On the first day of every week, each of you is to put something aside and store it up, as he may prosper. (1 Cor. 16:1-2)
>
> Now it is superfluous for me to write to you about the offering for the saints, for I know your readiness, of which I boast about you

to the people of Macedonia ... and your zeal has stirred up most of them. (2 Cor. 9:1-2)

St. Paul paints the picture of a local church so well known throughout the region for its charity to the poor and its generosity toward the whole Church that it moves others, not to envy nor complacency, but to greater zeal. The ancient Roman and Corinthian Christians present a model and a challenge to our modern parishes and dioceses.

Bread and Wine

Whatever else is offered, bread and wine are indispensible. In the words of Ven. Pope John Paul II, they bring a "unique contribution" to the sacrifice of the Mass, because "by means of the consecration by the priest they become sacred species" – that is, while retaining their appearance, they become the Precious Body and Blood of Christ. (*Dominicae Cenae* 9)

By the eleventh century, the procession with the bread and wine fell out of use in the Roman Rite, but it was restored to the Roman Rite in the Ordinary Form: "It is praiseworthy for the bread and wine to be presented by the faithful." (GIRM 73)[6]

As mentioned earlier, the bread and wine that are presented to the priest are gifts from God. The Eucharist is brought about through gifts that we return to God for Him to do with as He sees fit. The miracle of the multiplication of the fishes and loaves in the Gospel is rightly seen as a prefiguring of the Eucharist, because of Jesus' actions (taking, giving thanks, and distributing) and because of the superabundance of the food. But a third connection can be found: St. John points out that the bread and fish did not come from Jesus or His Apostles, but from a boy in the crowd. (cf. John 6:9) This is the case in the Mass as well.

A commentary by Theodore of Mopsuestia (died A.D. 428) on the Divine Liturgy describes the procession of bread and wine up to the altar as representing "Christ being ... led and brought to His Passion." As the elements are placed on the altar (representing the cross), this symbolizes Christ being "stretched on the altar [of the cross] to be sacrificed for us." (*Commentary on the Lord's Prayer, Baptism and the Eucharist*, Chapter 5) From

---

[6] Rev. Guy Oury, in his book *The Mass*, comments on the practice of some parishes to announce before Mass who will be presenting the gifts of bread and wine. He suggests, instead, announcing those *for whom the gifts are offered* instead! (cf. *The Mass*, p. 84)

that perspective, the unveiling of the chalice could be a representation of Christ being stripped of his clothes at the cross.

The bread in the Roman Rite is unleavened – wheat and water, with no yeast. In most of the Eastern Rites, leavened bread is used. These two traditions are both ancient and venerable; each has its own spiritual heritage and symbolism. It is likely (although not absolutely certain) that Jesus used unleavened bread at the Last Supper, which took place in very close proximity to the Passover and the Feast of Unleavened Bread. But even if the Lord did use leavened bread in the upper room, He certainly used unleavened bread when He broke bread with two of His disciples in Emmaus on Easter Sunday, because there would have been no leavened bread available for the week following the Passover.

The Western practice reflects a negative attitude toward leaven. This attitude was no doubt fashioned by the typical characterization of leaven in the New Testament as corrupt or sinful (with the notable exception of the heavenly leaven spoken of in Matthew 13:33). Bread *without* leaven is then a symbol of purity, virginity, sinlessness, and holiness. Connecting the sacrifice of Christ with the Passover, St. Paul wrote that we should rid ourselves of "the old leaven," a requirement for the celebration of the Passover in Exodus 12:13, because "Christ, our Paschal Lamb, has been sacrificed. Let us, therefore, celebrate the festival … with the unleavened bread of sincerity and truth." (1 Cor. 5:7-8) The unleavened bread of the Passover was called the "bread of affliction" (Deut. 16:3), so unleavened bread used for the Eucharist reminds us of our "afflicted" (Isa. 53:4, 7) Lord and His Passion and death. Finally, unleavened bread differs in appearance and taste from our daily bread; this contrast should lead us to recognize that the Eucharistic bread is no ordinary bread.[7]

The bread and wine are not merely physical elements, but they are richly symbolic. Ven. Pope John Paul II explained that the offering of bread and wine to the priest by the congregation is a symbolic exercise of their baptismal priesthood:

> Although all those who participate in the Eucharist do not confect
> the sacrifice as [the priest] does, they offer with him, by virtue of

---

[7] An apologetic for the use of leavened bread in the Eastern traditions is outside the scope of this book. Suffice to say, the reasons for its use are just as Christocentric and theologically sound as the Western tradition.

> the common priesthood, their own spiritual sacrifices represented by the bread and wine from the moment of their presentation at the altar. ... The bread and wine become in a sense a symbol of all that the eucharistic assembly brings, on its own part, as an offering to God and offers spiritually. (*Dominicae Cenae* 9)

As the bread and wine are brought to the altar, we should embark on an internal procession toward the altar of our hearts. We are required to use bread and wine because Jesus chose to use them,[8] but these gifts are also a fitting and sublime representation of that spiritual sacrifice we offer: our labors, our lives, our very selves.

First, consider with Pope Benedict XVI the historical, geographical, and cultural significance of bread and wine:

> There are four elements in creation on which the world of sacraments is built: water, bread, wine and olive oil. ... While water is the vital element everywhere, and thus represents the shared access of all people to rebirth as Christians, the other three elements belong to the culture of the Mediterranean region. In other words, they point towards *the concrete historical environment* in which Christianity emerged. (Homily at the 2010 Chrism Mass)

Bread and wine point to a particular culture, people, and place in history. Christians everywhere have cultivated wheat and grapes, in obedience to the Lord's example and in honor of the historical circumstances of His Incarnation. Pope Benedict went on to say how bread and wine depict different facets of human life: bread is a symbol of everyday life and of toil, while wine is a symbol of feasts and joy.

Second, consider how we get bread and wine. God gives us seeds. We cultivate them, collect them, work them, and form them into bread and wine. We are the good stewards of the talents received from God, which we invest and return to Him. (cf. Matt. 25:14-30) The manner in which wheat becomes bread and grapes become wine is a sign of how we are formed into the one Body of Christ: gathered from many grains into one loaf, from many grapes into one cup, from many members into one Body. Even the crushing of the grain and the grapes is a sign of how we must die to ourselves in Baptism, in order to be incorporated into Christ.

---

[8] Jesus was certainly acting within Jewish culture: the Passover meal, the *todah* offering of the Old Covenant, even as far back as the bread and wine offered by Melchizedek. (cf. Gen. 14:18-20) Jesus *could* have instituted the Eucharist under new signs, but He chose to used bread and wine.

Third, consider the words of our Lord: "I am the bread of life … the living bread which came down from heaven." (John 6:48, 51) "I am the vine, you are the branches." (John 15:5) Jesus calls Himself "bread" and "vine." He gives His Body and Blood to us as food for eternal life. What could be more fitting than for Him to manifest Himself under the forms of bread and of wine (the "blood" of the vine)? As the bread and wine are changed into His Body and Blood, we should pray that we, and all of humanity, will be more fully and perfectly changed into the Body of Christ.

Finally, consider their physical appearance. In his 1936 book *Calvary and the Mass*, Rev. Fulton Sheen described bread and wine as the two things in all nature that best represent the substance of life:

> Wheat is as the very marrow of the ground, and the grapes its very blood, both of which give us the body and blood of life. In bringing those two things, which give us life, nourish us, we are equivalently bringing ourselves to the Sacrifice of the Mass. We are therefore present at each and every Mass under the appearance of bread and wine, which stand as symbols of our body and blood.

We know they will become the Body and Blood of our Lord, but he sees them even before their consecration as symbols of *our* body and blood.

Preparation of the Gifts

As in the procession at the beginning of Mass, the procession of the gifts to the altar is not accompanied by vocal prayers (apart from the singing of a chant or hymn). Once the priest is back at the altar, holding in his hands the paten with the bread, the vocal prayers begin. Accompanying the external preparation of bread and wine is the interior preparation of our spiritual sacrifice. The early Christians recognized this, as explained in an essay in ZENIT's "The Spirit of the Liturgy" series by Rev. Juan José Silvestre Valór:

> This preparation came to be conceived not only as a necessary external action but as an essentially interior process. It was seen as related to the Jewish practice in which the head of the household lifted up the bread to God to receive it again from him, renewed. Eventually, understood in a deeper way, this gesture was associated with Israel's preparation for presenting herself before the Lord. In this way, the external gesture of the preparation of the gifts was more and more regarded as an interior preparation

before the nearness of the Lord, who seeks the Christians in their offerings.

The principal prayers said over the bread and wine in the Ordinary Form differ from those said in the Extraordinary Form.[9] To help come to a fuller understanding of this part of the Mass, we will use the prayers in the Extraordinary Form to give context to and supplement the prayers in the Ordinary Form.

Bread: "Blessed are you…"

The priest receives a paten with bread on it and brings it to the altar. There, holding it slightly above the altar with both hands,[10] he quietly says the following prayer. The paten with the bread should not be placed on the altar until after the prayer has been said. (GIRM 75)

**Benedíctus es, Dómine, Deus univérsi,
quia de tua largitáte accépimus panem, quem tibi offérimus,
fructum terræ et óperis mánuum hóminum:
ex quo nobis fiet panis vitæ.**

Blessed are you, Lord God of all creation,	*Tob. 8:5; Rom. 9:5*
for through your goodness we have received	*2 Cor. 9:8*
the bread we offer you:	*Gen. 14:18-20; Lev. 21:8*
fruit of the earth and work of human hands,	*Eccl. 3:13*
it will become for us the bread of life.	*John 6:33,35,48,51*

This prayer, and the corresponding one for the wine, can be said aloud if there is no singing taking place, and if the priest so chooses. This prayer describes the bread in four ways: a gift from God's "goodness," a "fruit of the earth," the "work of human hands," and the material to become the "bread of life."

We received the bread from God's goodness, His largesse (*largitate*) or bounty.[11] Now we offer it back to Him. The new translation supplies the word "you" after "bread we offer," which was absent from the old translation. It might seem a small and obvious thing, but it is crucial to remember that the Mass involves a sacrificial offering. As for the reason

---

[9] The Ordinary Form prayers are derived from prayers that would be said over bread and wine by Jews: "Blessed are You Who bring forth bread from the earth." (cf. Mishnah *Berekoth* 6:1)

[10] This gesture of *presentation* should not be confused with the elevations of the Host and chalice made during the Eucharistic Prayer. (cf. *CMRR* 273)

[11] The prayer over the bread is linked to a traditional prayer of blessing for a meal – "Bless us, O Lord, and these Thy gifts which we are about to receive from *Thy bounty (tua largitate)*…"

we offer God the bread, the prayer mentions one purpose: so that it will become "the bread of life." But there is another reason that deserves our attention, and for that, we turn to the prayer found in the Extraordinary Form:

Accept, O Holy Father, almighty and eternal God,
this spotless host, which I, Your unworthy servant,
offer to You, my living and true God,
to atone for my numberless sins, offenses, and negligences;
on behalf of all here present
and likewise for all faithful Christians living and dead,
that it may profit me and them as a means of salvation to life everlasting.
Amen.

Your first reaction to this prayer might be to ask why the bread is referred to as "spotless" – after all, this prayer is spoken over mere bread, not the Eucharist. The explicit sacrificial language is anticipatory.[12] The Offertory prayers in both forms of the Roman Rite have a twofold object: the present bread and wine, and the anticipated Body and Blood. The Roman Rite is very offering-oriented: from this part of the Mass onward, the prayers continually repeat the theme of making an offering (and praying for God to accept it). It needs to be said that the offering of mere bread and wine does not constitute the sacrifice of the Mass; only the Eucharist, the sacrifice of Jesus Christ Himself, is the real and true sacrifice, so do not let the language of the older prayers confuse you.

With that said, look again at the two prayers. While the Ordinary Form prayer emphasizes the bread becoming "the bread of life" (that is, *our* reception of the Eucharist in Holy Communion), the Extraordinary Form prayer emphasizes the bread becoming a "spotless host" (that is, *God's* reception of the Eucharist as the sacrifice of His Son). It is rather clear that the reason the Eucharist is offered to God is to atone for our sins, affirming that the Eucharist is the very same sacrifice that Christ offered on the cross (but presented mystically and without the shedding of blood). The older prayer also mentions the beneficial value that the Eucharist has for all faithful Christians, living and dead. This affirms that

---

[12] To see how such an anticipatory prayer can be proper, consider prayers such as the "Morning Offering" which consecrate and offer to Jesus all the thoughts and deeds of the coming day before they have been thought or done.

one can benefit from the offering of the Eucharist even without receiving Holy Communion, making a "spiritual Communion." That being said, Holy Communion is "a means of salvation to life everlasting," which the newer prayer affirms by calling the Eucharist the "bread of life."

The prayer over the bread should elicit in us a sense of profound gratitude to God, both for the gift of bread and for the surpassing gift of salvation through the self-giving sacrifice of His Son. (cf. *Catechism* 1333)

Mixing the Wine with Water

The next two prayers are associated with the chalice of wine. This first prayer is said quietly by the deacon or priest while he prepares the chalice by pouring in some wine and then adding a few drops of water:

Per huius aquæ et vini mystérium
eius efficiámur divinitátis consórtes,
qui humanitátis nostræ fíeri dignátus est párticeps.

By the mystery of this water and wine	*2 Macc. 15:39; John 19:34*
may we come to share in the divinity of Christ	*Rom. 5:2; 2 Pet. 1:4*
who humbled himself to share in our humanity.	*Phil. 2:8*

The simple act of pouring water into wine, and the prayer accompanying it, is a synthesis of the whole Mass, of the whole Catholic faith, and of all salvation history. In order to unearth the theological and doctrinal riches of this easily overlooked rite, we should first examine the history of the prayer that accompanies it.

Its oldest known ancestor is a Collect for the Nativity of our Lord from the Leonine Sacramentary, an ancient Mass-book dating back to the seventh century, if not earlier. Here is a translation of the Latin prayer:[13]

O God, Who wonderfully created the worthiness of man's nature,
and have more wonderfully renewed it,
grant, we beseech You,
that **we may be made partakers** of Your Son Jesus **Christ's divinity**
Who deigned to become a partaker of our humanity.

The first half of this Collect speaks of man's creation and then of his redemption and sanctification in Christ. The second half considers the Incarnation (celebrated especially on the Solemnity of the Nativity) by which Christ deigned (condescended) to share our humanity, and which

---

[13] The bold text is what is retained in the Ordinary Form prayer for the mingling.

enables us to share in His divinity, in the eternal life of God. This was an act of humility (cf. Phil. 2:8) by the Son, Who "emptied himself, taking the form of a servant, being born in the likeness of men." (Phil. 2:7) But the Incarnation was not simply God lowering Himself to our level; He also deemed human nature worthy of Himself and desired to raise it to a more wondrous dignity than it first knew.

This prayer was incorporated into the Roman Rite to accompany the mingling of water with wine in the chalice with a slight adaptation. Here is a translation of how the prayer appears in the Extraordinary Form:

> O God, Who wonderfully created the worthiness of man's nature,
> and have more wonderfully renewed it,
> grant that, **through the mystery of this water and wine,**
> **we may be made partakers of His divinity**
> **Who deigned to become a partaker of our humanity**,
> Jesus **Christ**, Your Son...

You can see that it is essentially the same as the ancient Collect, with the addition of the underlined clause concerning "the mystery of this water and wine."

Without this context, one might misinterpret the prayer as it exists in the Ordinary Form not as a prayer but merely as a commentary directed to the congregation (and therefore, as words that should be said aloud), but its history shows that these words are still a prayer addressed to God. So two questions remain: why is water mixed with the wine, and what has that to do with the Incarnation, with humanity and divinity?

Mixing water with wine was a cultural practice of Jesus' day, and Apostolic Tradition teaches us that Jesus followed this practice at the Last Supper. It was not a dishonest practice (as in Isaiah 1:22); rather, wine was thicker and more potent in those days, and it was necessary to temper the wine with water. (cf. 2 Macc. 15:39) Already in the first three centuries of the Church, there are numerous sources that confirm that the wine used at Mass was mixed with water: St. Justin Martyr's account of the Sunday liturgy (*First Apology* 65, 67), St. Irenaeus' references to a mixed cup (*Against Heresies* 4:32; 5:2), St. Clement of Alexandria's words that "the blood of the grape – that is, the Word – desired to be mixed with water" (*The Instructor* 2:2), and St. Cyprian's *Letter 62* (on the use of wine and water in the chalice) where he writes several times that it is a tradition of Christ Himself foretold in the book of Proverbs: "Wisdom has built her house … she has mixed her wine, she has also set her table. … She says, 'Come, eat of my bread and drink of the wine I have mixed.'" (Prov. 9:1-5)

But the wine used at Mass is no longer as thick or strong as the wine used two thousand years ago. What was once necessary gained a spiritual significance that has endured long after the necessity has ceased. The wine and water have four predominant symbolic interpretations.

First, they allude to **the piercing of Christ's heart** after His death. St. John records that one of the soldiers, to ensure that Christ was dead, "pierced his side with a spear, and at once there came out *blood and water.*" (John 19:34; cf. 1 John 5:6) This event itself was prefigured by Moses in the desert, when God commanded him to strike a rock with his rod so that water would flow forth. (cf. Ex. 17:5-6) St. Paul tells us that the rock was an allegory of Christ (cf. 1 Cor. 10:4); later Christians saw the rod of Moses as a foreshadowing of the cross. This event is seen sometimes as the birth of the Church, born out of the side of Christ while He slept in death; for Christ is the new Adam, and Eve was born out of the side of the sleeping Adam. (cf. Gen. 2:21-22) The water and blood represent the sacraments of the Baptism and Eucharist, which are the beginning and culmination of all the sacraments: "Water to cleanse, blood to redeem." (St. Ambrose, *De Sacramentis* Book V, 1:4)

This act is the basis for two popular devotions: the Sacred Heart of Jesus and Divine Mercy. Devotion to the Sacred Heart depicts His heart in this way: wounded and bleeding, aflame with charity, implanted with a cross, crowned with thorns, and radiant with divine light. The image of Divine Mercy devotion shows rays of red and white light streaming from His heart "as a fountain of mercy for us." Just as Moses saw a glimpse of God on Mount Horeb through a cleft in the rock (cf. Ex. 33:18-23), it is by the opening of Jesus' heart – the cleft in the Rock Who is Christ – that we see a glimpse of the extent and power of God's love for us.[14]

Second, they represent **Christ's divinity and humanity**: the wine points to His divinity, and the water to His humanity. Once the water and wine mingle, they cannot be separated; so too Christ's divinity and

---

[14] I owe this allegory to a brief lecture on the Sacred Heart by Rev. John Zuhlsdorf.

humanity, while distinct, are eternally joined in the Incarnation, which is why the original prayer was used on Christmas. Thus the prayer speaks of the "mystery of this water and wine." The Incarnation is the greatest act of "divine condescension," where God stoops down to our human level; it is the mystery and paradox of divine humility. "Christ who humbled himself to share in our humanity" alludes to St. Paul's words that Jesus "being found in human form he humbled himself and became obedient unto death, even death on a cross." (Phil. 2:8)

From the identification of the water with humanity comes the third symbolism: **the union of the faithful with Christ**. This too is drawn from the words of the prayer: "may we come to share in the divinity of Christ." The notion of sharing in the divine nature is not blasphemous; on the contrary, it is scriptural. It comes from St. Peter's second letter:

> His divine power has granted to us all things that pertain to life and godliness, through the knowledge of him who *called us to his own glory and excellence*, by which he has granted to us his precious and very great promises, that through these you may escape from the corruption that is in the world because of passion, and *become partakers of the divine nature*. (2 Pet. 1:3-4)

St. Paul alludes to this union as well, when he writes that through Jesus "we rejoice in our hope of *sharing the glory of God*." (Rom. 5:2) This was the ultimate purpose for which the Incarnation took place, so that after we are redeemed we might also be exalted by God:

> The Word became flesh to make us "partakers of the divine nature": "For this is why the Word became man, and the Son of God became the Son of man: so that man, by entering into communion with the Word and thus receiving divine sonship, might become a son of God." "For the Son of God became man so that we might become God." "The only-begotten Son of God, wanting to make us sharers in his divinity, assumed our nature, so that he, made man, might make men gods." (*Catechism* 460)

To receive the blood of Jesus Christ "is to become partaker of the Lord's immortality." (*The Instructor*, 2:2)

The union of divinity and humanity is a mystical marriage. Consider the first miracle of Jesus, changing water into wine at the wedding feast at Cana. (cf. John 2:1-10) This event, occurring at a wedding, points to the "marriage supper of the Lamb" (Rev. 19:9), of Christ and His Bride the Church. St. Paul wrote of this divine matrimony to the Corinthians and the Ephesians: "I betrothed you to Christ to present you as a pure bride to her one husband" (2 Cor. 11:2) and "Husbands, love your wives, as Christ loved the Church and gave himself up for her." (Eph. 5:25)

The drops of water added to the wine no longer exist of themselves but are caught up and incorporated into the wine. The water does not merely represent abstract humanity, but each of us concretely as humans: "we are the drop of water united with the wine." (*Calvary and the Mass*) This is an analogy for life in Christ: what Jesus has by nature (His divine Sonship), we receive by grace (divine adoption). We "are being changed into his likeness from one degree of glory to another" (2 Cor. 3:18), but this transformation will not be complete until we enter Heaven.

St. Cyprian wrote eloquently about the necessity of using both wine and water in the chalice. After identifying the wine with Christ and the water with those who make up the Church, he insists that

> in consecrating the cup of the Lord, water alone cannot be offered, even as wine alone cannot be offered. For if any one offer wine only, the blood of Christ is dissociated from us; but if the water be alone, the people are dissociated from Christ; but when both are mingled, and are joined with one another by a close union, there is completed a spiritual and heavenly sacrament.
>
> Thus the cup of the Lord is not indeed water alone, nor wine alone, unless each be mingled with the other; just as, on the other hand, the body of the Lord cannot be flour alone or water alone, unless both should be united and joined together and compacted in the mass of one bread; in which very sacrament our people are shown to be made one, so that in like manner as many grains, collected, and ground, and mixed together into one mass, make one bread; so in Christ, who is the heavenly bread, we may know that there is one body, with which our number is joined and united. (*Letter 62*, 13)

Notice how St. Cyprian draws attention to the imperceptible presence of water in the bread as well as in the wine? Both elements, then, attest to our participation in Christ in the sacrament of the Eucharist. This shows how it is we all participate in the Offertory: as we (water) are united to Christ (wine), we must unite our prayers and sacrifices to His sacrifice in the Eucharist. Just because these Offertory prayers are said quietly (for the most part) does not mean the faithful are mute spectators while the priest "does his thing." Instead, in that intimate silence is the setting for our deeply personal union with Christ and self-offering with Him.

The fourth symbolism is based on the ancient words of this prayer, lacking in the Ordinary Form, referring to **our creation and re-creation in Christ**. (cf. *Catechism* 1692) The water represents the purity of nature in which man was created: "little less than God," crowned with glory and honor, with dominion over the world and all therein. (cf. Ps. 8) But from such a lofty height our first parents fell into sin, and this purity was lost. We now live in hope of redemption through the blood of Christ, which has bestowed upon water the power to give us new birth, to make us "a new creation" in Christ. (2 Cor. 5:17) This re-creation is a greater work than the first creation and a foretaste of the future eternity where God will "make all things new." (Rev. 21:5) Therefore, let us pray that God may bring to completion the work of re-creation that He has begun in us. (cf. Phil. 1:6)

Do not be surprised that so much can be written about such a small prayer. The rite and its prayer are of exceptional significance, as they represent the totality of redemption, from the Incarnation to the Passion and beyond, to the Resurrection and our eventual sharing in the divine life of God in Heaven.

Wine: "Blessed are you..."

Once the chalice has been prepared, it can be offered:

Benedíctus es, Dómine, Deus univérsi,
quia de tua largitáte accépimus vinum, quod tibi offérimus,
fructum vitis et óperis mánuum hóminum,
ex quo nobis fiet potus spiritális.

Blessed are you, Lord God of all creation,	*Tob. 8:5; Rom. 9:5*
for through your goodness we have received	*2 Cor. 9:8*
the wine we offer you:	*Gen. 14:18-20*
fruit of the vine and work of human hands,	*Eccl. 3:13; Matt. 26:29*
it will become our spiritual drink.	*1 Cor. 10:4*

This prayer follows the same pattern as the prayer over the bread: what was said for that prayer applies to this prayer as well. The consecrated wine will become "our spiritual drink" – the Precious Blood of our Lord. The Israelites' spiritual drink was water from the side of the rock; for us, it is blood from the side of the Rock, Who is Christ. (cf. Ex. 17:5-6;

1 Cor. 10:4) The change that takes place in the bread and wine is not simply a spiritual change, but truly a substantial one. They change in their reality, not just in our perception of them. The following chapter will go into this mystery in more detail.

The prayer over the chalice in the Extraordinary Form can give us some additional context about the chalice and its contents:

> We offer unto You, O Lord, the chalice of salvation,
> entreating Your mercy that our offering may ascend
> with a sweet fragrance in the sight of Your divine Majesty,
> for our own salvation, and for that of the whole world.
> Amen.

As in the prayer over the bread, anticipatory language is used, calling it the "chalice of salvation" (Ps. 116:13) – we know that the contents of the chalice are of no avail until they are consecrated. This prayer expresses the scriptural belief that Jesus "is the expiation for our sins, and not for ours only but also for the sins of the whole world." (1 John 2:2) For this reason, the Church shares the desire of God for "all men to be saved and to come to the knowledge of the truth." (1 Tim. 2:4)

The chalice contains the wine and water, symbols of the Incarnation. That makes the chalice itself, in one sense, a symbol of the Blessed Virgin Mary, in whose womb the mystery of the Incarnation took place. Mary is a living sacred vessel specially consecrated by God to receive the Lord. And because God assumed human nature, He has given every man and woman the potential to be a sacred vessel capable of receiving Him in Holy Communion.

A final word should be said about the anticipatory character of the older prayers. If you recall from earlier in this chapter, the Offertory was interpreted as early as the fifth century as being a mystical re-presentation of Christ entering into His Passion. This view especially affected the language of the Offertory prayers, resulting in the bread and wine being called "holy" and being spoken of in highly sacrificial terms.

"With humble spirit..."

The priest now asks God to receive our offerings. The priest says this prayer for all the faithful ("May *we* be accepted"), but he says the prayer quietly, adopting a posture of humility, bowing profoundly before the altar. The words of this prayer remind him that, as a priest, he is "above all a servant of others" (*Sacramentum Caritatis* 23) and a servant of God.

In spíritu humilitátis et in ánimo contríto suscipiámur a te, Dómine; et sic fiat sacrifícium nostrum in conspéctu tuo hódie, ut pláceat tibi, Dómine Deus.

With humble spirit and contrite heart	*Ps. 51:17; Isa. 66:2*
may we be accepted by you, O Lord,	*Dan. 3:39*
and may our sacrifice in your sight this day	*Rom. 12:1; Eph. 5:2*
be pleasing to you, Lord God.	*Phil. 4:18; Col. 1:10*

This prayer evokes the words of King David and of Azariah, one of the three Israelites thrown into a fiery furnace by Nebuchadnezzar.

Psalm 51 was written by David after Nathan the prophet confronted him about his sin with Bathsheba, the wife of Uriah. David had seen and coveted her, committed adultery, and covered up the result by having Uriah killed in battle. (cf. 2 Sam. 11) David had broken three of the Ten Commandments! (cf. Ex. 20:13, 14, 17) The psalm reflects his true contrition and God's rich mercy:

> Have mercy on me, O God, according to your merciful love;
> > according to your abundant mercy blot out my transgressions.
> Wash me thoroughly from my iniquity, and cleanse me from my sin!
> . . .
> Create in me a clean heart, O God,
> > and put a new and right spirit within me.
> . . .
> For you take no delight in sacrifice;
> > were I to give a burnt offering, you would not be pleased.
> The sacrifice acceptable to God is a broken spirit;
> > *a broken and contrite heart*, O God, you will not despise.

(Ps. 51:1-2, 10, 16-17)

The prophet Isaiah receives similar words from the Lord at the very end of the book of his prophecies: "This is the man to whom I will look, he that is humble and contrite in spirit, and trembles at my word." (Isa. 66:2) Both David and Isaiah recognize that God does not accept an insincere sacrifice, a purely external sacrifice: "Outward sacrifice, to be genuine, must be the expression of spiritual sacrifice." (*Catechism* 2100) As the prophet Samuel explained to King Saul, "to obey is better than sacrifice." (1 Sam. 15:22) Obedience to God, the spiritual sacrifice of self-will, is the sign of "a broken spirit, a broken and contrite heart."

Several centuries later, after Israel had split in two and its people had gone into exile, three Israelite youths – Azariah, Mishael, and Hananiah – were being put to death by Nebuchadnezzar for refusing to bow down and worship the golden idol he had made. (cf. Dan. 3) He threw them into a blazing furnace, but God kept them safe from harm. In the midst of the flames, Azariah offered a prayer of thanks and contrition to God:

> At this time there is no prince, or prophet, or leader, no burnt offering, or sacrifice, or oblation, or incense, no place to make an offering before you or to find mercy.
>
> Yet *with a contrite heart and a humble spirit may we be accepted*, as though it were with burnt offerings of rams and bulls, and with tens of thousands of fat lambs; such *may our sacrifice be in your sight* this day, and may we wholly follow you, for there will be no shame for those who trust in you. (Dan. 3:38-40)

Azariah realizes that without access to the Temple and without priests, Israel cannot offer God the sacrifices legislated by the Mosaic covenant. While most sacrifices would require the death of a victim, Azariah offers himself and his companions as a living sacrifice. He asks God to accept them as a living sacrifice, "with a contrite heart and a humble spirit," and God preserved them from death. This is also true for us: Christ died for us to preserve us from death, so that we might offer ourselves to God as living sacrifices. (cf. Rom. 12:1) Rev. Valór writes that the biblical origin of this prayer "expresses the ultimate meaning" of the external offering of bread and wine: "the gift of the heart accompanied by the intimate disposition of personal sacrifice."

In Eucharistic Prayer III (as well as in the Prayer over the Offerings for Trinity Sunday), the priest prays to the Father, "May [Jesus] make of us an eternal offering to you." The bread and wine represent all that we have to offer, and the water mixed into the wine represents our offering being joined to that of Christ, but we properly participate in the offering of the Eucharist only if we are sincere about offering ourselves along with it. Pope St. Gregory the Great wrote eloquently about this in the late sixth century:

> Offer unto God the daily sacrifice of tears, and the daily sacrifice of His Body and Blood. ... But necessary it is that, when we do these things, we should also, *by contrition of heart, sacrifice ourselves unto almighty God*. For when we celebrate the mystery of our Lord's passion, we ought to imitate what we then do: for then shall it

truly be a sacrifice for us unto God, if we offer ourselves also to him in sacrifice. (*Dialogues IV*, 58-59)

This is what the Council Fathers at Vatican II had in mind when they wrote of the laity that

all their works, prayers and apostolic endeavors, their ordinary married and family life, their daily occupations, their physical and mental relaxation, if carried out in the Spirit, and even the hardships of life, if patiently borne – all these become "spiritual sacrifices acceptable to God through Jesus Christ." Together with the offering of the Lord's body, they are most fittingly offered in the celebration of the Eucharist. (LG 34)

All these prayers should serve as reminders that God can take our meager and sometimes imperfect sacrifices (represented by the bread and wine) and transform them by filling them with His grace.[15] Our whole lives should be one joyful and uninterrupted offertory.

At this point, the priest may bless the bread and wine and the altar with incense. The deacon or an altar server then censes him, and then the whole congregation will stand to be censed. If you recall from Chapter 2, incense is a visible sign of our prayers and sacrifices rising up to God with a pleasing aroma. All of us are censed because we are a "fragrant offering and sacrifice to God" (Eph. 5:2), but also because all of us, ordained or not, share in the one priesthood of Christ.

The grains of incense are consumed in fire and rise heavenward as a pleasing odor, symbolizing the change that will take place in the bread and wine by the fire of the Holy Spirit. The cloud of incense fills the church, indicating that the sacrifice of the Eucharist is meant for all the faithful and even the whole world. The priest and the congregation are censed directly, expressing the desire for God's blessing to descend in a special way on all who participate at Mass.

"Wash me, O Lord..."

The ancient practice of receiving bread and wine and other gifts from the congregation necessitated the priest washing his hands before continuing with the liturgy, not only for sanitary reasons, but also out of reverence for the Eucharist. This action gained a spiritual significance even before the presentation of the gifts became simplified.

---

[15] To that end, the Extraordinary Form follows this prayer with one asking the "Sanctifier" (the Holy Spirit) to bless the sacrifice that has been prepared for the glory of His name.

The rite and its meaning are found in the *Apostolic Constitutions* from the end of the fourth century: "let one of the sub-deacons bring water to wash the hands of the priests, which is a symbol of the purity of those souls that are devoted to God." (Book VIII, XI) A fuller explanation of the rite is found in the mystagogical catecheses of St. Cyril of Jerusalem:

> [This is] not at all because of bodily defilement; it is not that; for we did not enter the church at first with defiled bodies. But the washing of hands is a symbol that you ought to be pure from all sinful and unlawful deeds; for since the hands are a symbol of action, by washing them, it is evident, we represent the purity and blamelessness of our conduct.
>
> Did you not hear the blessed David opening this very mystery, and saying, "I will wash my hands in innocence, and so will compass Your Altar, O Lord"? The washing of hands is therefore a symbol of immunity from sin. (*Catechesis* XXIII, 2)

The purpose of this rite is to impress upon the priest and congregation the need for "interior purification" (GIRM 76) for the proper celebration of these sacred mysteries.[16] The rite is not to be omitted on the pretense that the priest's hands simply are not dirty.[17]

In the Ordinary Form, the priest says the following prayer quietly:

Lava me, Dómine, ab iniquitáte mea, et a peccáto meo munda me.

Wash me, O Lord, from my iniquity and cleanse me from my sin.   *Ps. 51:2*

We have already considered these words from Psalm 51, when we looked at the preceding prayer.

The Scripture used in the Ordinary Form differs from that which is used in the Extraordinary Form, Psalm 26:6-11, the psalm quoted by St. Cyril (and which is used in certain Eastern Rites). There is a different tone between Psalm 51:2 and Psalm 26:6. In the former, it is God Who washes: "Wash me, O Lord…" In the latter, it is the priest who washes: "I wash my hands…" While Psalm 26 is about recognizing the call to holiness and the importance of purity in exercising the priestly office, Psalm 51 is about admitting failure to live up to that holiness and purity. Psalm 26 contrasts the hands of the faithful priest with those of

---

[16] Complete inner purification is symbolized by washing only a part of the body. (cf. John 13:10)

[17] Traditionally, only the fingers of the priest's hands are washed, because they come into direct contact with the Blessed Sacrament; they are washed again in a special way after Communion.

evildoers, "in whose hands are evil devices, and whose right hands are full of bribes." (Ps. 26:10) The Extraordinary Form prayer does not imply that the priest is a faultless man who has no need of the mercy of God: the prayer ends by beseeching God, "Redeem me, and have mercy on me." (Ps. 26:11)

The point of both prayers is that, just as the holy sacrifice about to be offered is pure and spotless, so too the priest and people offering that sacrifice should be holy and without blemish. Of course, this state of sanctity does not come from ourselves, but from God.

Prayer over the Offerings

Once the preparation of the gifts is completed – and the preparation of the priest and people as well – the priest calls the congregation to prayer.

"Pray, brethren…"

Oráte, fratres: ut meum ac vestrum sacrifícium acceptábile fiat apud Deum Patrem omnipoténtem.

Pray, brethren (brothers and sisters), that my sacrifice and yours   *1 Pet. 2:5*
may be acceptable to God, the almighty Father.   *Heb. 13:16*

As the priest says these words, standing at the middle of the altar and facing the people, the congregation stands. The *Orate* is an elaborate form of the *Oremus* ("Let us pray") used for the Collect and the Post-Communion prayer. In place of the silence that would follow "Let us pray," the priest expresses what it is we are to pray for, and the congregation responds in vocal prayer: "May the Lord accept…"

The words of the priest take up once again the theme of offering, echoing the words of the earlier prayer that we, along with our sacrifice, might be accepted by God and found pleasing in His sight. The older translation rendered *meum ac vestrum sacrificium* as "our sacrifice," but the new translation is more accurate: "my sacrifice and yours." The use of this phrase not only unites the priest and congregation together in one common sacrifice, but also implies distinct roles and participation:

> As brethren, all Christians should, above all at the Eucharistic sacrifice and communion, have but one heart and one soul, and pray for and with one another. … The Eucharist is the sacrifice of the whole Church; it is not exclusively the priest's sacrifice, but the property of the faithful also. In different ways and in different

degrees they participate in the offering of the Eucharistic sacrifice, while the priest alone, in their name and for their benefit, completes the sacrificial action itself. Thus priest and people are at the altar bound together in a communion of sacrifice; and they offer not only the host and chalice, but themselves also. (*The Holy Sacrifice of the Mass*, pp. 590-591)

Ven. Pope Pius XII wrote at length about how the laity can truly be said to offer the sacrifice of the Mass in his landmark encyclical on the liturgy *Mediator Dei* (paragraphs 80-104). Vatican II synthesized this concept of participation in these words: "by offering the Immaculate Victim, not only through the hands of the priest, but also with him, [Christ's faithful] should learn also to offer themselves." (SC 48)

The congregation's response expresses the union of all the spiritual sacrifices of the faithful with the offerings of bread and wine, and with the Eucharist that will be offered from the hands of the priest himself. The words of this prayer (and of the prayer at the mingling of the water and wine) "express the character of the entire Eucharistic liturgy and the fullness of its divine and ecclesial content." (*Dominicae Cenae* 9)

Prayer over the Offerings

The priest then says another of the proper prayers of the Mass. This prayer, called the "Secret" in the Extraordinary Form, is known in the Ordinary Form by its more ancient designation, the *oratio super oblata*, the "Prayer over the Offerings." It is spoken audibly (unlike the Secret) and its purpose is to sum up the whole movement of the Offertory, just as the Collect sums up our prayer at the beginning of Mass.

What were first called God's gifts to us are now called our *offerings* to God. In the Prayer over the Offerings, the priest asks God to accept the offerings of bread and wine on the altar and to "restore them to us with the increase which He alone can bestow that they may become the source of our life." (*The Splendour of the Liturgy*, p. 143) The bread and wine will ultimately become the Body and Blood of our Lord, and that is the general theme of the prayer.

The Prayer over the Offerings consistently includes two petitions: that God would accept our offerings, and that we would receive graces in return. Like the Collect, it makes frequent use of juxtaposition. Here is an example, from the First Sunday of Advent:

Súscipe, quaesumus, Dómine,
múnera quae de tuis offérimus colláta benefíciis,
et, quod nostrae devotióni concédis éffici temporáli,
tuae nobis fiat praemium redemptiónis aetérnae.

Per Christum…

Accept, we pray, O Lord, these offerings we make,   *Petition of offering*
gathered from among your gifts to us,
and may what you grant us to celebrate devoutly here below
gain for us the prize of eternal redemption.   *Petition of receiving*

Through Christ our Lord.

In the example above, the human element ("the offerings *we* make") is derived from the divine element ("*your* gifts to us"), and the temporal celebration of the Eucharist has as its goal our "eternal redemption."

The Order of the Mass is the same week after week, but the proper prayers change. We do not hear them over and over, so we owe it to ourselves to pay greater attention to them, so they do not go in one ear and out the other. These prayers can provide us with fruitful meditation for the whole day, allowing the Mass to truly set the tone for our daily lives. In this way, the Mass becomes a prayer that lasts more than just an hour: it is interiorized and integrated into our lives, and our lives become a continual prayer of reverence, gratitude, and offering to God.

The Offertory is not simply an interlude between the Liturgy of the Word and the Liturgy of the Eucharist. The two parts of the Mass "are so closely connected with each other that they form but one single act of worship." (SC 56; cf. GIRM 28) Because of this connection, "a person should not approach the table of the Bread of the Lord without having first been at the table of His Word." (*Inaestimabile Donum* 1)

The theme of the Offertory is the "wonderful exchange" by which earthly things are "taken from the sphere of nature into the higher order of grace … to become holy things." (*The Holy Sacrifice of the Mass*, p. 553) As the prayer said during the mixing of wine and water makes clear, this exchange is true not only of the bread and wine, but of us as well. In one of his catechetical lectures, St. Cyril of Jerusalem quoted Psalm 23:5 and related it to this part of the liturgy: "When the man says to God, 'You have prepared before me a table,' what other does he indicate but that mystical and spiritual Table?" (*Catechesis* XXII, 7)

Before Mass, the priest began his preparation by putting on sacred vestments and praying. Upon reaching the altar, this preparation took on a more penitential character. During the Liturgy of the Word, the priest was prepared to speak the words of the Gospel by listening to Scripture and praying for a clean heart and lips. Now in the Offertory, he prepares for the Holy Sacrifice of the Mass: praying over the bread and the wine, recalling his need for purity of soul, and seeking God's approval of all that is offered to Him. With all this preparation behind him the priest will begin the Eucharistic Prayer, in which the miracle of the Mass takes place.

Questions for Reflection: Priests

1) **Interpret:** What exchanges have taken place between God and man throughout salvation history? (e.g. Gen. 2:21-22) What are the reasons for these exchanges, and what do they teach us about the exchanges that take place in the Mass?

2) **Interpret:** Why might Jesus have used *bread* and not *lamb* at the Last Supper as the sign of His Body?

3) **Interpret:** What did Jesus send two of His Apostles to do before they celebrated the Last Supper, and how does this relate to the Offertory?

4) **Explain:** Which of the interpretations provided for the mixing of the water and wine speaks to you as a priest the most? What other symbolism can you see in this rite?

5) **Explain:** Consider the things the Church blesses with incense. What do they all have in common?

6) **Explain:** How can you approach the washing of your hands as a real liturgical act of prayer?

7) **Relate:** How can you help your parishioners to intentionally and actively present themselves – their work, their joys, their sorrows, and their trials – through the bread and wine on the altar?

8) **Relate:** How do you encourage your parishioners to be generous in their contributions for the Church and the poor?

9) **Relate:** How do the Offertory prayers remind you of the role of the virtue of humility in your priesthood and in Christian life in general?

10) **Relate:** When during the liturgy do you call to mind those people or intentions for which you are offering the Mass?

Questions for Reflection: Laity

1) **Interpret:** How did the Israelites prepare for the sacrifice of the Passover? (cf. Ex. 12:1-11) How do you prepare for the sacrifice of the Eucharist?

2) **Interpret:** The prayers over the bread and wine in the Ordinary Form are inspired by Jewish *berakah* prayers that bless and thank God for His gifts of creation (like bread and wine). Why does the preparation of the bread and wine include thanking God for them?

3) **Interpret:** How is the Paschal mystery (the Passion, Death, Resurrection, and Ascension of Christ) prevalent in the prayers and actions of the Offertory?

4) **Explain:** Why are the altar furnishings handled with such care? What does this say about the importance of the bread and wine prior to their consecration?

5) **Explain:** The Offertory prayers in the Extraordinary Form use anticipatory language. Which prayers in the Ordinary Form are anticipatory, and why is this language appropriate?

6) **Relate:** Your heart will soon be lifted up to the Lord. What do you bring to Mass to offer to the Lord on the altar of your heart? Is your daily life worthy of being consecrated to the Lord?

7) **Relate:** One of the five precepts of the Church is "to provide for the needs of the Church." (*Catechism* 2043) How generous are you in your almsgiving? Do you give to God out of your surplus or out of your livelihood?

8) **Relate:** Can you see yourself in the drops of water added to the wine? Are you willing to offer yourself in and with Christ?

"From the rising of the sun to its setting my name is great among the nations, and in every place incense is offered to my name, and a pure offering; for my name is great among the nations, says the LORD of hosts."
(Malachi 1:11)

I received from the Lord what I also delivered to you, that the Lord Jesus on the night when he was betrayed took bread, and when he had given thanks, he broke it... In the same way also the chalice, after supper...
(1 Corinthians 11:23-25)

6

Eucharistic Prayer

T HE PRECEDING CHAPTER began by breaking the Liturgy of
the Eucharist into three parts: the Offertory, the Eucharistic
Prayer, and the Communion Rite. In this chapter, it might help
to turn to the words of the Roman Canon (Eucharistic Prayer I) to look
at the Liturgy of the Eucharist in another way: "He took bread in his holy
and venerable hands [Offertory], and with his eyes raised to heaven to
you, O God, his almighty Father, giving you thanks [Preface], he said the
blessing [Consecration], broke the bread [Fraction], and gave it to his
disciples [Communion]." These five movements guide us through the
actions taking place during the Liturgy of the Eucharist.

We tend to think of the Eucharistic Prayer as only the prayer spoken
by the priest between the "Holy, Holy, Holy" and the "Through him, and
with him, and in him" doxology. However, the GIRM establishes that
the Eucharistic Prayer actually begins with the dialogue between the
priest and the congregation that takes place immediately after Prayer over
the Offerings:

> Now the center and summit of the entire celebration begins:
> namely, the Eucharistic Prayer, that is, the prayer of thanksgiving
> and sanctification. The priest invites the people to lift up their

hearts to the Lord in prayer and thanksgiving; he unites the congregation with himself in the prayer that he addresses in the name of the entire community to God the Father through Jesus Christ in the Holy Spirit. (GIRM 78)

As the GIRM explains, the Eucharistic Prayer is addressed to God the Father, not to the congregation. Except for the opening dialogue, when the priest uses the words "we" or "us," he is not speaking to the people, but rather to God on behalf of the people. The Eucharistic Prayer is also Trinitarian: it is simultaneously thanksgiving and praise to the Father, the sacrificial memorial of the Son, and the substantial presence of Christ through His Word and the power of the Holy Spirit. (cf. *Catechism* 1358)[1]

In the Ordinary Form, there are many Eucharistic Prayers that the priest may use, including the Roman Canon, the only Eucharistic Prayer used in the Extraordinary Form.[2] Instead of providing the text for each of these Eucharistic Prayers, this chapter will look at their general form and content, focusing on the elements they have in common, especially the words of consecration.[3]

Parts of the Prayer

There are eight basic elements that are found in all Eucharistic Prayers. They do not always appear in the same order, nor are they given the same emphasis and attention, but they are always present. (GIRM 79)

Thanksgiving is expressed particularly in the Preface, in which the priest glorifies and thanks the Father for the whole work of salvation, or for some particular aspect of it that relates to the feast day or liturgical season. Some Prefaces focus on a specific mystery of the faith or on the saint(s) being celebrated that day. At the end of the Preface comes an **acclamation**: the *Sanctus* ("Holy, Holy, Holy"). This hymn evokes the unending song of the angels around the throne of God in Heaven.

---

[1] Paragraphs 1322-1419 of the *Catechism of the Catholic Church* cover the Eucharist in detail.

[2] The Roman Canon has been in constant use in the Roman Rite since at least the sixth century, and parts of it are quoted in *De Sacramentis* written by St. Ambrose in the fourth century. From the time of Pope St. Gregory the Great (A.D. 590-604) until the 1960s, the Roman Canon was the only Eucharistic Prayer used in the Roman Rite and its text was seldom altered. The first change to the text since the Council of Trent was the addition of St. Joseph's name in 1962.

[3] There are at several Eucharistic Prayers approved for use in the dioceses of the United States of America. These six Eucharistic Prayers are treated in the third volume of this series, *Praying the Mass: The Eucharistic Prayer*.

The Eucharistic Prayer eventually reaches the **epiclesis** where the priest extends his hands over the bread and wine and invokes the Holy Spirit to come down upon them so that, by the words of our Lord, they may become His Body and Blood. This followed by the **consecration**, also called the "institution narrative" or "words of institution," by which Christ's sacrifice is made present on the altar.

Immediately after this comes the **anamnesis**, in which the Church keeps the memorial of Christ's sacrifice, recalling his command, "Do this in remembrance of me." (Luke 22:19) Then comes the **offering** of the Eucharist, the spotless Victim, to God the Father. The Church earnestly desires that we would offer ourselves with Christ, so that all we are and do may be consecrated to God the Father, through Christ our mediator, in the power of the Holy Spirit: "the entire congregation of the faithful should join itself with Christ in confessing the great deeds of God and in the offering of Sacrifice." (GIRM 78)

Throughout the Eucharistic Prayer are **intercessions**, asking that the Holy Sacrifice would be beneficial for the Church and would advance the salvation of the whole world. We remember and honor the saints, especially the Blessed Virgin Mary, and we pray for the souls of the dead. This great prayer concludes with a Trinitarian **doxology** in which the priest confesses that all glory and honor is due to God.

Now that we know the basic structure of the Eucharistic Prayer, we can look at specific parts of the prayer in more detail.

Preface

The Preface is the first part of the Eucharistic Prayer, which begins with a dialogue between the priest and people, continues in a prayer of thanks to God the Father, and ends by invoking the choirs of angels.

We might interpret the name "Preface" in a purely secular way, as if it refers to a preamble or introduction before the main part of the prayer, but the early Christians thought very differently. What we generally think of as the Eucharistic Prayer or Canon, they called the *praefatio* or Preface for two reasons, owing to the Latin etymology of the word. This prayer, more than all the other prayers of the Mass, is spoken (*fati*) before (*prae-*) God; that is, it is spoken in His presence. (*A Commentary on the Prefaces and the Eucharistic Prayers of the Roman Missal*, p. 3) More specifically, we are speaking before (*prae-*) the face (*facie*) of God. (*Living and Loving the Mass*, p. 66) Because our hearts have been lifted up to God, we are before His throne, amid His heavenly court of angels and saints, and we address Him with words of praise and thanksgiving.

The dialogue that begins the Preface is present in some form in every ancient liturgy; it has been a part of the Latin Church since at least the early fourth century. It clearly situates the action of the liturgy in Heaven above, "before the face of God." It evokes the experience of St. John's mystical revelation: he heard a voice summoning him to "Come up here" (Rev. 4:1), and instantly found himself before God's throne, amid the ceaseless singing of "Holy, holy, holy!" (Rev. 4:8)

The dialogue consists of three calls from the priest and responses from the congregation — a greeting, an exhortation, and an invitation — each of which invokes "the Lord."

"The Lord be with you."

The priest greets the faithful with the familiar "The Lord be with you," and the congregation responds, "And with your spirit." There is one important difference between this greeting and the others given by the priest throughout the Mass: if the Liturgy of the Eucharist is being celebrated *ad orientem* (Chapter 2, p. 56), the priest does not turn around to face the people when he says these words.[4] Not until the priest again says "The Lord be with you," offering them the peace of Christ, will he face the congregation. Why is this?

Commentaries on the older form of the Mass explain that because the Eucharistic Prayer is the most solemn part of the Mass, the priest no longer diverts his gaze from the altar until the sacrifice of Christ has been made present and duly offered to the Father. (*Glories of the Catholic Church*, p. 237) Rev. Gihr compares the priest at the altar to Moses, who communed with God "face to face" in the cloud of glory that signified God's presence: "henceforth he has eyes and mind directed only to the altar" so as not to disturb his contemplation of the sacred mysteries. (*The Holy Sacrifice of the Mass*, p. 599; cf. Ex. 33:9-11)

---

[4] The rubrics for this dialogue (cf. GIRM 148), unlike other dialogues (cf. GIRM 124, 146, 154, 157, 165, 185), make no mention of facing or turning to face the people. (cf. CMRR 281)

"Lift up your hearts."

Next, just as St. John was told to "come up," the priest raises his hands toward Heaven and exhorts the faithful:

Sursum corda.

Lift up your hearts. *Lam. 3:41*

The congregation replies, "We lift them up to the Lord" (*Habemus ad Dominum*). After we have prayed for the Lord to be in our presence, we pray that we might be in the presence of the Lord, before His face.

The priest's words come from Jeremiah's book of Lamentations, and the gesture of the priest stands in for the missing words: "Let us lift up our hearts and hands to God in heaven." (Lam. 3:41) In their context, these words were an admonition from Jeremiah to the people of Israel: "Let us test and examine our ways, and return to the LORD!" (Lam. 3:40) In the context of the Mass, we have examined ourselves in the Penitential Act, and now we (re)turn to the Lord; as St. Augustine said at the end of many of his sermons, "Let us turn to the Lord" (*Conversi ad Dominum*).[5] The raised hands of the priest represent the lifting of our hearts, as if he held them aloft as an offering to God:

> The priest raises his hands, in order by this gesture to manifest and accentuate the inward soaring of the mind and his desire to give himself wholly to the Lord. By this movement of the hands is expressed the longing for that which is above us, that which is heavenly and eternal. (*The Holy Sacrifice of the Mass*, p. 599)

The Latin words of the priest are very succinct: *Sursum corda* (literally "upward hearts"). They could be translated as a statement ("Our hearts are raised up.") or as a question ("Are your hearts with God?"), but our English translation renders them as a call to action, and their response as a resolute, affirmative response. These words are filled with passion and should not be mumbled feebly as just some rote ritual dialogue.

So what does it mean for us to have our hearts with the Lord? It means that we are united with God in a communion that transcends time and space. It means that we are striving to conform ourselves to Christ. It means that the Holy Spirit is operating in our lives. At this particular

---

[5] This is yet another reason why it is fitting to celebrate the Liturgy of the Eucharist *ad orientem*, facing the east: the external sign (our orientation) expresses the internal direction (our spiritual attitude).

moment in the liturgy, it means that we are meditating on heavenly things rather than earthly things. This is how liturgical commentators through the centuries have interpreted this exhortation. St. Cyprian wrote this in the third century:

> Let all carnal and worldly thoughts pass away, nor let the soul at that time think on anything but the object only of its prayer. For this reason also the priest [says] "Lift up your hearts," so that upon the people's response, "We lift them up unto the Lord," he may be reminded that he himself ought to think of nothing but the Lord. (*Treatise* 4, 31)

St. Cyril of Jerusalem, a century later, interpreted these words similarly:

> For truly ought we in that awesome hour to have our heart on high with God, and not below, thinking of earth and earthly things. ... Let no one come here, who could say with his mouth, "We lift up our hearts unto the Lord," but in his thoughts have his mind concerned with the cares of this life. At all times, rather, God should be in our memory but if this is impossible by reason of human infirmity, in that hour above all this should be our earnest endeavor. (*Catechesis* XXIII, 4)

These Church Fathers were expounding upon what St. Paul had written to the Colossians: "If then you have been raised with Christ, seek the things that are above. ... Set your minds on things that are above, not on things that are on earth." (Col. 3:1-2) It is not easy to do so (as St. Cyril admits) but it is what we should aspire to, especially in the Mass.

We are to "have our hearts on high with God" because the earthly Liturgy of the Eucharist is a doorway through which we enter into the eternal liturgy of Heaven. The word "door" appears three times in quick succession in the book of Revelation:

> "Behold, I stand at the door and knock; if any one hears my voice and opens the door, I will come in to him and eat with him, and he with me." ... After this I looked, and behold, in heaven an open door! (Rev. 3:20; 4:1)

After seeing this open door – which Jesus had just described as a sign of His desire to "come in" and "eat" – St. John has a heavenly vision that culminates in "the marriage supper of the Lamb." (Rev. 19:9) It defies description, but it is a mystical reality that must be confronted: "We are no longer on earth," wrote Rev. Jean Danielou, S.J., "but in some way transferred to heaven." (*The Bible and the Liturgy*, p. 135) For several centuries, churches were built and decorated to remind people of this:

stained-glass windows depicting the lives of Jesus and the saints, images of angels, the high altar with its surroundings reaching toward a vaulted ceiling, incense, candles, vestments, golden vessels… the list goes on. It is as if at every Mass, the book of Revelation is brought to life; or rather, we are brought into the life described in the book of Revelation.

Finally, it profits us to know what the priest says at this point in the Greek liturgies. The words of the priest are *Ano schomen tas kardias* ("may we hold up our hearts"). The word *ano* comes from the Greek prefix *an(a)-* meaning "up" or "back" (not the prefix *a(n)-* meaning "not"). This prefix is also present in the name that the early Christians gave to the Eucharistic Prayer: the *anaphora*, the "offering up" or the "giving back." This returns us to the idea of the Mass as a great exchange between God and man, and leads into the last part of the dialogue.

"Let us give thanks to the Lord our God."

The priest, lowering his hands, concludes with an invitation to worship:

Grátias agámus Dómino Deo nostro.

Let us give thanks to the Lord our God.   *1 Chr. 16:34; Jdth. 8:25; Isa. 12:4*

We already said that we are offering up our hearts to the Lord, expressing our intention to be living sacrifices; now we say we are giving thanks to the Lord. Now the true offering of the *anaphora* is named: "thanks." Or, as the Greeks would say, "Eucharist." These words of the priest in the Greek liturgies are *Eucharistisomen to Kyrio*. The word "Eucharist" means "thanksgiving."

Thanksgiving should be our immediate response to the gratuitous love that God has for us, which He demonstrated by sending His only-begotten Son among us, not only to teach and instruct us in the way of righteousness and peace, but to give His life for ours and redeem us from our sins. St. Cyril says that it is our duty to give thanks owing to the fact "that He called us, unworthy as we were, to so great a grace; that He reconciled us when we were His foes." (*Catechesis* XXIII, 5)

The priest declares to the faithful "his intention to offer a prayer of thanksgiving, the Preface, over the Eucharistic table in acknowledgment of God's gifts to men, most of all the gift which those present have come to celebrate." (*A Commentary on the Prefaces and the Eucharistic Prayers of the*

Roman Missal, p. 8) The priest is inviting us to "do this in memory" of Jesus, to "do" the Eucharist.

Notice that the priest, who first spoke to the congregation as *you* – "The Lord be with *you*. Lift up *your* hearts." – now says *we* – "Let *us* give thanks." The Eucharist is not the private act of the priest, but the public act "performed by the Mystical Body of Jesus Christ, that is, by the Head and His members." (SC 7) Although the efficacious words are spoken by the priest *in persona Christi* and the offering is made at his hands, the faithful are joined in the act of offering by virtue of their being priestly members of the Body of Christ through Baptism.

When we hear of the Mass (or more specifically the Eucharist) as a "sacrifice of praise" or "thanksgiving" (*Catechism* 1330, 1360, 2643), we should not imagine this is a merely verbal offering. On the contrary, the Eucharist is the fulfillment and perfection of the Jewish "thank offering" found in the Old Testament. The major categories of sacrifice defined in the Mosaic law (cf. Lev. 1-7) are burnt offerings, cereal offerings, sin offerings, guilt offerings, and peace offerings. One of the peace offerings was called the *todah*, the Hebrew word for "thanksgiving" (like the Greek *eucharist*). One of Jacob's sons was named Judah because his mother said "I will praise the LORD" at his birth. (Gen. 29:35) This name, *Yehudah* in Hebrew, is *todah* as a verb. How fitting that Jesus is of the tribe of Judah.

The *todah* offering involved sacrificing a lamb, consecrating bread, eating the meat and bread with wine, and singing songs of thanksgiving. The occasion of the *todah* was deliverance from extreme peril, and the *todah* psalms tell a story of suffering and salvation.[6] They begin with a lament in which the psalmist retells his plight and calls upon the Lord, and they end with words of thanks and praise to God, often including language like "My *vows* to you I must perform, O God; I will render *thank offerings* to you." (Ps. 56:12)[7]

One important *todah* psalm is Psalm 22, which Jesus invoked from the cross by crying aloud its first line, "My God, my God, why have you forsaken me?" (Matt. 27:46) If you have never read the whole psalm, you

---

[6] Examples of the *todah* in the Old Testament are Jonah (cf. Jon. 2), King Hezekiah (cf. Isa. 38), and King David. (cf. 1 Chr. 16)
[7] Some *todah* psalms are 16, 18, 21, 32, 65, 100, 107, 116, 124, and 136.

may not be aware that it moves from laments of distress (verses 1-18) to a confident call upon the Lord (verses 19-21), and ends with promises to praise God among the congregation, then among all Israel, even among all the nations. (verses 22-31) The psalmist promises "my vows I will pay before those who fear [God]" (Ps. 22:25) and says that "the afflicted shall eat and be satisfied" (Ps. 22:26), that those in distress will partake of the sacrificial *todah* meal because they have been delivered.

How does the *todah* relate to the Eucharist? There is an ancient rabbinic teaching that in the Messianic age, "all sacrifices will cease, but the thank offering [*todah*] will never cease." (*Catholic for a Reason III*, p. 68) Christians have long regarded the Eucharist as the fulfillment of the Passover, but it is only recently that biblical scholars have considered how the Passover matches the description of the *todah*; Dr. Tim Gray calls it "Israel's corporate *todah*." (*Catholic for a Reason III*, p. 75) He does this because, in addition to the description of the Passover sacrifice and the ritual meal it involves, the overall narrative of the Exodus is like a *todah* psalm: Israel cries out to God in their oppression (cf. Ex. 2:23-25), He hears their cry and answers them (cf. Ex. 6:5-7), and after the defeat of Pharaoh's army the Israelites sings a hymn of praise. (cf. Ex. 15:1-18)[8]

This is the great "thanks" we offer at Mass. The faithful voice their assent and participation not with the customary Hebrew *Amen*, but with a Greco-Roman expression, "It is right and just." This was a formula of approval used by a populace ratifying an election or another matter put before them. (*A Commentary on the Prefaces and the Eucharistic Prayers of the Roman Missal*, p. 9) With these words, the people affirm the moral and juridical character of the matter at hand. The priest then enters into the Preface prayer, repeating the words spoken by the people.

Preface Prayer

The Preface is one of the propers of the Mass, varying by the liturgical season or feast day. From the eleventh century until the twentieth, there were only eleven Prefaces in the Roman Rite. Between 1919 and 1929 four more were added, and after the Second Vatican Council many more

---

[8] For more on the relationship between the *todah* and the Eucharist, I recommend Dr. Tim Gray's essay "From Jewish Passover to Christian Eucharist: The Todah Sacrifice as Backdrop for the Last Supper" in *Catholic For a Reason III*, as well as Card. Ratzinger's *Feast of Faith*, pp. 33-60.

were composed.[9] The Ordinary Form now has more than fifty Prefaces. This multitude of Prefaces exists "to bring out more fully the motives for thanksgiving within the Eucharistic Prayer and to set out more clearly the different facets of the mystery of salvation." (GIRM 364)

While examining each Preface is beyond the scope of this book, we can look at them in more generally: the opening phrase, the tone and purpose of the body of the prayer, and the conclusion that leads into the angelic hymn.[10] The Preface begins with words similar to these, from the typical Preface for Eucharistic Prayer II:[11]

Vere dignum et iustum est, æquum et salutáre,
nos tibi, sancte Pater, semper et ubíque grátias ágere
per Fílium dilectiónis tuæ Iesum Christum…

It is truly right and just, our duty and our salvation,
always and everywhere to give you thanks, Father most holy,   *1 Th. 5:18*
through your beloved Son, Jesus Christ…   *Rom. 7:25*

Here the priest repeats and elaborates upon the congregation's response. It is "right and just" to give God thanks because it is His due, and thus it is "our duty." It is also beneficial for us: it is salutary, "our salvation." In his letters, St. Paul repeatedly stressed the importance of "always and for everything giving thanks in the name of our Lord Jesus Christ to God the Father." (Eph. 5:20; cf. Phil. 4:6; Col. 3:17; 1 Th. 5:18) He also began many of his letters by thanking God for the faith of those to whom he was writing. St. Paul certainly knew the worth of heartfelt and constant thanksgiving to God!

The body of the Preface follows this sage advice; it "gives thanks to the Father, through Christ, in the Holy Spirit, for all his works: creation, redemption, and sanctification." (*Catechism* 1352) It is usually a deeply scriptural prayer, evoking the early Christian "hymns" found in the letters of St. Paul. (cf. Col. 1:15-20; Phil. 2:6-11; 1 Tim. 6:15-16) It concludes by expressing the desire for our voices to be joined with those of the saints

---

[9] The Preface of St. Joseph and the Preface for the Dead were added in 1919. The Mass of Christ the King and its proper Preface were added in 1925. The Mass of the Sacred Heart and its proper Preface were added in 1929.

[10] One excellent and thorough (albeit out-of-date) catechesis is *A Commentary on the Prefaces and the Eucharistic Prayers of the Roman Missal* by Msgr. Louis Soubigou from 1969.

[11] Eucharistic Prayer II has its own Preface, but other Prefaces can be used instead.

and angels in Heaven, singing their unending hymn of praise, with words like these:

**Et ídeo cum Angelis et ómnibus Sanctis
glóriam tuam prædicámus, una voce dicéntes:**

And so, with the Angels and all the Saints   *Ps. 103:20-22; Heb. 12:22-23*
we declare your glory, as with one voice we acclaim: *Rev. 5:8-12; 19:1*

Sanctus

When we sing the *Sanctus*, the words that angels sing unceasingly in Heaven are placed on our lips. If the words of the priest in the Preface are not enough to remind us of that, consider the words of this familiar hymn:

> Hark! the loud celestial hymn angel choirs above are raising,
> Cherubim and seraphim in unceasing chorus praising;
> Fill the heavens with sweet accord: "Holy, holy, holy, Lord!"
>
> *(Holy God, We Praise Thy Name*, verse 2)

Because our hearts are raised to Heaven, it is only fitting that we praise God with truly heavenly words.

This hymn is an example of the communion of saints in action. You may think you have come to a Sunday Mass at your local parish, but you have really come "to Mount Zion and to the city of the living God, the heavenly Jerusalem, and to innumerable angels in festal gathering, and to the assembly of the first-born who are enrolled in heaven, and to a judge who is God of all, and to the spirits of just men made perfect, and to Jesus." (Heb. 12:22-24)

After the singing of the *Sanctus* the faithful listen and pray in reverent silence (GIRM 78) and "associate themselves with the priest in faith" (GIRM 147) as the priest continues to offer praise to the Father.[12]

Epiclesis

Our hearts are in Heaven, "where Christ is" (Col. 3:1), and we are seated with Christ "in the heavenly places" (Eph. 2:6), so our offering should be made heavenly too. The priest asks God to sanctify the bread and wine, the final step of their preparation. (cf. *Catechism* 1105, 1353) This is "the

---

[12] In the Extraordinary Form, the priest prays the Eucharistic Prayer inaudibly; in the Ordinary Form, he is directed to pray it "in a loud and clear voice." (GIRM 32)

most perfect blessing imaginable" for the bread and wine, to "become Christ's body and blood offered in sacrifice," which are sources of life and salvation for us. (*The Holy Sacrifice of the Mass*, p. 572)

Invoking the Holy Spirit

This part of the Eucharistic Prayer is called the *epiclesis* (meaning "to call down") because the priest calls down, or asks the Father to send down, the Holy Spirit.[13] The sanctification of the bread and wine is universally attributed to the Holy Spirit; two Church Fathers who attest to this are St. Cyril of Jerusalem and St. John of Damascus. St. Cyril wrote:

> Having sanctified ourselves by these spiritual Hymns, we beseech the merciful God to send forth His Holy Spirit upon the gifts lying before Him; that He may make the Bread the Body of Christ, and the Wine the Blood of Christ; for whatsoever the Holy Ghost has touched, is surely sanctified and changed. (*Catechesis* XXIII, 7)

Why does the Church associate the Holy Spirit with the change of the bread and wine into the Eucharist? Here is how St. John of Damascus explained it:

> "How shall this be," said the holy Virgin, "seeing I know not a man?" And the archangel Gabriel answered her: "The Holy Spirit shall come upon you, and the power of the Highest shall overshadow you."
>
> And now you ask how the bread became Christ's body and the wine and water Christ's blood. And I say unto you, "The Holy Spirit is present and does those things which surpass reason and thought." (*De Fide Orthodoxa* IV, 13)

In other words, the role of the Holy Spirit in the Consecration of the Eucharist is related to His role in the Incarnation of the Word.

The mystical connection between the Incarnation and the Eucharist is a profound one, based upon Scripture. Consider that Jesus, the Bread of life, was born in Bethlehem (from the Hebrew *beit lehem*, "house of bread") and placed in a feeding trough for animals, a manger (from the French *manger*, "to eat"). Many Church Fathers wrote commentaries about this connection. For example, St. John Chrysostom wrote that the altar "takes the place of the manger, for the body of the Lord is laid upon the holy table, not as before, wrapped in swaddling clothes, but clothed

---

[13] *Epiclesis* comes from *epi-* ("over, upon") and *kaleo* ("to call"). The root *kaleo* is also found in the Greek word *ekklesia*, which means "the called-out," which we translate as "church."

on every side with the Holy Spirit." (*De beato Philogonio*)   More recent commentaries have drawn comparisons as well:

> The Incarnation is, in a manner, renewed and enlarged in the Eucharistic consecration. For the same reason the miracles of the Incarnation and consecration are ascribed to the efficacy of the Holy Ghost: both mysteries … have a special resemblance to the peculiar character of the Holy Ghost, who is personal love and sanctity. (*The Holy Sacrifice of the Mass*, pp. 572-573)

What the Holy Spirit began in the Incarnation – the substantial presence of the Word-made-flesh among us – is continued in the Eucharist.

In Eucharistic Prayer III, the priest acknowledges that God gives life to all things and makes them holy "by the power and working of the Holy Spirit." In the epiclesis he prays, "*by the same Spirit* graciously make holy these gifts we have brought to you for consecration." As we profess in the Nicene Creed, the Holy Spirit is the "giver of life" by Whom the Son was incarnate in the womb of the Virgin Mary; it is this same Spirit Who "changes the inanimate elements of bread and wine into Christ's body and blood." (*The Holy Sacrifice of the Mass*, p. 573)

The connection between the Incarnation and the Consecration is expressed in various liturgical ways. In the preparation of the bread and wine in the Divine Liturgy of St. John Chrysostom, an instrument called an "asterisk" is placed over the bread. This device is made of two arcs of metal at right angles to one another, joined at the top; it looks like the frame of a simple cage. Its purpose is to prevent the veil that is placed over the bread from coming into contact with the bread. But this device has a symbolic purpose as well, as indicated by its appearance, and its name which comes from the Greek *aster*, meaning "star." It represents a sign of the Incarnation – the star that indicated to the Magi where they could find Jesus – and as the priest places it over the bread, he prays words alluding to Matthew 2:9: "And the star came and stood over the place where the child was."

This connection is represented in the design of some tabernacles. Because the dove is a symbol of the Holy Spirit, some churches have a tabernacle in the form of a dove. (cf. *Catechism* 701) St. Basil, bishop of Cappadocia in the late fourth century, had a dove of gold suspended over the altar for a tabernacle.

Fire from Heaven

In addition to the dove, fire is another symbol associated with the Holy Spirit. (cf. *Catechism* 696) St. John Chrysostom saw the fire which Elijah called down atop Mount Carmel (cf. 1 Kgs. 18:30-39) to be a type of the Holy Spirit. In his treatise on the priesthood, he compared the priest to Elijah, and the Holy Spirit to the fire from Heaven, at the moment of the epiclesis:

> There stands the priest, not bringing down fire from Heaven, but the Holy Spirit: and he makes prolonged supplication, not that some flame sent down from on high may consume the offerings, but that grace descending on the sacrifice may thereby enlighten the souls of all, and render them more refulgent than silver purified by fire. (*On the Priesthood* III, 4)

Sights and Sounds

The epiclesis is signaled by a number of audio and visual clues.

The priest extends his hands, palms facing down, over the bread and wine as he begins the invocation of the Holy Spirit. At his ordination, the palms of the priest's hands were anointed with oil, because his hands will be used for blessing and offering sacrifice. The gesture he uses was explained earlier: an Old Testament priest placed his hands on the head of an animal to consecrate it as a sacrifice, and on the head of a man to consecrate him as a living sacrifice. (Chapter 2, pp. 40, 43)

It is customary to ring a bell as the priest extends his hands over the offerings, and at the elevations of the Host and the chalice. (GIRM 150) The ringing of bells "enhances and accentuates the solemn moments of the sacred action." (CMRR 113) Bells appear in the Old Testament as an element of Aaron's priestly dress:

> You shall make ... bells of gold ... round about on the skirts of the robe. And it shall be upon Aaron when he ministers, and its sound shall be heard when he goes into the holy place before the LORD, and when he comes out, lest he die. (Ex. 28:33-35)

The initial purpose of those bells was to let the other priests know if he had died while in the Holy of Holies, into which only the high priest was allowed access. But there was a less macabre purpose to those bells, as recounted in the book of Sirach: the high priest was encircled with golden bells "to send forth a sound as he walked, to make their ringing heard in the temple *as a reminder* to the sons of his people." (Sir. 45:9)

The sound of the bells served as a holy reminder to the people of Israel of the duty of the priest in the Temple, of the sacrifice he offered for them, and of the glory and majesty of almighty God.

As the priest extends his hands and the bell rings forth to remind us of the awesome sacrifice being prepared on the altar, the deacons kneel and remain kneeling until after the Consecration. (GIRM 179) The posture of the congregation during the Eucharistic Prayer varies from country to country, but the universal rule is that *all* (except priests and bishops) are to kneel from the epiclesis until the end of the Consecration. In the United States, the norm is to kneel from the end of the *Sanctus* until after the *Amen* at the end of the Eucharistic Prayer. (GIRM 43)

Finally, at the end of the epiclesis, as the priest says the words "the Body and Blood," he withdraws his hands from over the bread and wine and traces the Sign of the Cross over them with his right hand.

A Second Epiclesis

The epiclesis has a dual purpose: not only does the Holy Spirit sanctify the bread and wine so that they may become the Body and Blood of our Lord, but He also sanctifies the faithful who partake in the Eucharist so that we may be "gathered into one body [and] become a living sacrifice in Christ" to the glory of God. (Eucharistic Prayer IV) This purpose is expressed in another epiclesis of sorts after the Consecration.

Consecration

There has been mere bread and wine in the sacred vessels on the altar from the Offertory until now, but these are inadequate as a sacrifice to God. The real sacrifice is Christ Himself, and it is the Eucharistic Prayer that effects this change, specifically at the Consecration. Immediately following the epiclesis comes the "institution narrative," words by which the priest recounts the actions of Christ at the Last Supper. At the core of the institution narrative are the words of institution that consecrate the bread and wine as the Body, Blood, Soul, and Divinity of our Lord. The language used in the institution narrative differs from one Eucharistic Prayer to the next, but the words of Consecration remain the same.[14]

---

[14] It should be pointed out that the words of Consecration in the Ordinary Form differ slightly from the words in the Extraordinary Form, but the most essential words – "This is my Body" and

The Church does not call this a narrative in the sense that the priest is merely narrating the events of Holy Thursday (along with the words of our Lord), as if telling a story to God. Nor does she mean that the priest is narrating the events to the congregation; remember that the priest is not speaking to the faithful but to the One in Whom our faith is placed. Nor is the priest copying the actions of Jesus as he narrates those actions; that is, he does not break the bread when he says that Jesus broke the bread, he does not give it to the congregation when he says that Jesus gave it to His disciples, and so on.

If you recall the model for the Liturgy of the Eucharist from the beginning of this chapter, the Eucharistic Prayer is about the "giving thanks" (at the Preface) and the "blessing" (at the Consecration) that Jesus pronounced over the bread and wine; the "breaking" and the "giving" occur later. The priest *does* speak to the Father about what Jesus did at the Last Supper, but it is done in a manner similar to that found in the Collect. In the Collect, the priest addresses God by recollecting something about Him; the Eucharistic Prayer does much the same thing. Here is an excerpt from the Roman Canon containing the transition from the epiclesis to the Consecration:

... ut nobis Corpus et Sanguis fiat dilectíssimi Fílii tui, Dómini nostri Iesu Christi. Qui, prídie quam paterétur, accépit panem...

so that it may become for us the Body and Blood of your most beloved Son our Lord Jesus Christ. On the day before he was to suffer, he took bread...

The Latin word *qui* means "who." The priest is essentially praying, "may it become for us the Body and Blood of Jesus Christ, *Who* on the day before He was to suffer took bread..." What might appear to be simple narration is really still prayer.

The prayer reaches its apex when the priest lends his voice to Christ. In the words of Rev. Valór in his contribution to ZENIT's series, "The Spirit of the Liturgy," the Consecration is "a divine action that is realized through human discourse." Priests are not mere messengers of the Lord, simply repeating His words. On the contrary, they are "ambassadors for Christ, God making his appeal through [them]." (2 Cor. 5:20) They are

---

"This is ... my Blood" – are unchanged. The words are based on the four accounts of the Last Supper: Matthew 26:26-28, Mark 14:22-24, Luke 22:19-20, and 1 Corinthians 11:23-25.

"ministers of a new covenant" (2 Cor. 3:6), ministers of Jesus Christ "in the priestly service of the gospel of God." (Rom. 15:16) Priests speak the words of Consecration with the authority of the One in Whose name they have been sent. (*The Glories of the Catholic Church*, p. 250)

Given the extreme importance of the words of Consecration, the *Roman Missal* instructs priests to pronounce them "clearly and distinctly, as their meaning demands." Ven. Pope John Paul II's 1980 Letter on the Eucharist said that our worship of God matures and grows

> when the words of the Eucharistic Prayer, especially the words of consecration, are spoken with great humility and simplicity, in a worthy and fitting way, which is understandable and in keeping with their holiness; when this essential act of the Eucharistic Liturgy is performed unhurriedly; and when it brings about in us such recollection and devotion that the participants become aware of the greatness of the mystery being accomplished and show it by their attitude. (*Dominicae Cenae* 9)

The authority to say these words efficaciously (so as to bring about the Consecration) comes from the *Head* of the Church, Jesus Christ Himself, through the sacrament of Holy Orders. (*Feast of Faith*, p. 94)

Transubstantiation

The Catholic Church has perennially professed and taught that Jesus is really and substantially present in the Eucharist. Jesus Christ is spiritually present to His Church in many ways, but His presence in the Eucharist is unique. Therefore, before looking at the actual words of Consecration, it is necessary to lay a doctrinal groundwork.[15]

In 1965, Pope Paul VI wrote an encyclical in which he presented a summary and synthesis of the Church's doctrine on the Eucharist, and refuted some erroneous opinions. After describing other ways in which Christ is present, he referred to the Church's teaching at the Council of Trent, explaining what is meant by the expression "the real presence":

> This presence is called "real" not to exclude the idea that the [other presences] are "real" too, but rather to indicate presence *par excellence*, because it is substantial and through it Christ becomes present whole and entire, God and man. (*Mysterium Fidei* 39)

---

[15] The hymns composed by St. Thomas Aquinas for the Feast of Corpus Christi contain a wealth of doctrine about the Most Blessed Sacrament of the Eucharist: *Adoro Te devote, Lauda Sion, Pange lingua, Sacris solemniis,* and *Verbum supernum.*

This means that Jesus is present in the Eucharist in His complete substance: His humanity is present with His divinity, so we speak of the Eucharist as the "Body, Blood, Soul, and Divinity" of Jesus Christ. It is this sacramental presence of Christ that makes the Eucharist a true sacrifice, but before we consider the Eucharist as a sacrifice, we should consider the Eucharist in and of Itself.

The Church does not teach that Jesus becomes bread and wine, but the exact opposite: bread and wine become Jesus. That they *become* Jesus means that a change takes place, not that the Church simply considers them to represent Jesus. The Church does not call this a "trans*form*ation" because that word denotes a change of *form*, and it is precisely the form of the bread and wine that does not change at the Consecration, and only as long as the appearance of bread and wine remain does the Real Presence remain.

Instead, we use the word "trans*substanti*ation" to describe a change in the *substance* of the bread and wine. The substance is the true essence or identity of a thing: bread comes in all shapes and sizes and colors and textures, but none of those physical attributes makes bread *bread*. In the Consecration of the bread and wine, their substance – what makes bread *bread* and wine *wine* – is changed into the complete substance of Christ, without changing their appearance. This means that a consecrated Host, if examined under a microscope, would appear to be made up of the molecules that make up normal unleavened bread. The change is only perceptible by the soul, by faith.[16]

St. Cyril of Jerusalem addressed this mystical change in the course of his catecheses. To the doubting or questioning neophyte, he says:

> Since then He Himself declared and said of the Bread, This is My Body, who shall dare to doubt any longer? And since He has Himself affirmed and said, This is My Blood, who shall ever hesitate, saying that it is not His blood? He once in Cana of Galilee, turned the water into wine, akin to blood, and is it incredible that He should have turned wine into blood? ...
>
> [Be] fully assured that the seeming bread is not bread, though sensible to taste, but the Body of Christ; and that the seeming

---

[16] "Let faith provide for the defect of the senses" (*praestet fides supplementum sensuum defectui*), from *Pange lingua*, verse 5.

wine is not wine, though the taste will have it so, but the Blood of Christ… (*Catechesis* XXII, 1, 2, 9)

St. John of Damascus made a similar argument for the creative power of the word of God:

If then the Word of God is quick and energizing, and the Lord did all that He willed; if He said, Let there be light and there was light, let there be a firmament and there was a firmament; if the heavens were established by the Word of the Lord and all the host of them by the breath of His mouth; if the heaven and the earth, water and fire and air and the whole glory of these, and, in truth, this most noble creature, man, were perfected by the Word of the Lord; if God the Word of His own will became man and the pure and undefiled blood of the holy and ever-virginal one made His flesh without the aid of seed, can He not then make the bread His body and the wine and water His blood? (*De Fide Orthodoxa* IV, 13)

Support for this belief is found throughout the Church Fathers.[17] One of the earliest professions of faith in the Eucharist as the true flesh of our Lord, outside of Scripture, is from St. Ignatius of Antioch. As he was being carried off to Rome to be martyred near the beginning of the second century, he wrote letters to various churches, offering instruction, encouragement, and admonitions. Writing to the Smyrnaeans, he warned them about certain men who denied that Jesus had a true physical body. Because of their error, they did not receive the Eucharist "because they confess not the Eucharist to be the flesh of our Savior Jesus Christ, which suffered for our sins, and which the Father, of His goodness, raised up again." (*Letter to the Smyrnaeans* 7)

Consider for a moment how sensitive Christ is to our sensibilities by allowing us to receive His Body and Blood under the form of food. If He gave us His Body and Blood under Their own forms, who would be able to consume Them? Who would not be scandalized and offended by such a gesture? Indeed, that was the reaction of many of His disciples when He presented this "hard saying" to them. (cf. John 6:52-66)

Concomitance

The dogma of transubstantiation carries with it the belief that Christ is completely and substantially present under both the form of bread *and*

---

[17] See St. Ambrose, *De Mysteriis* IX, 50-54; and *De Sacramentis* IV, 14-16; V, 21-23. A collection of quotes from St. Hilary, St. Ambrose, and St. Augustine is found in the *Summa Theologiae* III, Q. 75.

the form of wine. Thus, even though we tend to call the Host the "Body of Christ" and the contents of the chalice the "Blood of Christ," each is the Body *and* the Blood of Christ. This is called "concomitance," from a Latin word meaning "association."

St. Thomas Aquinas expressed this doctrine in the hymn *Lauda Sion*:

Caro cibus, sanguis potus:	Flesh is food, Blood is drink:
manet tamen Christus totus	yet the whole Christ abides
sub utraque specie.	under either appearance.

(*Lauda Sion*, verse 7)

The Church defined this belief with clarity at the Council of Trent:

> Immediately after the consecration, the veritable body of our Lord, and his veritable blood, together with his soul and divinity, are under the species of bread and wine …

This is the first statement of belief: that Jesus is present – Body, Blood, Soul, and Divinity – in the Eucharist under the forms of bread and wine. But He is not divided among the two forms:

> … the body indeed under the species of bread, and the blood under the species of wine, by the force of the words,[18] but the body itself under the species of wine, and the blood under the species of bread, and the soul under both, by the force of that natural connection and concomitancy whereby the parts of Christ our Lord, who hath now risen from the dead, to die no more, are united together…

Quoting St. Paul (cf. 1 Cor. 6:9), the Council explained that Jesus cannot suffer separation anymore: His Body and His Blood are eternally united, so where one is, the other must also be. The Council includes His Soul, because Christ is alive, and a living human has a body and a soul. The Council also includes His Divinity, because the human and divine natures of Christ are also eternally united in His one Person:

> … and the divinity, furthermore, on account of the admirable hypostatical union thereof with his body and soul.

Based on this complete and inseperable presence of Christ in the Eucharist, the Council concludes thus:

> Wherefore it is most true, that as much is contained under either species as under both; for Christ whole and entire is under the species of bread, and under any part whatsoever of that species;

---

[18] "By the force of the words" means "because Jesus said 'body' over the bread and 'blood' over the wine."

likewise the whole Christ is under the species of wine, and under the parts thereof. (Session 13, Chapter 3)

What this means in simple terms is that since the resurrected, glorified Christ cannot suffer division (of Body from Blood, of Soul from Body, or of divinity from humanity), wherever His Body is present, there too is His Blood, Soul, and Divinity. Thus the consecrated bread contains the whole Christ, as does the consecrated wine.

Let us now look at the words of Consecration and consider their consequences: what does it mean for the Body and Blood of Jesus Christ to be made present on the altar?

"This Is My Body…"

As the priest recalls how Jesus took bread, broke it, and gave it to His disciples, he picks up the Host from the paten and, bowing slightly, says the following words:[19]

ACCÍPITE ET MANDUCÁTE EX HOC OMNES:
HOC EST ENIM CORPUS MEUM, QUOD PRO VOBIS TRADÉTUR.

TAKE THIS, ALL OF YOU, AND EAT OF IT,	*Matt. 26:26*
FOR THIS IS MY BODY,	*Mark 14:22*
WHICH WILL BE GIVEN UP FOR YOU.	*Luke 22:19; 1 Cor. 11:24*

By these words, bread from the earth becomes the Bread from Heaven. The priest does not say "This is *His* Body," but "This is *my* Body." He is not speaking of his own body, but of the Body of the High Priest Jesus. He is speaking *in persona Christi*.

The bread, both before and after its consecration, is called the *Host*, from the Latin *hostia* ("sacrificial victim"). In Chapter 3, we considered Christ as the altar of sacrifice at Mass. He is the priest and victim as well, and these two roles are encountered in the words "This is my Body," because the Jesus Who is the High Priest saying those words is the same Jesus Whose Body is being offered by those words. This dual nature is found in some common hymns, such as "Alleluia! Sing to Jesus!" and "At the Lamb's High Feast We Sing."

> Thou within the veil hast entered, robed in flesh, our great High Priest;
> Thou on earth both priest and victim in the Eucharistic feast.
>
> (*Alleluia! Sing to Jesus!*, verse 4)

---

[19] In the Extraordinary Form, the words are just *Hoc est enim corpus meum* ("For this is my body").

Praise we Him, whose love divine gives His sacred blood for wine,
Gives His body for the feast, Christ the Victim, Christ the Priest.

(At the Lamb's High Feast We Sing, verse 1)

If you look at the accounts of the Last Supper in the Bible, you will note that the words of Consecration (in Latin or in English) are not an exact quote. They are not meant to be; these words are not a narrative but a "sacramental formula" (like "I baptize you in the name..."). The priest by saying these words accomplishes what they signify: the bread is changed into the true Body of the Lord.

The priest lifts up the Host for the congregation to see and adore. (This will be discussed in detail below.) After he gently places the Host back onto the paten, he genuflects in private adoration. (GIRM 274)[20]

"This Is the Chalice of My Blood..."

The priest continues the institution narrative, taking the chalice, bowing slightly, and praying:[21]

ACCÍPITE ET BÍBITE EX EO OMNES:
HIC EST ENIM CALIX SÁNGUINIS MEI NOVI ET ÆTÉRNI TESTAMÉNTI,
QUI PRO VOBIS ET PRO MULTIS EFFUNDÉTUR
IN REMISSIÓNEM PECCATÓRUM.

HOC FÁCITE IN MEAM COMMEMORATIÓNEM.

TAKE THIS, ALL OF YOU, AND DRINK FROM IT,	*Matt. 26:27*
FOR THIS IS THE CHALICE OF MY BLOOD,	*Luke 22:20*
THE BLOOD OF THE NEW AND ETERNAL COVENANT,	*Heb. 12:24; 13:20*
WHICH WILL BE POURED OUT FOR YOU AND FOR MANY	*Mark 14:24*
FOR THE FORGIVENESS OF SINS.	*Matt. 26:28*
DO THIS IN MEMORY OF ME.	*1 Cor. 11:25*

The sixteenth-century Roman Catechism following the Council of Trent advised pastors to meditate frequently upon the words of Consecration in order to better understand the many mysteries that lay beneath their surface. We will try to do the same, focusing specifically on the changes between the old translation and the new one.

The Latin word *calix* is translated as "chalice" instead of "cup." This is done to impress upon us the grandeur and majesty, not of the chalice

---

[20] Concelebrating priests do not genuflect, but make a profound bow. (cf. GIRM 222c)
[21] In the Extraordinary Form, the Consecration of the wine begins with *Hic est* ("For this is..."), includes *mysterium fidei* ("the mystery of faith"), and does not include *Hoc facite...* ("Do this...").

itself, but of what it contains. The word "chalice" is an example of the sacral or elevated language which is appropriate in vernacular translations of the Mass, according to *Liturgiam Authenticam* 47 and 50. It is evocative of a ritual sacrifice rather than just a meal.

The word *aeterni* describing the New Covenant is now translated as "eternal" instead of "everlasting." The covenant is not simply *everlasting* (without end) but *eternal* (without beginning or end). It was described as such in the letter to the Hebrews, which speaks of Christ's blood as "the blood of the *eternal* covenant." (Heb. 13:20) Because participation in the New Covenant is participation in the eternal life of the Holy Trinity and in the eternal self-offering of the Son to the Father, we can speak of the covenant as eternal, even though we can point to a moment in time when Jesus instituted it.

Instead of saying "shed for you," the priest now says "poured out for you." The words "poured out" can be used of both the Blood of Christ and the contents of the chalice. As Rev. Paul Turner puts it, "you can pour out a chalice, but you cannot shed a chalice." The expression "so that sins may be forgiven" is retranslated as "for the forgiveness of sins." These phrases might sound identical, but the new wording is a tighter translation that more directly relates the words of Christ in the Gospel of St. Matthew.

For You and For *Many*

It seems that the most controversial change in the minds of many people (Catholic or not) is that of the word "all" to the word "many." The old translation stated that Christ's Blood was shed "for you and *for all* so that sins may be forgiven." This is an accurate theological statement: Christ is "the expiation for our sins, and not for ours only but also for the sins of the whole world." (1 John 2:2) But it was not so accurate a translation of the Latin. So now, when the priest says "for you and for *many*," some might wonder if the Church is denying that Christ died for everyone. If we know that Christ died for *all*, how can we say that He poured out His Blood only for *many*? To address this issue properly, we need to examine the Latin and Scripture more closely.

First, the Latin word in the prayer is *multis*, which means "many" and not "all." (The word *omnibus* means "all," but that word has never been used for the Consecration of the wine in the Roman Rite.) Second, you will find that Jesus used the word "many" and not the word "all" in the Gospel: "for this is my blood of the covenant, which is poured out for *many* for the forgiveness of sins." (Matt. 26:28) There is not one major English translation of the Bible that uses the word "all" in this verse. The priest is simply saying what Jesus said.

Why did Jesus use the word "many" on this occasion? To answer that, we need to consider Who Jesus is, and how He made His identity known to the people around Him. All four evangelists connect John the Baptist with the voice crying out in Isaiah 40:3, and Isaiah 40 marks the beginning of the "book of consolation," those prophecies in Isaiah that deal with the relief and consolation that God would send Israel in their time of persecution and exile. A primary agent of this consolation is the "Suffering Servant," of whom Isaiah 52:13–53:12 is a clear prophecy. At the end of this prophecy, God speaks of His servant in these words:

> By his knowledge shall the righteous one, my servant, make *many* to be accounted righteous; and he shall bear their iniquities. ... He *poured out* his soul to death, and was numbered with the transgressors; yet he bore *the sin of many*, and made intercession for the transgressors. (Isa. 53:11-12)

Jesus was surely thinking of this prophecy, and how He was fulfilling it, when He spoke to His Apostles about the pouring out of His blood "for many." So while Jesus died for all, on this particular occasion He used the word "many." The reason can perhaps be explained by St. Paul in a passage where he uses the expression "for all."

> For the love of Christ urges us on, because we are convinced that one has died *for all*; therefore all have died. And he died *for all*, that those who live *might live no longer for themselves* but for him who for their sake died and was raised. (2 Cor. 5:14-15)

While Christ died for all, salvation is not brought without our individual willing participation. By dying for all of us, Christ has presented us with the potential to live no longer for ourselves but for Him, but this is not automatically guaranteed for everyone. We can truthfully say (as the old translation did) that the Blood of Christ was shed for all, so that sins *may* be forgiven. But not all *will* have their sins forgiven, and so we can also say truthfully (as the new translation does) that His Blood was poured out for many for the forgiveness of (their) sins. It is with this in mind that the Church uses "for many" and not "for all." In fact, the Roman Catechism from the sixteenth century explained the use of *pro multis* instead of *pro omnibus* in just that way:

> Looking to the *efficacy* of the passion, we believe that the Redeemer shed his blood for the salvation of *all* men; but looking to the advantages, which mankind derive from its efficacy, we find, at once, that they are not extended to the whole, but to a large proportion of the human race. ... With great propriety therefore, were the words, *for all*, omitted, because here *the fruit* of the passion is alone spoken of, and to the elect only did his passion bring the fruit of salvation. (p. 155)

Remembrance

At the end of the Consecration of the wine we hear the words that the priests of the Church repeat and fulfill day after day, week after week, until the Lord comes again: "Do this in memory of me." These words attest to the "memorial" aspect of the Eucharist. But we must ask, what was it that Jesus was asking the Apostles to do, and how is it that in doing so they "remember" Jesus?

To answer this question, we should first look at the institution of the Passover. The Lord told Moses, "This day shall be for you a memorial day." (Ex. 12:14) The concept of memorial (*zikkaron*) in Judaism is more than just remembering something in the past, but making that past event present, re*member*ing it – becoming a member of it. The Passover was to be eaten in a certain manner, not only on the day of its institution, but every year, as if those who were eating it were themselves being liberated from Egypt that very night. (cf. *Catechism* 1363) More will be said about the memorial aspect of the Eucharist when we get to the *anamnesis*.

Although the Latin text of the Consecration uses verbs in the future tense – "*will be* given up" and "*will be* poured out" – the Greek of the New Testament uses verbs in the present tense: "which *is* given ... which *is* poured out." (Luke 22:19-20) What Jesus was telling the Apostles to do in the future was not simply to remember fondly what Jesus would be doing for them the next day. Jesus was making present the very sacrifice He would offer on the cross. It is this "making present" of His one sacrifice that He commanded His Apostles to do. He applied the Jewish concept of memorial to the "giving up" and "pouring out" of His Body and Blood under the sacramental signs of bread and wine. You could say that Jesus *pre*-presented or anticipated before the Crucifixion what is now *re*-presented after the Crucifixion.

Finally, two hymns written by St. Thomas Aquinas include verses describing the enduring nature of what Christ did at the Last Supper, and what He instructed His Apostles to do:

Quod in coena Christus gessit,	What Christ carried out at the Supper,
faciendum hoc expressit	He also instructed to be done
in sui memoriam.	in His memory.
Docti sacris institutis,	Taught by His sacred precepts,
panem, vinum in salutis	we consecrate bread and wine
consecramus hostiam.	into the saving Victim.

(*Lauda Sion*, verse 5)

Sic sacrificium istud instituit,	Thus He instituted this sacrifice,
cuius officium committi voluit	and willed to entrust this duty
solis presbyteris,	to the priests alone,
quibus sic congruit,	to whom it was fitting to do thus:
ut sumant, et dent ceteris.	that they partake, and give unto the others.

(*Sacris Solemniis*, verse 5)

From these two hymns, we see that what Christ did, and what His priests do in His memory, is not simply distribute bread and wine around a table for a meal. By changing the bread and wine into His very Self, He made Himself, the sacrificial victim of our salvation, present under the form of a sacrament. As Christ made the sacrifice present, so too do His priests.

The Elevation

While some theologians may debate about when the exact moment of transubstantiation is, we know from the liturgical practice of the Roman Rite that the priest lifts up the Host and the chalice so that they can be seen and adored by the congregation. We would not dare adore bread or wine, so the Church is demonstrating her faith that by the time the sacred elements are lifted up, they are no longer bread and wine, but the very Body and Blood of Christ. This action is called the "elevation." As Jesus was "lifted up" on the cross at His Crucifixion (John 3:14), now at Mass He is once more lifted up to "draw all men" to Himself. (John 12:32)

The gesture of elevation should be "gracious and unhurried" so as to allow for genuine adoration and devout reverence. (CMRR 301) It is not an act of offering the Host or chalice to God; rather, as is stated in the rubrics, it is a "showing" of the Host or chalice to the congregation. It is a moment of personal adoration for the priest and the congregation, who may offer private prayers in the silence of their hearts. We all look upon Him Who was pierced (cf. Zech. 12:10; John 19:37; Rev. 1:7) and offer a silent prayer of thanksgiving or contrition, or even an affirmation of faith like St. Thomas: "My Lord and my God!" (John 20:28) The elevation probably originated as a liturgical response to heresies that denied the Real Presence of Christ in the Eucharist, such as that of Berengarius in the eleventh century. The elevation was established in French liturgies by the twelfth century and spread to other areas during the thirteenth. (*The Holy Sacrifice of the Mass*, pp. 678-679)[22]

St. Gregory the Great wrote that "in the very hour of the sacrifice, at the words of the Priest, the heavens [are] opened, and the choirs of Angels are present in that mystery of Jesus Christ," that "high things are accompanied with low, and earthly joined to heavenly, and that one thing is made of visible and invisible." (*Dialogues* IV, 58) It is another point of contact between the Incarnation and the Consecration: "After the birth of Christ, heaven and earth sent adorers to the crib at Bethlehem; after the consecration heavenly adorers again surround the Eucharistic Saviour on the altar." (*The Holy Sacrifice of the Mass*, p. 679-680)

Just as at the epiclesis, according to local custom a bell can be rung at the elevation of the Host and of the chalice. (GIRM 150) This is not only a reminder to the congregation of what has taken place and Who it is they are beholding, but in some churches the bell-tower rings as well, signaling to all within hearing of the church that the Consecration has just taken place. The use of church bells to call people to prayer is an old tradition, one which has found expression in a nineteenth century painting by Jean-François Millet, *Angelus*. It depicts a farmer and his wife with their heads bowed in prayer around sunset, as the evening Angelus bells toll from a distant church steeple.

Depending on the style of vestment being worn by the priest, there may be an altar server kneeling near him to lift the back of his chasuble

---

[22] Incense can also be used at the elevation, not only to show honor to God but also to symbolize the sweet fragrance of a pure offering. The use of incense at the elevation is recorded by the end of the fourteenth century.

as he raises the Host. This is functional – helping to relieve some of the weight of the chasuble as the priest raises his arms – but I can also see in it (whether by design or coincidence) an allusion to the act of faith made by a woman in the Gospel. She had been suffering from a hemorrhage for twelve years, and when she heard that Jesus was near, she came near and touched the hem of His garment and was healed. (cf. Luke 8:43-44)

Why would she have believed that she could be healed by touching the hem of Jesus' clothing? The garment He was wearing was most likely the traditional Jewish prayer-cloak called a *talit*, from which hung knotted fringes or tassels, with one knot for each of the 613 commandments in the Torah. These fringes were called *tzitzit*, and they hung from the four *kanaph* ("corners" or "wings") of the *talit*. Maybe the woman, seeing with the eyes of faith, perceived Jesus to be the "sun of righteousness" rising "with healing in its wings" prophesied in Malachi 4:2.[23] That desire to be close to Jesus, to reach out and touch Him, and to be healed by Him, could be represented by the holding of the priest's chasuble as he lifts up Christ in the Eucharist. This implicit desire for healing is made explicit later in the Mass, when the congregation asks Jesus to "say the word" and heal their souls.

The Eucharist as a Sacrifice

The Church speaks of the Eucharist as a true sacrifice because it makes present again the one and only sacrifice of Jesus Christ on the cross. The Eucharist *re*-presents (not to be confused with the word "represents") the sacrifice of Christ. Quoting the 22nd Session of the Council of Trent, the *Catechism* explains the relation this way:

> The sacrifice of Christ and the sacrifice of the Eucharist are *one single sacrifice*: "The victim is one and the same: the same now offers through the ministry of priests, who then offered himself on the cross; only the manner of offering is different." "And since in this divine sacrifice which is celebrated in the Mass, the same Christ who offered himself once in a bloody manner on the altar of the cross is contained and is offered in an unbloody manner... this sacrifice is truly propitiatory." (*Catechism* 1367)

---

[23] Similar healings took place through the Apostles. People sought healing by the mere shadow of St. Peter (cf. Acts 5:15) and from clothing that St. Paul had worn. (cf. Acts 19:11-12)

The *Catechism* uses the word "unbloody" to describe the Eucharist. How can a sacrifice be unbloody, and how can the Eucharist be said to be the same sacrifice of Christ on the cross when that sacrifice *was* bloody?

Jesus' Body and Blood were separated in the course of His Passion, resulting finally in His death. His Body and Blood can no longer be separated, for "Christ being raised from the dead will never die again." (Rom. 6:9) But then how do we demonstrate the death of the Lord by receiving Communion, as St. Paul states? (cf. 1 Cor. 11:26) The answer is in the separate consecration of the bread and wine. The consecration of the wine (the visible sign of His Blood) apart from the bread (the visible sign of His Body) "places before our eyes ... his passion, crucifixion, and death." (*The Catechism of the Council of Trent*, p. 155) This same explanation is espoused by virtually every commentary on the separate consecration.[24] The consecration of the wine apart from the bread represents the death of the Lord, and we shall see that His Resurrection is represented as well in an almost imperceptible moment of the Communion Rite.

The last question to consider about the Eucharist as a sacrifice is: how can Christ's "once and for all" sacrifice be presented again? Are we *re*-sacrificing Christ?

The Church is clear in her teaching that Christ is not sacrificed again. But His sacrifice, as all sacrifices, has two elements: the immolation (or death) of the victim, and the oblation (or offering) of the victim. Jesus still bears the wounds of His Passion: Jesus proved His identity to the disciples by showing them His hands and feet and side (cf. Luke 24:39; John 20:20), and St. John saw Jesus in Heaven as "a Lamb *standing*, as though it had been *slain*." (Rev. 5:6) So Jesus, in the eternity of Heaven, is always showing forth His sacrifice; He is eternally presenting Himself to the Father.

The letter to the Hebrews confirms this, for it says that Jesus "holds his priesthood permanently" (Heb. 7:24) and that "it is necessary for this priest also to have something to offer." (Heb. 8:3) If Jesus is no longer offering a sacrifice, then He is no longer acting as a priest. In his essay

---

[24] For example, see Rev. Fulton Sheen's *Calvary and the Mass*, and Rev. Nicholas Gihr's *The Holy Sacrifice of the Mass*, p. 677.

"He Died Once, but His Sacrifice Lives On" in *Catholic For a Reason III*, Thomas Nash explains this seeming paradox:

> Because Jesus holds His priesthood permanently, there must be a way for Him to continue offering His once-for-all sacrifice. The earthly, historical aspects (suffering, death, Resurrection) are completed – events never to be repeated. However, the heavenly aspect of His sacrifice, which encompasses and completes what He did on the Cross, never ends – thus the image of the Lamb standing triumphantly in heaven. ...
>
> Jesus the Son of God doesn't suffer, die, and rise again at each and every Mass, as some Protestant Christians misunderstand. Rather, the completed sacrifice of the Lamb, who was slain, transcends time itself and thus is celebrated forever in heaven. Therefore, every time we "remember" Jesus at Mass, we are able to become present to, and to re-present anew to the Father, from our perspective, the never-ending and eternally life-giving Offering of His Son. (*Catholic For a Reason III*, pp. 58-59, 61)

Thus, Christ's eternal sacrifice is re-presented in time. This should not surprise us if we remember that, beginning with the Preface Dialogue, we have been brought up mystically to the heavenly courts. In the liturgy, Heaven and earth meet, and we might sometimes forget where we are. St. John Chrysostom describes it thus:

> When you see the Lord sacrificed, and laid upon the altar, and the priest standing and praying over the victim, and all the worshippers empurpled with that precious blood, can you then think that you are still among men, and standing upon the earth? Are you not, on the contrary, straightway translated to Heaven, and casting out every carnal thought from the soul, do you not with disembodied spirit and pure reason contemplate the things which are in Heaven? (*On the Priesthood* III, 4)

"The mystery of faith."

At the conclusion of the words of Consecration, after the priest has had a moment for private adoration of the Precious Blood, the priest says the following words:

Mystérium fídei.

The mystery of faith.   *1 Cor. 4:1; 1 Tim. 3:9,16*

The old translation of these two Latin words included an embellishment: "*Let us proclaim* the mystery of faith." The new translation respects the words as they stand, just like translating "*Verbum Domini*" as "The word of the Lord" and "*Corpus Christi*" as "The Body of Christ." Furthermore, the old translation emphasized the acclamation of the faithful, but are we really proclaiming "the mystery of faith" to which the priest is referring?

The words *mysterium fidei* appear in the context of the Consecration of the wine as early as the sixth and seventh centuries, even though there is no Scriptural evidence of Christ using those words at the Last Supper.[25] The phrase was borrowed from one of St. Paul's letters to St. Timothy, where it occurs in a different context: "Deacons ... must hold *the mystery of the faith* with a clear conscience." (1 Tim. 3:8-9) Rev. Josef Jungmann proposed that these words became "associated with the Consecration of the chalice by reason of the fact that responsibility for the chalice was the deacon's task." (*The Mass*, p. 193) This responsibility, attested to in some ancient liturgical texts, is still present in the Roman Rite today: during the doxology at the end of the Eucharistic Prayer, the priest holds the paten, but a deacon (if there is one) holds the chalice.

What is the mystery of faith to which the Church is drawing our attention by these words? A cursory look at magisterial documents from the past century[26] shows that the phrase is used virtually exclusively for the Eucharist. Pope Benedict XVI wrote that by saying these words, the priest "expresses his wonder before the substantial change of bread and wine into the body and blood of the Lord Jesus, a reality which surpasses all human understanding." (*Sacramentum Caritatis* 6) The mystery of faith is precisely that imperceptible change which takes place on the altar.

These words came to be included in the Consecration of the wine because such an awesome mystery is placed before our human reason: "the Son of God, God and man, suffered death for our redemption, a death signified by the Sacrament of his blood." (*The Catechism of the Council of Trent*, p. 155) And now in the unbloody sacrifice of the Eucharist, His Blood is mystically made present: "the God-Man did shed His blood for

---

[25] In the Extraordinary Form, the words *mysterium fidei* occur within the formula of Consecration for the wine.

[26] See Pope Leo XIII, *Mirae Caritatis* 7; Vatican II, *Sacrosanctum Concilium* 47-48; Pope Paul VI, *Mysterium Fidei* 1, 15; Sac. Cong. of Rites, *Eucharisticum Mysterium* 15; Pope John Paul II, *Dominicae Cenae* 2; *Ecclesia de Eucharistia* 11, 54; *Mane Nobiscum Domine* 11; Cong. for Divine Worship and the Discipline of the Sacraments, *Redemptionis Sacramentum* 40; and Pope Benedict XVI, *Sacramentum Caritatis* 6.

us on the cross [and] again sheds it for us in a mystical manner on the altar." (*The Holy Sacrifice of the Mass*, p. 676)

Pope Innocent III (died A.D. 1216), writing to someone who asked about the inclusion of the words *mysterium fidei* in the Roman Canon, gave the following two-part explanation in his response. First, he corrected an erroneous interpretation of the words:

> Certain people [say] that in the sacrament of the altar the truth of the body and blood of Christ does not exist, but only the image and species and figure, inasmuch as Scripture sometimes mentions that what is received at the altar is sacrament and mystery and example. But such run into a snare of error…

The error he is opposing is that, according to some, what is believed to be present (the Body and Blood of Christ) is not truly present. Against this erroneous opinion, he says that the phrase *mysterium fidei* is used

> … since something is *believed* there other than what is *perceived*; and something is perceived other than is believed. For the species of bread and wine is perceived there, and the truth of the body and blood of Christ is believed. (*Cum Marthae circa*)

So the Body and Blood, although not perceived by the senses, are still truly present. This is a great mystery that can only be believed through the humility of faith.

Anamnesis and Offering

After the acclamation by the faithful, the next two movements of the Eucharistic Prayer come in quick succession, and it is possible, if you are not paying attention, to miss what makes the Mass a genuine sacrifice to God, and not a mere factory for producing Holy Communion for us.

First comes the *anamnesis*, which began, in a way, with the last words of the Consecration: "Do this in memory of me." This is another Greek word; it means "memorial" or "remembrance." It is a double-negative meaning "to not forget": to not (*an-*) not (*a-*) remember (*mnesis*). All four major Eucharistic Prayers use the language "celebrate the memorial" to describe what we are doing. Now that Christ's sacrifice has been made present on the altar, we can truly remember it in the Jewish sense of the word. (cf. *Catechism* 1357)

According to St. Thomas Aquinas, the Eucharist is "the perfect sacrament of our Lord's Passion, as containing Christ crucified." (*Summa*

Theologiae III, 73, 5) But it is not just the sacrament of His Passion; it also includes "his wondrous Resurrection and Ascension into heaven" and it orients us toward "his second coming." (Eucharistic Prayer III) All these mysteries are remembered in the Eucharist. (cf. *Catechism* 1354)

But the priest and congregation are not the only ones remembering Christ's sacrifice. The priest is, in effect, asking the Father to remember it too. When God remembers a covenant, it means He re-confirms its validity and guarantees its effects. (cf. Gen. 9:15; Luke 1:72) When the good thief asked Jesus on the cross to "remember" him (cf. Luke 23:42), he was not asking Him just to reminisce about the time they both spent being crucified; the thief wanted Jesus to *act* upon His memory.

That is what the priest is asking of God. The sacrifice of Christ on the cross was *propitious*; that is, God looked upon it favorably and granted forgiveness for sins because of it. The Church teaches that the sacrifice of the Mass is also propitious, because it is the same sacrifice that Christ offered on the cross. (cf. *Catechism* 1367) In Eucharistic Prayer III, the priest prays to God, "we offer you in thanksgiving this holy and living sacrifice." Then the priest prays that God will recognize in it the same "sacrificial Victim by whose death you willed to reconcile us to yourself." Clearly, the Church sees in the Eucharist the very same historical and eternal sacrifice of Christ on the cross... and so does God.

With these words (rather than with the elevation of the Host and chalice after their consecration), we come to the oblation, the offering of the sacrifice. Long before the priest or people receive the Eucharist in Holy Communion, it is offered back to God in a continuation of that "wonderful exchange." The bread and wine that the priest presented to God have been changed into the Body and Blood of His Son, and the priest immediately offers Them back to God, Who in His goodness will return Them to us as a sacred banquet.

In offering to God the same sacrifice that His Son offered, the priest is asking God to remember – to validate and renew – the Covenant instituted in Christ's Blood. In Eucharistic Prayer IV, the priest speaks of "the sacrifice acceptable to [God] which brings salvation to the whole world." The Constitution on the Sacred Liturgy from Vatican II affirms the efficacious nature of the sacrifice of the Eucharist, "through which the work of our redemption is accomplished." (SC 2) Thus the Eucharist gains for us the grace and mercy of God. This teaching is not new; it is what the Church Fathers wrote centuries earlier. Consider these strong words of Pope St. Gregory the Great:

> Offer unto God the daily sacrifice of tears, and the daily sacrifice of his body and blood. For this sacrifice does especially *save our souls* from everlasting damnation, which in mystery does renew unto us the death of the Son of God: who although being risen from death, does not now die any more, nor death shall not any further prevail against him: yet living in himself immortally, and without all corruption, he is again sacrificed for us in this mystery of the holy oblation: for there his body is received, there his flesh is distributed *for the salvation of the people*: there his blood is not now shed amid the hands of the unfaithful, but poured into the mouths of the faithful. (*Dialogues* IV, 58)

The priest is not only offering the Eucharist to God, but we are all joined with Him in that offering. We have all united our own personal sacrifices and offerings to Christ in the Offertory; we "offer the Divine Victim to God, and offer [our]selves along with It." (*Lumen Gentium* 11) These "spiritual sacrifices" are "acceptable to God" when we offer them "through Jesus Christ." (1 Pet. 2:5) All who are baptized can make these sacrifices by virtue of their share in the priesthood of Christ, Who is operating in them. (cf. 2 Cor. 13:5; Gal. 2:20) Christ is in us, offering Himself to the Father, and bringing us along with Him. We are imitating Christ, as we have been told to do. (cf. 1 Cor. 11:1; Eph. 5:1-2; 1 Th. 1:6)

In addition to Jesus Himself, we have been given another model to imitate in the Eucharistic offering. While Jesus is the model *par excellence*, especially for ordained priests, His mother is an excellent model as well.

Offering Christ with Mary

Just as Mary can be our model for prayerful reception of the word of God (treasuring and encountering it), she can be our model for prayerful offering the Eucharist. Our contemplation of Mary in this way begins at the foot of the cross, where St. John tells us she stood. (cf. John 19:25)[27]

In the Offertory, the priest is presented with gifts from God, and in the Eucharistic Prayer they are offered to God. Mary experienced this

---

[27] Recall the Prayer to the Blessed Virgin Mary (p. 34), one of the priest's prayers before Mass. *Stabat Mater*, a thirteenth century hymn, begins: "The sorrowful mother stood near the cross."

first-hand: she received the Word as a "gift" from God and offered Him back to God on the cross. This theme occurs in some papal documents from the past few centuries, such as Pope Leo XIII's 1894 encyclical on the Rosary:

> As we contemplate [Jesus] in the last and most piteous of those [Sorrowful] Mysteries [of the Rosary], there stood by the Cross of Jesus *His Mother*, who, in a miracle of charity, so that she might receive us as her sons, *offered* generously to Divine Justice *her own Son*, and died in her heart with Him, stabbed with the sword of sorrow. (*Iucunda Semper Expectatione* 3)

The role of Mary in offering Christ to the Father was also described in Ven. Pope Pius XII's encyclical on the Mystical Body of Christ:

> It was [Mary], the second Eve, who, free from all sin, original or personal, and always more intimately united with her Son, *offered Him on Golgotha* to the Eternal Father... (*Mystici Corporis Christi* 110)

More recently, Ven. Pope John Paul II reflected on Marian aspects of the Eucharist at the end of his encyclical on the Eucharist and the Church:

> Mary, throughout her life at Christ's side and not only on Calvary, made her own the sacrificial dimension of the Eucharist. ... In her daily preparation for Calvary, Mary experienced a kind of "anticipated Eucharist" – one might say a "spiritual communion" – of desire and of oblation, which would culminate in her union with her Son in his passion... (*Ecclesia de Eucharistia* 56)

Mary does not represent the priest at the crucifixion, for Jesus is the priest, victim, and altar of His sacrifice; so what role does that leave for her? Mary is a figure of the Church (cf. *Catechism* 967, 972), so in her is represented all the faithful who offer the sacrifice *with* the priest. She joined her suffering with that of her Son (cf. Luke 2:34-35); she offered Him, even as He offered Himself. Thus Mary is a surpassing model for the lay faithful at Mass, she who inaugurated the exercise of the common priesthood by assisting at the first "Mass" on Calvary.

Intercessions

Interspersed throughout the Eucharistic Prayer are various intercessions: for the Church, for the living and the deceased, for unity and peace, and for the salvation of the world. (cf. *Catechism* 1353)

St. Cyril of Jerusalem lists the following intercessions:

> After the spiritual sacrifice, the bloodless service, is completed, over that sacrifice of propitiation we entreat God for the common

peace of the Churches, for the welfare of the world; for kings; for soldiers and allies; for the sick; for the afflicted; and, in a word, for all who stand in need of succor we all pray and offer this sacrifice. (*Catechesis* XXIII, 8)

The local bishop and the Pope are always included in these intercessions, because the local parish celebration of the Eucharist is never in isolation from the "particular church" (the diocese) of which the bishop is the pastor, nor the "universal church" of which the Pope is the supreme pastor. (cf. *Catechism* 833)

The intercessions for unity usually have a character of an epiclesis to them, asking the Holy Spirit to bring to perfection that unity which our participation in Holy Communion both represents and builds up.

As the Offertory prayers in the Extraordinary Form make clear, the Eucharist is also offered "for those departed in Christ but not yet fully purified." (Council of Trent, Session 22, Chapter 2; cf. *Catechism* 1371) If this sounds like mere superstition, consider these words of the mother of St. Augustine, St. Monica, before her death:

Put this body anywhere! Don't trouble yourselves about it! I simply ask you to *remember me* at the Lord's altar wherever you are. (*Catechism* 1371; cf. *Confessions* IX, 11, 27)

St. Cyril taught the newly baptized about prayers for the deceased as well:

I know that many say, what is a soul profited, which departs from this world either with sins, or without sins, if it be commemorated in the prayer? ... When we offer to Him our supplications for those who have fallen asleep, though they be sinners, [we] weave no crown, but offer up Christ sacrificed for our sins, *propitiating our merciful God for them* as well as for ourselves. (*Catechesis* XXIII, 10)

The Eucharistic Prayers usually provide an opportunity for the priest and congregation to call to mind the names of their deceased loved ones.

Along with these intercessions are commemorations of the saints, especially the Blessed Virgin Mary (Pope Paul VI, *Marialis Cultus* 10) and whichever saint's memorial or feast day is being celebrated.[28] In the third Eucharistic Prayer, the priest speaks of how important the saints are to us, "on whose constant intercession in [God's] presence we rely for unfailing help." These commemorations were already part of the Divine Liturgy in the time of St. Cyril:

---

[28] The Roman Canon contains two sets of intercessions containing lists of saints dear to Rome.

Then we commemorate also those who have fallen asleep before us, first Patriarchs, Prophets, Apostles, Martyrs, that *at their prayers and intercessions* God would receive our petition. Then on behalf also of the Holy Fathers and Bishops who have fallen asleep before us, and in a word of all who in past years have fallen asleep among us, believing that *it will be a very great benefit to the souls*, for whom the supplication is put up, while that holy and awesome sacrifice is set forth. (*Catechesis* XXIII, 9)

Doxology

The Eucharistic Prayer ends by recalling that God gives us all that is good through His Son. This is followed by the "minor doxology" (the *Gloria* being the "major doxology"). If there is a deacon, the priest hands him the chalice and the priest holds the paten; otherwise the priest holds the paten and the chalice. (GIRM 151, 180) They are lifted up to signify their sacrificial character. (CMRR 318) The priest (and him alone) then prays these words:

Per ipsum, et cum ipso, et in ipso,
est tibi Deo Patri omnipoténti, in unitáte Spíritus Sancti,
omnis honor et glória per ómnia sæcula sæculórum.

Through him, and with him, and in him,	*2 Cor. 1:20; Col. 3:17; Heb. 13:15*
O God, almighty Father,	*Ps. 115:1; Rom. 11:36; Rev. 11:17*
in the unity of the Holy Spirit,	*Eph. 2:18; 4:4*
all honor and glory is yours, for ever and ever.	*1 Tim. 1:17; Jude 25; Rev. 5:13*

The congregation responds with a hearty *Amen*, which is uttered through and with and in Jesus Christ, to the glory of God. (cf. 2 Cor. 1:20)

The word "doxology" comes from the Greek *doxa-* ("glory, praise") and *logos* ("word, speech"), meaning "words of praise." This doxology is a synthesis of the numerous acclamations and hymns of praise scattered throughout the Bible, only a dozen of which are listed in the annotations above. As the Eucharistic Prayer has a Trinitarian structure, so too the doxology is Trinitarian: through, with, and in the Son, in union with the Holy Spirit, to the Father.

Are the words "through... with... in" repetitive? No; rather, they highlight Christ's role as "mediator between God and men" (1 Tim. 2:5) with "a wealth of language which recalls the concentrated rapture of St. Paul's Christology." (*The Splendour of the Liturgy*, p. 87) Jesus has a twofold nature: He is God *and* Man. In considering these two natures, we see how all honor and glory is given to God the Father. (*The Holy Sacrifice of the Mass*, pp. 724-725)

The Father is honored and glorified *through* Jesus, first of all, by His sublime self-sacrifice. The Son of God, in obedience to His Father's will and out of His love for the Father and for us, offered Himself for our redemption. The second way in which all honor and glory go to God through His Son is precisely because, as a man, He is our mediator, so whatever praise we offer the Father goes through Jesus.

But because the three Persons of the Trinity are one God, Jesus is honored and glorified *with* His Father and the Holy Spirit. We profess this in the Creed when we say that the Holy Spirit "with the Father and the Son is adored and glorified." The Eucharist, although offered to the Father specifically, is a sacrifice of praise and thanksgiving directed to all three Persons of the Trinity. As a man, Jesus obeyed the Commandment to love and serve God, so when we honor and glorify the Father, we are doing so alongside Jesus.

The Father is honored and glorified *in* Jesus because the Persons of the Trinity are one in essence and eternally "in" one another.[29] Whatever honor and glory is rendered to the Son is received by the Father and the Holy Spirit as well. We honor and glorify God in Christ as a man insofar as we unite ourselves to His offering of His Body and Blood.

The "unity of the Holy Spirit" refers not only to the unity of Persons in the Trinity, but also to the unity with God which is ours through the Holy Spirit dwelling in us. (cf. Rom. 8:9; 1 Cor. 3:16; 6:19) It is through the Spirit that God's love has been poured into our hearts (cf. Rom. 5:5), so it is in the unity of that same Spirit that we return that gift of love to Him.

In the Eucharistic Prayer we find all the "ends" of the Mass: adoration in the words of the angels, and in our personal acts of devotion to Jesus in the Eucharist; contrition in recognizing our sinfulness, and in offering

---

[29] This is called the "perichoresis" or "divine circumincession," the eternal communion between the Father, Son, and Holy Spirit.

the "Sacrifice of our reconciliation" (Eucharistic Prayer III); thanksgiving especially in the Preface, but present most wondrously in the Eucharist Itself; and supplication for our Church, our world, our loved ones, and especially our faithful departed. Although most of the words come from the mouth of the priest, they should all resound in our hearts: we should be able to say *Amen* with true conviction as the priest concludes this most solemn prayer.

In the rite of priestly ordination, the bishop says to the men about to be ordained, "Know what you are doing, and imitate the mystery you celebrate: model your life on the mystery of the Lord's cross." In the Eucharistic Prayer, that mystery of the Lord's cross is made present again under the form of a sacrament, but each of us is imitating that mystery in our lives, in our vocations, and in the universal vocation to holiness. The priest too can be a model for the laity to follow, by offering the Eucharist with devotion and zeal for souls, with contrition and humility. Then it will be more and more that he lends his voice to Christ, allowing himself to decrease so that the Lord might increase. (cf. John 3:30)

It is sometimes said that Mass brings us back to Calvary, but in *The Credo of the People of God*, Pope Paul VI wrote that "the bread and wine consecrated by the priest are changed into the body and blood of Christ enthroned gloriously in heaven." It is the risen and glorified Christ Who re-presents His self-offering to the Father, so perhaps it is more accurate to say that the Mass brings us, like Calvary brought Mary and the beloved disciple, to Jesus eternally giving Himself to the Father in Heaven. This eternal self-gift of love could only be perfectly manifested in time and space as obedience unto death, but Christ is risen and dies no more, so we do not witness a physical, bloody death but a mystical, unbloody offering as it is in Heaven. We are witnesses to this offering and part of it as well, belonging to His Mystical Body and Bride, the Church. And so now the marriage banquet of the Lamb and His Bride is prepared.

Questions for Reflection: Priests

1) **Interpret:** How do Christ's actions at the Last Supper serve as a model for the Liturgy of the Eucharist?

2) **Interpret:** How is the Eucharist like other ways of giving thanks? How does it surpass them?

3) **Interpret:** What are some of the great deeds of God mentioned in the Prefaces and Eucharistic Prayers? Why are these particular works named?

4) **Interpret:** Why has Christ commanded His Church to "do this in remembrance" of Him?

5) **Explain:** What impact might the *ad orientem* posture have on your perception (or your congregation's perception) of the Eucharist as a sacrifice?

6) **Explain:** How does the Church acknowledge the communion of of saints in the Eucharistic Prayer?

7) **Explain:** The Trinity is invoked in the concluding doxology of the Eucharistic Prayer. When else is the Trinity invoked during the Mass? How are these parts of the Mass related?

8) **Relate:** How can the Eucharistic Prayer be a model for all your daily offerings to God?

9) **Relate:** How do you "lift up your heart to the Lord" in your pastoral work?

10) **Relate:** How do you teach your parishioners what it means to offer themselves with the Divine Victim? (*Lumen Gentium* 11)

Questions for Reflection: Laity

1) **Interpret:** Why does the priest exhort us to lift up our hearts, rather than our voices, to God? (Consider Isa. 29:13.)

2) **Interpret:** Read one of the *todah* psalms listed in footnote 7 on page 154. How does it correspond to the Paschal mystery?

3) **Interpret:** What do the Gospels record as actions of the Holy Spirit? How are these related to the role of the Holy Spirit in the Eucharistic Prayer?

4) **Interpret:** The Divine Liturgy of St. John Chrysostom connects the birth of Christ to the Eucharist, through the reference to the start of Bethlehem. What other events of Christ's life are seen in the Eucharistic Prayer?

5) **Explain:** What other parts of Mass are preceded by a dialogue between the priest and the people? What purpose might these dialogues serve?

6) **Explain:** Why does the posture of the congregation (and of the deacon) differ from the posture of the celebrant(s) during most of the Eucharistic Prayer?

7) **Explain:** Why does the priest speak the words of institution in the first person (as Christ) rather than in the third person?

8) **Relate:** How do you lift up your heart to the Lord and give Him thanks through your daily work?

9) **Relate:** How can the Eucharistic Prayer be a model for personal prayer?

10) **Relate:** How does your participation in the Eucharist, offered for the sins of the whole world, motivate you to be a missionary for Christ?

11) **Relate:** How can you learn to offer yourself with Christ in the sacrifice of the Eucharist, so that your participation during the Eucharistic Prayer is more than mere listening?

You prepare a table before me in the presence of my enemies.
(Psalm 23:5)

We have an altar from which those who serve the tent have no right to eat.
(Hebrews 13:10)

7

Communion Rite

THUS FAR IN THE MASS, the priest, in imitation of Jesus, has taken bread (and wine), given thanks, and blessed it. The last two "movements" are for it to be broken and eaten. These two actions take place in the Communion Rite, which begins with the praying of the Our Father and ends with the Post-Communion prayer.

For the Israelites, an integral step in the offering of a sacrifice was to consume a portion of it.[1] The first official sacrifice of the Israelites was the Passover. To be protected from the final plague that God sent upon Egypt, every family had to acquire a lamb, kill it, and smear its blood upon their doorposts. But it was not sufficient to be symbolically "covered in the blood" of the lamb on the door: you also had to eat its flesh. (cf. Ex. 12:7-8) Eating a meal was also part of the act of sealing a covenant. After Moses had read the book of the covenant to the Israelites and ritually sprinkled them with the blood of the covenant, he and Aaron and seventy-two elders of the Israelites went up Mount Sinai and ate and drank in the presence of God. (cf. Ex. 24:7-11)

---

[1] The sacrifices of the Old Covenant contributed greatly to the sustenance of the priests of Israel, because they consumed a portion of every sacrifice offered to God. The *todah* happened to be one of the few sacrifices of which non-priests also ate a portion.

Because the Eucharist is the Christian Passover, the perfect and perpetual sacrifice of the New Covenant, the Eucharistic rite includes the eating of the sacrifice. After it has been consecrated and offered to God in the Eucharistic Prayer, the priest consumes a portion of it and then offers it to the congregation to receive. To call the Eucharist a *meal*, though, does not do justice to the sublimity and supernatural quality of Eucharist as food. No, the Eucharist is much more than a meal; it is a sacrificial repast and a marriage banquet.

A common image used to portray the coming Messianic kingdom in the days of Jesus was that of a feast. Jesus Himself told a parable in which He compared the Kingdom of Heaven to "a marriage feast" held by a king for his son. (cf. Matt. 22:1-14) His parable contained a very important warning for any who might enter that banquet ill-prepared: when the king found a guest improperly dressed, he had the man cast out. So the Church requires that those faithful who desire to partake of the Lord's Body and Blood be properly disposed; part of that preparation is carried out in the Communion Rite. (GIRM 80)

The Eucharist is spiritual nourishment, but it cannot be thought of apart from the sacrifice of Christ. In receiving Holy Communion, we are participating in His sacrifice and receiving the effects of that sacrifice: in the words of St. Gregory of Nazianzen, "The Eucharist is the unbloody sacrifice by which we communicate in the sufferings and in the divinity of Christ." (*Oration* IV) There is no Communion without the Sacrifice of the Mass, and just as we have prepared for the sacrifice, so too we must prepare for the Communion.

"At the Savior's command…"

Our preparation for Communion begins with the Our Father, which has a long history of liturgical use. In the Greek liturgies, it was prayed after the *anaphora* by the fourth century. (*Catechesis* XXIII, 11) In the Roman Rite, its location has changed over time. Pope St. Gregory the Great placed it in its present location, directly after the Eucharistic Prayer. It seemed to him "very unsuitable that we should say over the oblation a [Eucharistic] prayer which a scholastic had composed, and should not say the very prayer which our Redeemer composed over His body and blood." (*Epistles* IX, XII) In Pope Gregory's day, the Our Father was not said by the congregation, but by the priest alone.[2]

This prayer is considered a preparation for Communion because of its petition for "daily bread," understood spiritually by numerous early Christian writers (e.g. Origen, Tertullian, St. Cyprian) to be referring to the Eucharist. This petition is the hinge between the first three petitions dealing with rendering honor and glory to God – which is most perfectly achieved in the offering of the Eucharist – and the last three petitions dealing with the conditions for and the fruits of receiving the sacrament worthily. This makes the prayer a beautiful transition from the offering of the sacrifice to the communion in the sacrifice, "so that what is holy may, in fact, be given to those who are holy." (GIRM 81)

The priest introduces the Our Father with the following words:

Præcéptis salutáribus móniti, et divína institutióne formáti, audémus dícere:

At the Savior's command	*Matt. 6:9; Luke 11:1-2*
and formed by divine teaching,	*Luke 10:22; Rom. 8:15; 15:16; Gal. 4:6*
we dare to say:	*2 Cor. 3:12; Eph. 3:12; Heb. 4:16*

This phrase may be very ancient, as St. Cyprian alludes to it – or at least uses very similar vocabulary – in his treatise on the Lord's Prayer:

> Among the rest of His salutary admonitions and divine precepts [*salutaria sua monita et praecepta divina*] wherewith He counsels His people for their salvation, He also gave a form of praying – Himself advised and instructed [*monuit et instruxit*] us what we should pray for. (*De Oratione Dominica* 2)

This introduction tells us three things: we are praying this in obedience to Christ, we are using the words He taught us, and we are being bold in doing so.[3] We should contemplate this boldness when we say this prayer.

Why do we "dare to say" the Our Father? Simply put, it is because we are presuming to call God our *Father*. We are part of God's family, adopted sons and daughters through Christ our Lord, with Whom we are

---

[2] This is still the case in the Extraordinary Form, except that the congregation says the very last words, "*sed libera nos a malo*" ("but deliver us from evil").

[3] The old translation (at least in the United States) provided four options for this introduction, but two of them were completely new texts that failed to capture the sense of daring present in the Latin text; they were simply previews of the prayer: "Let us ask our Father to forgive our sins and to bring us to forgive those who sin against us." "Let us pray for the coming of the kingdom as Jesus taught us."

"fellow heirs" (Rom. 8:17), and in Whom "we have boldness and confidence of access" to God. (Eph. 3:12) It is through Baptism that we receive the grace to call upon God as Father, and it is through the encouragement of the Lord's command to pray this way that we continue to do so, despite our sinfulness. The *Catechism* calls this "filial boldness." (*Catechism* 2610, 2777) The Collect for the 19th Sunday in Ordinary Time uses similar words: "Almighty ever-living God, whom ... we dare to call our Father..." The prayer goes on to ask God to perfect in our hearts the spirit of adoption. Despite our human dignity, in the flesh and without Christ, we were "children of wrath" (Eph. 2:3), but brought to life in the Holy Spirit and united to Christ, our human dignity is raised even higher.[4] And, as we are about to receive His Son, it is fitting that we should acknowledge God as Father.

It is a quite a privilege we have, as baptized Christians, to call God our Father. Do we take this for granted? Dr. Scott Hahn relates a story about a debate he was scheduled to have with a Muslim scholar on the topic of the Trinity.[5] Some time before the debate, the two of them had the opportunity to sit down for breakfast and converse. Dr. Hahn made the mistake of referring to Jesus as the "Son of God," a title which offended the Muslim scholar greatly: "You have blasphemed: Allah has no sons." Dr. Hahn found it very difficult to discuss the Trinity without using the words "Father" and "Son."

Finally, the Muslim explained that God is not a father because He does not love like a father loves, but as a master, using analogy from his own life: "I have a dog. I love my dog. But I am moving soon to a new apartment, and they do not allow pets. Before I move, I will take that dog that I love, and I will kill it." Dr. Hahn sat confused, expecting a punch line. "With love like that, who needs enemies?" he thought. The conversation did not last much longer. Afterward, as Dr. Hahn was sitting in his car with his brother in the restaurant parking lot, the two

---

[4] "In Christian antiquity the Our Father was regarded as really and exclusively the 'prayer of the faithful'; for the baptized alone had the right to address God as Father." (*The Holy Sacrifice of the Mass*, p. 729, footnote 1)

[5] Dr. Hahn told this story in his talk "Living the Mysteries" at a two conference with Dr. John Bergsma at Immaculate Conception Church in Somerville, NJ, called "The Mystery of Faith: Called to Conversion and Communion." (April 23-24, 2010)

realized what an honor and privilege it is to be able to pray, "Our Father, who art in heaven" and "Glory be to the Father, and to the Son, and to the Holy Spirit."

"Deliver us, Lord..."

The priest prays the Our Father with the congregation, his arms out-stretched. We should all dare to say (or sing) this prayer with that "filial boldness" but also with humility, remembering that we are not bold because of ourselves, but only because of the grace of Christ which has made us truly God's children. (St. Ambrose, *De Sacramentis* IV, 19)

At the conclusion of the Our Father, the priest prays aloud:

**Líbera nos, quǽsumus, Dómine, ab ómnibus malis,
da propítius pacem in diébus nostris, ut, ope misericórdiæ tuæ adiúti,
et a peccáto simus semper líberi et ab omni perturbatióne secúri:
exspectántes beátam spem et advéntum Salvatóris nostri Iesu Christi.**

Deliver us, Lord, we pray,	*1 Chr. 16:35; Ps. 6:4; 2 Cor. 1:10*
from every evil,	*1 Sam. 26:24; Ps. 140:1; Gal. 1:4; Col. 1:13*
graciously grant peace in our days,	*John 14:27; 16:33; Phil. 4:6-9; 2 Th. 3:16*
that, by the help of your mercy,	*Titus 3:5; 1 Pet. 1:3; Heb. 4:16*
we may be always free from sin	*Gen. 20:6; John 8:11; Rom. 6: 22; Rev. 1:5*
and safe from all distress,	*Ps. 18:6; 118:5; Phil. 4:6; 1 Pet. 5:7*
as we await the blessed hope	*Ps. 62:5; Gal. 5:5; Titus 2:13*
and the coming of our Savior, Jesus Christ.	*Acts 1:11; 1 Th. 5:23; Rev. 22:20*

This prayer (known as an *embolism*, a Greek word meaning "insertion") was probably introduced into the liturgy by Pope St. Gregory as well, when he moved the Our Father from just after the Fraction Rite to just after the Eucharistic Prayer. (*The Splendour of the Liturgy*, p. 213)

This prayer, the *Libera nos*, expands upon the last petition of the Our Father: deliverance from evil. (GIRM 81) The word *libera* (translated as "deliver") literally means "liberate" or "loosen," as if evil were binding us in chains. This cry to God to be loosed from the bonds of evil can be found throughout the Scriptures, especially in the psalms. (cf. Ps. 6:4; 2 Cor. 1:10) Deliverance is an essential theme of the *todah* psalms, especially that *todah* sung when the Ark of the Covenant was brought to Jerusalem. (cf. 1 Chr. 16:1, 7, 35)

In the Extraordinary Form, this prayer explicitly asks for deliverance from all evils, "past, present, and to come" (*præteritis, præsentibus, et futuris*).

Although these words are not present in the Ordinary Form, the intent is still there: "When we ask to be delivered from the Evil One, we pray as well to be freed from all evils, present, past, and future, of which he is the author or instigator." (*Catechism* 2854) We are concerned with past evil because sins often have lasting effects which we long to be freed of. At present, we are beset by evil on all sides – even from within the Church – from which we wish to be delivered. And the future is uncertain to us, so we earnestly desire to be spared from whatever ill designs the Enemy seeks to set against us.

Praying for Peace

Among the sorts of evil we desperately seek deliverance from, war and persecution were among the foremost in the minds of early Christians. The first generations of Christians were persecuted by the likes of Herod and Saul, and later by the Emperor of Rome. Until the fourth century, being openly Christian practically guaranteed you a martyr's death. Even today, Christians are persecuted and killed for their faith. Especially in the Middle East, and in countries that are predominantly Muslim, it is not uncommon for Christians to be mocked, harassed, threatened, assaulted, imprisoned, tortured, or executed for their faith.

But, as St. Paul asked, "Shall tribulation, or distress, or persecution, or famine, or nakedness, or peril, or sword" separate us from the love of Christ? (Rom. 8:35) No; instead, "in all these things we are more than conquerors through him who loved us." (Rom. 8:37) In suffering for the name of Christ, we are sharing in His sufferings. The trials that I listed and that St. Paul listed are a summary of the life and Passion of Christ; so long as we suffer such things in Him, we are "more than conquerors."

All the same, we do pray to be delivered from such evils, and so we pray above all that God would "graciously grant peace in our days." Peace is a common theme in the Gospels, indeed, throughout the whole Bible. We should be "peacemakers" (Matt. 5:9), we are told to "be at peace with one another" (Mark 9:50), we want our feet guided "into the way of peace" (Luke 1:79), and most of all, we want peace "not as the world gives" it but as Christ gives it. (John 14:27) God is, after all, the "God of love and peace." (2 Cor. 13:11; cf. Phil. 4:6-9)

Eschatological and Eucharistic Preparation

The priest prays that we might "be always free from sin" by God's mercy (cf. Heb. 4:16) as we await the "blessed hope and the coming of our Savior, Jesus Christ." This final clause, about awaiting the coming of Christ, is an addition to this prayer found in the Ordinary Form.

The old translation blurred the scriptural reference present in this clause, rendering it "as we *wait in joyful hope for* the coming of our Savior" instead of "as we *await the blessed hope and* the coming of our Savior." The old translation was right in that we should await the Lord's return in joyful hope (cf. Luke 21:25-28), but it was not an accurate translation of the text, and so it obscured the clear allusion to St. Paul's letter to Titus:

> For the grace of God has appeared for the salvation of all men, training us to renounce irreligion and worldly passions, and to live sober, upright, and godly lives in this world, *awaiting our blessed hope, the appearing of* the glory of our great God and *Savior Jesus Christ*, who gave himself for us to redeem us from all iniquity and to purify for himself a people of his own who are zealous for good deeds. (Titus 2:11-14)

This desire to be free from sin at our Lord's advent is directed not only to His coming at the end of time (cf. *Catechism* 2760), but also His coming in the Eucharist. (cf. *Catechism* 1404) The Eucharist is the sign of unity, the bond of charity, the symbol of concord: it is "the sacrament of peace." (*Sacramentum Caritatis* 49; cf. *Catechism* 1323) The Communion Rite is a time of preparation for receiving the Eucharist, so we pray to receive the sacrament of peace worthily, and the absence of mortal sin is a prerequisite for the worthy reception of Holy Communion.

Rite of Peace

The prayers which follow this request for "peace in our days" continually call to mind the need for peace as only Jesus Christ can give it. In the Rite of Peace, the Church asks for peace and unity, not only for herself but for all humanity. (GIRM 82)

Unlike the vast majority of the prayers of the Mass, these prayers are addressed directly to Jesus, not to His Father and ours. Because of this, the priest in the Extraordinary Form is directed to say these prayers with his eyes focused upon the Blessed Sacrament on the altar; this rubric is absent in the Ordinary Form, but some commentaries still recommend the practice. (CMRR 321; *The How-to Book of the Mass*, p. 195; *The Bible and the Mass*, p. 91)

"Lord Jesus Christ, who said…"

The priest begins by praying to Jesus, in the familiar manner of a Collect:

Dómine Iesu Christe, qui dixísti Apóstolis tuis:
Pacem relínquo vobis, pacem meam do vobis:
ne respícias peccáta nostra, sed fidem Ecclésiæ tuæ;
eámque secúndum voluntátem tuam pacificáre et coadunáre dignéris.
Qui vivis et regnas in sǽcula sæculórum.

Lord Jesus Christ, who said to your Apostles:	
Peace I leave you, my peace I give you;	*John 14:27*
look not on our sins,	*John 8:11; Rom. 5:8; Gal. 2:17*
but on the faith of your Church,	*Acts 16:5; Eph. 5:25-27*
and graciously grant her peace and unity	*John 16:33; 17:11,21-22; 20:19,21*
in accordance with your will.	*1 John 5:14*
Who live and reign for ever and ever.	*Luke 1:32-33; Rev. 11:15; 22:5*

This prayer calls to mind the Last Supper discourse that Jesus held with His Apostles: "Peace I leave with you; my peace I give to you; not as the world gives do I give to you. … I have said this to you, that in me you may have peace. In the world you have tribulation; but be of good cheer, I have overcome the world." (John 14:27; 16:33)

The preceding prayer had called attention to our sins and anxieties and imperfections, but this prayer shifts the focus from our sins to the faith of the Church.[6] The Church is a paradox: she is sinless, while her members on earth are not; her faith is perfect, while her members on earth waver and doubt. (cf. *Catechism* 825-827) By setting our minds on the peace and unity that Christ wills for His Church, we can be more receptive to that grace which enables us to carry out His perfect will in each of our lives.

This peace of Christ is unlike the world's peace. Christ gives us an interior peace of soul with God and with ourselves, and an exterior peace with our neighbors. It is the rest for which all men long, as St. Augustine wrote in his confessions: "You have made us for yourself, O Lord, and our hearts are restless until they rest in you." (*Confessions* I, 1) It is not a

---

[6] The Roman Canon includes a similar prayer: "Admit us, we beseech you, into [the saints'] company, not weighing our merits, but granting us your pardon, through Christ our Lord."

mere placation attained by amassing worldly possessions, honors, and pleasures, for these are fleeting, and often serve as obstructions to peace which comes from following Christ. (cf. Mark 10:21-22) True peace is a satisfaction of the whole person, body and soul, found only in God, which then overflows to love for others, even for those who persecute or insult us. (cf. Luke 6:27-28) We can learn about this peace by reading the Acts of the Apostles and the epistles, which give witness to the concord and unity of the Church in her earliest days.

"The peace of the Lord..."

The priest offers the congregation peace, just as Jesus did to His Apostles on the day of His Resurrection. (cf. John 20:19-21)[7] The priest extends and joins his hands (turning to face the congregation for the first time since before the Preface, if he has been celebrating *ad orientem*), saying:

Pax Dómini sit semper vobíscum.

The peace of the Lord be with you always. *Phil. 4:7; Col. 3:15; 2 Th. 3:16*

In offering you "the peace of the Lord," the priest is expressing his desire that "the Lord of peace" (2 Th. 3:16) would be with you always as well.

"Let us offer each other..."

Then the priest (or deacon, if he is present) may invite the congregation to offer that peace one to another, although this sharing of the peace by the congregation is an optional part of the Mass:

Offérte vobis pacem.

Let us offer each other the sign of peace. *Rom. 16:16; 1 Th. 5:26; 1 Pet. 5:14*

Ironically, the Sign (or Kiss) of Peace is a rather controversial part of Mass in the Ordinary Form. Pope Benedict XVI addressed the concern of the bishops in their 2005 Synod on the Eucharist, who discussed whether there should be "greater restraint in this gesture, which can be exaggerated and cause a certain distraction in the assembly just before the reception of Communion." (*Sacramentum Caritatis* 49)

How can it be a distraction? Sometimes the sobriety of the moment is lost by the commotion of people walking around the church to try and

---

[7] Greetings of peace are found in nearly every epistle in the New Testament, with the exceptions of Hebrews, James, and 1 John.

give the sign of peace to as many others as possible. Some priests do this with regularity, despite being expected to remain within the sanctuary, "so as not to disturb the celebration." (GIRM 154)[8] The Sign of Peace is a liturgical action, a ritual exchange, not an informal greeting. The intimacy that is intrinsic to offering peace to another is still present, but in proper measure: "It should be kept in mind that nothing is lost when the sign of peace is marked by a sobriety which preserves the proper spirit of the celebration, as, for example, when it is restricted to one's immediate neighbors." (*Sacramentum Caritatis* 49)

The Location of the Peace

One way to resolve the issue of distraction just before the reception of Holy Communion is to omit the sharing of the Sign of Peace by the congregation, a legitimate option in the Ordinary Form. (GIRM 154) But another resolution suggested by some of the bishops at the Synod was to reconsider the placement of the Sign of Peace in the Mass; Pope Benedict XVI explicitly mentioned this in a footnote:

> Taking into account ancient and venerable customs and the wishes expressed by the Synod Fathers, I have asked the competent curial offices to study the possibility of moving the sign of peace to another place, such as before the presentation of the gifts at the altar. (*Sacramentum Caritatis* 49, footnote 150)

The rationale for this suggestion invariably quotes Matthew 5:23-24: "So if you are offering your gift at the altar, and there remember that your brother has something against you, leave your gift there before the altar and go; *first be reconciled* to your brother, and *then come and offer* your gift." Indeed, in the Eastern liturgies, the Kiss of Peace takes place before the presentation of the bread and wine at the altar. Many ancient witnesses to liturgical worship[9] attest to this placement, including the second century account of St. Justin Martyr:

> Having ended the prayers, we salute one another with a kiss. There is then brought to the president of the brethren bread and a cup of wine mixed with water... (*First Apology* 65)

These witnesses also usually allude to Matthew 5:23-24.

---

[8] The priest has also *already* given the peace to the congregation.
[9] See the *Didache* 14; the *Apostolic Constitutions* II, 57; and St. Cyril of Jerusalem, *Catechesis* V, 3.

In the Roman Rite, however, the Sign of Peace has traditionally been given *after* the Eucharistic Prayer, not before it.[10] This tradition has a long pedigree, as Pope St. Innocent I defended and explained it in a letter from the early fifth century to Bishop Decentius of Gubbio (in Italy):

> You assert that some persons recommend the kiss of peace to the congregation before the completion of the Mysteries [when it] should be given only after [the Eucharistic Prayer] is over, that by it may be revealed that the congregation give their consent to all that has been done in the mysteries and celebrated in the church, and to prove by this sign of the concluding kiss of peace the completion of the celebration of reconciliation. (*The Holy Sacrifice of the Mass*, pp. 757-758)

From the Roman perspective, the Kiss of Peace is not a preparation for the offering of the sacrifice, but a sign of consent after the sacrifice of reconciliation has been completed; that is, the Kiss of Peace flows from the Eucharist.

This is expressed in the Extraordinary Form by the priest kissing the altar before he offers the peace, a gesture not present in the Ordinary Form. Recall how the altar is kissed at the beginning of Mass as a sign of solidarity with Christ (and those saints whose relics are in the altar) before the congregation is greeted. The same symbolism is at work in the Extraordinary Form: the priest has just prayed to Jesus for peace, and the Prince of Peace is present on the altar in the Eucharist, and so he kisses the altar to express, in the words of Rev. Jungmann, that peace "come[s] from the altar and [is] passed on as a blessing emanating from there." (*The Mass*, p. 210)

The Meaning of the Peace

In this light, we can see that the Kiss of Peace in the Roman Rite "does not have the connotation either of reconciliation or of a remission of sins" – which is what Confession and the Penitential Act are for – "but instead signifies peace, communion, and charity before the reception of the Most Holy Eucharist." (*Redemptionis Sacramentum* 71) It is not a kiss of merely natural affection, but of that Christian brotherly love that ought to be among all who will receive the Body and Blood of the Lord.

---

[10] For an excellent analysis of the history and purpose of the Kiss of Peace in the Roman Rite, I recommend the essay "A Crisis of Meaning in the Sign of Peace" by Michael Foley.

The Kiss of Peace also has a Paschal character to it. Judas betrayed Christ with a kiss, and this is precisely the sort of kiss we wish to avoid; at the same time, Jesus greeted His Apostles after His Resurrection by saying "Peace be with you." This connection between the Kiss of Peace and the Resurrection is even clearer in the Extraordinary Form, where the rite of mingling the Precious Body and Blood precedes the Kiss, whereas in the Ordinary Form it follows the Kiss. The significance of the mingling rite will be explained shortly.

Fraction Rite

After the Rite of Peace, the congregation begins the singing of the *Agnus Dei* while the priest begins the Fraction, the *fractio panis* or "breaking of the bread."

The *Agnus Dei*

It was probably Pope St. Sergius I toward the end of the seventh century who introduced the singing of the *Agnus Dei* during the Fraction Rite. This ancient hymn invokes Christ as the "Lamb of God" and asks Him to "have mercy on us" and "grant us *peace*" – yet another prayer for peace directed to Jesus.

In the Old Testament, the lamb is a clear sign of sacrifice, and Isaiah uses the lamb as an image of the Suffering Servant-Messiah. (cf. Isa. 53:7) In the New Testament, this symbolism is continued most clearly in the preaching of St. John the Baptist, who identified Jesus as "the Lamb of God, who takes away the sin of the world." (John 1:29) In his book of Revelation, St. John the Apostle calls Jesus a lamb more than two dozen times, including his most stunning vision of "a Lamb standing, as though it had been slain." (Rev. 5:6)[11]

The *Fractio Panis*

As the congregation sings, the priest "breaks the bread." This rite should be carried out with due reverence, but it should not become a spectacle nor be unnecessarily prolonged. (GIRM 83) Because of the reverence due to the Eucharist, the priest (and any deacons or priests assisting him)

---

[11] Jesus is not only the Lamb; He is also "the Good Shepherd" (John 10:11) Who gives up His life for His sheep, and "the Lion of the tribe of Judah" (Rev. 5:5) Who conquers death.

should take care to avoid the scattering of fragments when the Host is divided.

It is important to remember that, although the substance of the Eucharist is Christ, the physical characteristics remain those of bread and wine. Thus, when the priest breaks the Host, he is not "breaking" Christ; on the contrary, the doctrine of concomitance reminds us that "Christ is present whole and entire in each of the species and whole and entire in each of their parts, in such a way that the breaking of the bread does not divide Christ." (*Catechism* 1377) This point of doctrine was so important to St. Thomas Aquinas that he included it in the hymn *Lauda Sion*:

Fracto demum sacramento,	Finally, the sacrament being divided,
ne vacilles, sed memento	do not falter, but remember:
tantum esse sub fragmento,	there is just as much in a fragment
quantum toto tegitur.	as is hidden in the whole.
Nulla rei fit scissura:	None of the substance is divided,
signi tantum fit fractura,	but only the sign is broken,
qua nec status, nec statura	that what is signified is not diminished
signati minuitur.	in either state or stature.

(*Lauda Sion*, verse 10)

You might recall that the Israelites were instructed not to break any bone of their Passover lambs. (cf. Ex. 12:46) This precept was in fact a prophecy of the manner of Christ's death:

So the soldiers came and broke the legs of the first, and of the other who had been crucified with him; but when they came to Jesus and saw that he was already dead, they did not break his legs. … For these things took place that the Scripture might be fulfilled, "Not a bone of him shall be broken." (John 19:32-36)

We know that Christ broke bread at the Last Supper, and it was by this action that the disciples on the way to Emmaus come to recognize Him. (cf. Luke 24:30-31, 35) St. Paul said that the "bread which we break [is] a participation in the body of Christ." (1 Cor. 10:16)

But if the bones of the Passover lamb and of the Lamb of God were not broken, why is the Eucharistic bread broken? St. John Chrysostom explained that "what He suffered not on the cross, this He suffers in the oblation for your sake, and submits to be broken, that He may fill all men." (*Homily on First Corinthians* XXIV) For the ancient practice was that a single piece of bread was consecrated, and thus it would need to be divided in order to distribute it to the faithful. But as is the case with virtually every facet of the liturgy, a functional act like the Fraction soon acquired a wealth of symbolic meanings.

The earliest meaning had to do with the unity of the faithful in the one mystical Body of Christ, as St. Paul taught the Corinthians: "Because there is one bread, we who are many are one body, for we all partake of the one bread." (1 Cor. 10:17; cf. GIRM 83) Around the end of the fourth century, Theodore of Mopsuestia (modern Turkey) interpreted the fraction as pertaining to the multiple appearances of the Lord after His Resurrection. (Jungmann, *The Mass*, p. 207) Eventually, the breaking of the Host came to represent the violence of Christ's Passion and death, the "bruising" of the Suffering Servant, the chastisement that makes us whole. (cf. Isa. 53:5; *Summa Theologiae* III, 83, 5)

The gesture also has to do with the Eucharist as spiritual food, for it is by the "breaking of the bread" that it is prepared for distribution to the faithful. And finally, it is related to the Eucharist as the sacrament of peace, because the phrase "to break bread" implies that there is a peace between people.

Fraction of the Chalice?

As Communion under both kinds became more and more popular in the decades following Vatican II, some priests and liturgists were concerned about how to retain the sign value of a single bread and a single chalice on the altar during the Eucharistic Prayer, while still allowing the faithful to receive the Precious Blood from multiple chalices. One solution was to consecrate the wine in the chalice and in another, larger vessel like a decanter or a pitcher, and then to pour the Precious Blood into multiple chalices at the Fraction Rite. A major drawback of this solution is that it increases the likelihood that the Precious Blood might be spilled; it could also, in conjunction with the sort of vessels used for distribution, cause people to treat the Precious Blood as mere wine.

In 2004, the Vatican Congregation responsible for the regulation of the liturgy made it clear that this practice is not to be done:

> The pouring of the Blood of Christ after the consecration from one vessel to another is completely to be avoided, lest anything should happen that would be to the detriment of so great a mystery. Never to be used for containing the Blood of the Lord

are flagons, bowls, or other vessels that are not fully in accord with the established norms. (*Redemptionis Sacramentum* 106)

Where Communion under both kinds is desired, and the faithful are to receive directly from a chalice, it seems that the best solution is simply to consecrate wine in multiple chalices on the altar.[12]

"May the mingling..."

Closely related to the Fraction Rite is the mingling of the Body with the Blood in the chalice. (GIRM 83) The priest quietly says these words:

Hæc commíxtio Córporis et Sánguinis Dómini nostri Iesu Christi fiat accipiéntibus nobis in vitam ætérnam.

May this mingling of the Body and Blood	*John 6:55; 1 Cor. 10:16*
of our Lord Jesus Christ	
bring eternal life to us who receive it.	*John 6:27,54; Rom. 6:22; 1 John 5:11*

By these words, the priest prays that the Eucharist might be effective in our lives as the "medicine of immortality," as it was called by St. Ignatius of Antioch in the early second century. (*Catechism* 1331, 1405) A simple but profound action accompanies this prayer: the priest takes a small piece of the Host and places it in the chalice, thus mingling the two species of bread and wine.

Although the faithful in the congregation are singing while all this is taking place, everyone should be aware of what is happening and of its great significance. The priest is praying not only for himself but for all who partake of the Body and Blood of our Lord. He is, in effect, praying that we have properly prepared ourselves for Holy Communion; he will pray specifically for himself in a moment.

This mingling has accrued several interpretations over the centuries, seven of which we will consider, each derived from the physical action of uniting the two species of the Eucharist (bread and wine) in the chalice.

The Unity of the Sacrament

The earliest documents that explain the meaning of this union describe it as a declaration that these two species constitute a single whole, that it is one sacrament (Jungmann, *The Mass*, p. 208), signifying "the unity of the

---

[12] Another solution to allow Communion under both kinds is called *intinction*, where the priest or deacon dips the Host into the Precious Blood and then places the Host directly on the tongue of the communicant.

Body and Blood of the Lord in the work of salvation." (GIRM 83) This point of doctrine has been made by many commentators on the liturgy. Theodore of Mopsuestia explains three times in his liturgical commentary that "although these elements are two, they are nevertheless one in power." St. Thomas Aquinas addresses the question of "whether the Eucharist is one sacrament or several" in his *Summa Theologica*, and states that because the Eucharist is the sacrament of the Church's unity and a sacrament "bears the likeness of the reality of which it is the sacrament," thus the Eucharist is one sacrament, as the Church is one. He concludes that although "the bread and wine are materially several signs," the sacrament Itself is "formally and perfectively one." (*Summa Theologiae* III, 73, 2) To put it plainly, the Eucharist is not two sacraments, but one sacrament made present under two forms.

This interpretation does not challenge the doctrine of concomitance (which states that the whole Christ is received under the form of bread or under the form of wine). Instead, it confirms this doctrine by physically displaying the inherent unity of the two forms.

A Symbol of the Resurrection

It was only a short theological step from that first meaning to this second one. If the consecrated bread is a sign of the Body of the Lord, and the consecrated wine is a sign of His Blood, and the separate consecration of both was a sign of His death... what event is represented by their union? His Resurrection, of course! This makes the mingling the continuation of the liturgical re-presentation of the Paschal mystery. Having witnessed His Passion and death in the Offertory and Consecration, we now behold His Resurrection. This union is hidden from our view by the chalice, for no one witnessed the very moment of that glorious and ineffable mystery of the Resurrection.

What this means is that the Body that we receive in the Eucharist is the "living and glorious" – that is, resurrected and glorified – "Body of Jesus Christ." (GIRM 83) His Body is not injured or torn apart when we receive Him in Communion, because glorified bodies enjoy *impassibility* – from the Latin *im-* ("not") and *passio* ("suffer"), meaning "unable to suffer." (*Summa Theologiae* III, 81, 3)

Participation in Christ's Suffering

Although Christ no longer suffers, He certainly did endure great pains in His Passion. In the Garden of Gethsemane, He asked the Father, "if it be possible, let this chalice pass from me." (Matt. 26:39; cf. 26:42) The cup is a common Old Testament image symbolizing the wrath of God which is being poured out or drunk. (cf. Ps. 75:8; Isa. 51:17; Jer. 25:15)

Whatever other symbolism the cup in Jesus' prayer in Gethsemane has, it also represents the great sorrow and suffering that Jesus would bear. To that end, the chalice used at Mass (which contains the Precious Blood that was poured out in the Passion) can be seen as Christ's "cup of sufferings." (*Douay Catechism*, p. 133) Because the mingling (a sign of the Resurrection) takes place *in* the chalice (a sign of the Passion), the *Douay Catechism* gives the interpretation that we cannot share in the fruits of the Resurrection unless we are willing to share in His suffering as well, as St. Paul wrote to the Romans. (cf. Rom. 8:17)

The Unity of the Church

The fourth interpretation is based upon two ancient (but discontinued) Roman customs, called the *sancta* and the *fermentum*, named for the two fragments of the Eucharistic bread used in these rites which attested to the unity of the Church across time and space. (*Ordo Romanus Primus*, pp. 106-109)

In the *sancta* (meaning "holy"), the Pope would place in the chalice a portion of consecrated bread, reserved from a previous Mass he had celebrated. This signified that the Eucharist was one sacrifice throughout all time, uniting the communicants at this Mass with those from the previous Mass down through the weeks, months, and years.

In the *fermentum* (meaning "leavening"), the Pope sent a portion of the consecrated bread to priests throughout the city for them to put into the chalice at their next Mass. Pope St. Innocent I describes this practice in the same letter to Decentius mentioned above. The *fermentum* signified that the Eucharist is one sacrifice through all space, and that those priests were celebrating the Eucharist in union with the Pope. Union with the local bishop is an important part of the celebration of the Eucharist, as expressed by St. Ignatius of Antioch in two of his letters from the second century: "Let that be deemed a proper Eucharist, which is administered either by the bishop, or by one to whom he has entrusted it." (*Epistle to the Smyrnaens* 8) "There is one flesh of our Lord Jesus Christ, and one cup to show forth the unity of His blood; one altar; as there is one bishop, along with the presbytery and deacons, my fellow-servants." (*Epistle to the Philadelphians* 4)

The Members of the Church

Varying interpretations were given to the traditional three pieces[13] into which the Host was divided: Christ's Body alive, buried, and resurrected; the piercing of His Body in His hands, feet, and side; the Persons of the Holy Trinity. But a prevailing interpretation was that they stood for the three divisions of the Church: triumphant in Heaven, militant on earth, and suffering in Purgatory. (*Summa Theologiae* III, 83, 5; *The Glories of the Catholic Church*, pp. 260-261)

A Guarantor of Peace

In the Extraordinary Form, the mingling comes before the Sign of Peace. Because the mingling represents the Resurrection, and peace was the first gift given by Jesus to His Apostles after He was raised from the dead, the two rites (the mingling and the Sign of Peace) were seen to be mystically connected. (*The Glories of the Catholic Church*, p. 262) The mingling is then the guarantor of that peace: Christ, being raised, assures us of His lasting peace.

Manifesting the *Agnus Dei*

Another mystical interpretation of the mingling sees that it corresponds to the three verses of the *Agnus Dei*. While it is permissible to repeat the first two verses as long as necessary until the Fraction Rite is finished (GIRM 83), its traditional form is two verses ending with "have mercy on us" and one verse ending with "grant us peace."

As mentioned above, the two Eucharistic species (bread and wine) represent "the unity of the Body and Blood of the Lord in the work of salvation" which gained us God's *mercy*. (GIRM 83) They come together

---

[13] The long-standing tradition of the Roman Rite (at least since the 9th century) was to divide the Host into three portions – two large particles and a third small particle to be placed in the chalice – all of which were consumed by the priest. This strict division into three portions is not required in the Ordinary Form, where the primary Host can be large enough to be divided into portions that the faithful receive. (cf. GIRM 321)

as one in the chalice, representing the Resurrection, which guarantees our *peace*. Thus the mingling mirrors our sung supplication to the Lamb of God that "appropriately concludes with the *twofold* cry for *mercy* and the *single* cry for *peace*." (*The Holy Sacrifice of the Mass*, p. 750)

Preparation for Communion

After the Fraction Rite and the mingling, the priest prepares himself for his reception of Holy Communion. Consuming the Body and Blood is the conclusion of the sacrifice; it is when the sacrifice to God becomes a sacrament for us. Christ means for the Eucharist to be eaten, not only to be offered and adored; after all, He gave it to us under the forms of food and drink. Before we can receive Jesus in the Eucharist, we must be properly prepared, lest we receive Him unworthily. The more carefully and thoughtfully and fervently we prepare ourselves for Communion, the more fruitful and effective it will be in our lives.

In many Eastern liturgies, the priest or deacon cries out "Holy things to the holy!" St. Cyril of Jerusalem explains that this acclamation speaks of the action of the Holy Spirit, Who sanctifies not only the offerings of bread and wine, but us as well at our Baptism and Confirmation. The Eucharist is holy by nature, for it is Jesus Christ; we are holy, not by our nature, but by our participation in Christ. (*Catechesis* V, 19)

Discerning the Body

Do we know what we are getting ourselves into and what we are getting into ourselves? The same Lord we praised in the Gloria and professed in the Creed, we will receive into our bodies. Dr. Scott Hahn compares and contrasts the Eucharist with electricity and fire: if we know that these awesome powers of nature must be handled with care, how much more respectfully should we treat the divine life and divine power that come to us in the Eucharist? (*The Lamb's Supper*, p. 159)

St. Paul, after warning that whoever "eats the bread or drinks the cup of the Lord in an unworthy manner will be guilty of profaning the body and blood of the Lord" (1 Cor. 11:27), gives us a rule by which to measure if we are prepared to receive Holy Communion:

> Let a man *examine himself*, and so eat of the bread and drink of the cup. For any one who eats and drinks without *discerning the body* eats and drinks judgment upon himself. (1 Cor. 11:28-29)

"Discerning the body" can mean many things. In the immediate context of examining yourself, it means to perform an examination of conscience to see whether you are living according to the flesh, instead of according to the spirit. (cf. Rom. 8:5-14)

But if we read it in its wider context, starting at 1 Corinthians 11:17, we see that St. Paul is writing about the manner in which the Corinthians treated the Lord's Supper. If eating and drinking the consecrated bread and wine "proclaim[s] the Lord's death" (1 Cor. 11:26), then we need to discern the body – that is, we must recognize what we are receiving: the very Body of Christ.[14] St. Augustine offers this interpretation:

> Let them who already eat the Flesh of the Lord and drink His Blood, *think what it is* they eat and drink, lest, as the Apostle says, "They eat and drink judgment to themselves." (St. Augustine, *Sermon* LXXXII, 1)

Opening our Eyes

St. John Chrysostom took St. Paul's warning about eating and drinking judgment differently:

> The disciples [on the road to Emmaus] knew Him not, except "in the breaking of bread." And truly he that eats and drinks not judgment to himself in the breaking of bread does know Christ. (St. John Chrysostom, *Homily II on 1 John*, 1)

He directs our attention to the encounter on the road to Emmaus, which paralleled an event that took place many centuries earlier.

In the third chapter of the book of Genesis we find the first account of people sharing food and its consequences. No sooner had Eve and Adam eaten the fruit of the Tree of the Knowledge of Good and Evil, than "the *eyes* of both *were opened*, and *they knew* that they were naked." (Gen. 3:7) They ate this food in direct disobedience to God's command: "of the tree of the knowledge of good and evil *you shall not eat*, for in the day that you eat of it *you shall die*." (Gen. 2:17)

Thousands of years later God gave a new command: "Take, *eat*," for "if any one eats of this bread, *he will live* for ever." (Matt. 26:26; John 6:51) Then, on the very day of His Resurrection, two of Jesus' disciples ate of the fruit of the cross, the true Tree of Life:

---

[14] This interpretation is supported by a variant found in some Greek manuscripts that reads "discerning the body *of the Lord*." This is present in the Douay-Rheims translation.

[Jesus] took the bread and blessed and broke it, and gave it to them. And their *eyes were opened* and *they recognized* him; and he vanished out of their sight. They said to each other, "Did not our hearts burn within us while he talked to us on the road, while he opened to us the Scriptures?" ... Then they told [the Apostles] what had happened on the road, and how he was known to them in the breaking of the bread. (Luke 24:30-35)[15]

The encounter of Cleopas and an unnamed disciple on the road to Emmaus is often used to summarize the mystery and movement of the Mass: Jesus comes to us in the Scriptures, our hearts burn for Him, and then He is made known to us in "the breaking of the bread," a name for the Eucharist dating back to the first days of the Church. (cf. Acts 2:42; 20:7) Jesus disappears from the disciples' sight because they recognize Him (and His presence) in the Eucharist; what they perceived without understanding by eyes of flesh, they now perceived with understanding by eyes of faith: they truly discerned His Body.

The Summit of the Sacraments

The Eucharist is "the source and summit of the Christian life" (*Catechism* 1324) because it is not only a means of grace, it contains the Author of grace; thus we call the Eucharist the "Most Blessed Sacrament." All the other sacraments derive their power from the One Who is contained in the Eucharist, but there is a particularly strong connection between the Eucharist and the sacraments of Baptism and Penance.

There is a special unity between Baptism and the Eucharist: just as Baptism is a participation in Christ's death and Resurrection, dying to sin and rising to new life in Him, so too is the Eucharist, because it is the sacrament of His sacrificial death in which He gives us His glorified Body and Blood as food. This is one reason why the Church does not offer Holy Communion to those who are not baptized.

Just as there is no Communion without the Consecration, there should be no Communion without discernment. (cf. 1 Cor. 11:29) Thus, there is a unity between Penance and the Eucharist. Ven. Pope John Paul II, in his encyclical *Redemptor Hominis*, described this link:

The Christ who calls to the Eucharistic banquet is always the same Christ who exhorts us to penance and repeats his "Repent."

---

[15] The Greek (and Latin) vocabulary and structure of Luke 24:31 clearly parallel Genesis 3:7.

Without [constant] conversion, partaking of the Eucharist would lack its full redeeming effectiveness… (*Redemptor Hominis* 20)

This is one reason why the Church does not knowingly administer Holy Communion to someone in a state of mortal sin.

The Priest's Prayers

The priest prepares for Communion by quietly saying one of two prayers. This quiet recollection helps prevent Communion from being a mere external act, and more a moment of blessed silence in the presence of the Lamb. (*The Spirit of the Liturgy*, pp. 213-214) In the Extraordinary Form he prays both prayers, but in the Ordinary Form he chooses one.[16] As they are addressed to Jesus, it is appropriate for the priest to pray these prayers while gazing upon the Lord in the sacrament.

These prayers are suitable for use by the laity as well, who are also encouraged to make a similar act of preparation. (GIRM 84)

"Lord Jesus Christ, Son of the Living God…"

The first prayer, from the ninth century, echoes St. Peter's confession and recalls the work of the Trinity in our redemption. The priest prays to be kept far from sin and close to Christ by the Eucharist:

Dómine Iesu Christe, Fili Dei vivi, qui ex voluntáte Patris, cooperánte Spíritu Sancto, per mortem tuam mundum vivificásti: líbera me per hoc sacrosánctum Corpus et Sánguinem tuum ab ómnibus iniquitátibus meis et univérsis malis: et fac me tuis semper inhærére mandátis, et a te numquam separári permíttas.

Lord Jesus Christ, Son of the living God,	*Matt. 16:16; John 11:27*
who, by the will of the Father	*Acts 2:23; 3:18*
and the work of the Holy Spirit,	*Rom. 8:11; Heb. 9:14*
through your Death gave life to the world,	*John 3:16; 6:33; Rom. 5:18*
free me by this, your most holy Body and Blood,	*Acts 13:39; Heb. 9:14*
from all my sins and from every evil;	*Eph. 1:7; 2 Tim. 4:18*
keep me always faithful to your commandments,	*John 15:10; 1 Cor. 7:19*
and never let me be parted from you.	*Rom. 8:35-39*

When St. Peter confessed Jesus to be "the Christ, the Son of the living God" (Matt. 16:16), he only saw a man standing before him, yet he

---

16 "The priest's reception of Holy Communion is preceded by two very beautiful and profound prayers, from which, to avoid the silence being too long, he is to choose one. Perhaps we shall again one day take the time to use both." (Cardinal Ratzinger, *The Spirit of the Liturgy*, p. 213)

did not hesitate to profess His divinity. Standing at the altar, the priest sees neither Christ's divinity or humanity, but with rock-like conviction and faith, he confesses both. (*The Holy Sacrifice of the Mass*, p. 762)

This prayer succinctly reminds us that our redemption, as well as the liturgy, is the work of the Most Holy Trinity. (cf. *Catechism* 1073) It may be unpleasant to consider (and unpopular among some modern schools of theology), but it really was the will of the Father that His Son suffer and die on the cross for our sins. (cf. Isa. 53:10; Phil. 2:8) And it was through the Holy Spirit, Who formed Christ's body in the womb of the Virgin Mary, that Christ offered Himself to the Father. (cf. Heb. 9:14)

The blessed fruit of Jesus' sacrificial death is that He brought new life to a world dead in sin; what Jesus did for the world, the priest asks Him to do personally in his own life. First he prays to be freed from all his sins and all evils, which is the effect of the Eucharist as a sacrifice. (cf. *Catechism* 1393-1395) Then he prays for the grace to keep Christ's commandments and to abide in Him, which are effects of the Eucharist as a sacrament. (cf. John 15:10; *Catechism* 1391, 2053)

"May the receiving of your Body and Blood..."

The other prayer is a composition from the tenth century, although it has an ancestor in the *Apostolic Constitutions* of the late fourth century.[17] The priest prays for a worthy reception of Holy Communion:

Percéptio Córporis et Sánguinis tui, Dómine Iesu Christe, non mihi provéniat in iudícium et condemnatiónem: sed pro tua pietáte prosit mihi ad tutaméntum mentis et córporis, et ad medélam percipiéndam.

May the receiving of your Body and Blood, Lord Jesus Christ,	*John 6:53-56*
not bring me to judgment and condemnation,	*1 Cor. 11:27-29*
but through your loving mercy	*Ps. 25:6; Luke 1:78; Jude 21*
be for me protection in mind and body	*Ps. 91:14; 1 Th. 5:23; 1 Pet. 2:25*
and a healing remedy.	*Sir. 34:17; Rev. 22:2*

In the Extraordinary Form, this prayer is slightly longer, containing the words "which I, though unworthy, presume to receive" after "Lord Jesus

---

[17] "Let us give thanks to Him who has thought us worthy to partake of these His holy mysteries; and let us beseech Him that it may not be to us for condemnation, but for salvation, to the advantage of soul and body, to the preservation of piety, to the remission of sins, and to the life of the world to come." (*Apostolic Constitutions* VIII, XIV)

Christ." This may have been removed from the Ordinary Form because the priest expresses the same sentiment moments later when saying "Lord, I am not worthy to receive you…" with the congregation. But if we all admit to being unworthy to receive Communion, what does it mean to say that we should avoid receiving the Lord unworthily?

> If a man has done all in his power, if he has prepared himself as carefully as possible, then indeed we say, and justly, that he is worthy to receive Holy Communion. But this does not prevent his regarding and confessing himself as unworthy of so great a grace; it is precisely this humble avowal of his own unworthiness that is required to make him in some degree worthy of Holy Communion. (*The Holy Sacrifice of the Mass*, p. 765)

With this in mind, the priest asks that the Eucharist not be a source of condemnation. (cf. 1 Cor. 11:27-29) St. Cyril of Jerusalem taught that if we are "deemed worthy" of these mysteries, we "become of the same body and blood with Christ" (*Catechesis* IV, 1), so perhaps the analogy can be made to an organ transplant. When a body receives a new organ, it may not be compatible with the body resulting in a "condemnation" of sorts; but if the organ is "of the same body and blood" as the body, it is received as "a healing remedy." This comparison may not be perfect, but it leads us to ask: "Am I the body and Christ is the organ? Or is *Christ* the body and *I* am the organ?" We find the right orientation in the words of Christ and St. Paul: "I am the vine, you are the branches" (John 15:5), "We are members of his body." (Eph. 5:3; cf. 1 Cor. 6:15; 12:27)

Those who receive Communion daily (such as priests) have all the more reason to pray fervently for a worthy reception. We are creatures of habit, and frequent reception of the Eucharist can turn into a routine, leading to that sort of thoughtlessness and carelessness that paves the way to an unworthy Communion. Furthermore, this sacrificial banquet is our affirmation of the New Covenant; when we receive the Eucharist, we are swearing an oath to God to be faithful to His Covenant. We must not swear this oath falsely. (*Swear to God*, pp. 144-145)

The priest asks for "protection in mind and body" on account of the spiritual combat we endure in this world. (cf. *Catechism* 409; 1 Pet. 2:11) Satan seeks to darken our intellect and weaken our wills to coerce us into sin; he "prowls around like a roaring lion, seeking some one to devour." (1 Pet. 5:8) Communion refreshes our souls and strengthens the life of grace. (cf. *Catechism* 1392) It gives us the grace to avoid mortal sin and wipes away venial sin (cf. *Catechism* 1393-1395), thus protecting us and serving as "a healing remedy." As the "medicine of immortality," it is our pledge of the integral healing and restoration of body and soul to take place in the resurrection. (cf. *Catechism* 1405)

"Behold the Lamb of God..."

After his preparation, the priest genuflects in adoration. Then he holds the Host over the paten or the chalice, facing the people. (GIRM 157) Then he says these words recorded by St. John the Apostle:

Ecce Agnus Dei, ecce qui tollit peccáta mundi.
Beáti qui ad cenam Agni vocáti sunt.

Behold the Lamb of God,	*John 1:36*
behold him who takes away the sins of the world.	*John 1:29; 1 John 3:5*
Blessed are those called to the supper of the Lamb.	*Rev. 2:7; 3:20; 19:9*

At the Offertory, as the priest mixed a little water with wine, he prayed that we might come to share in the divinity of Christ. That prayer is now being answered, by the call to share in the supper of the Lamb. These words, together with their response – "Lord, I am not worthy..." – made by the priest and congregation, form our final act of preparation before actually presenting ourselves to receive Communion. St. Cyril exhorts us: "Deprive not yourselves, through the pollution of sins, of these Holy and Spiritual Mysteries." (*Catechesis* V, 23) This invitation to participation in the Eucharist is similar to Jesus' promise to "give some of the hidden manna" to those who endure (Rev. 2:17) and to invite those who open the door to dine with him. (cf. Rev. 3:20)

The old translation rendered *Ecce* as "This is" instead of "Behold," obscuring the quote of St. John the Baptist's bold proclamation from the shores of the Jordan. It made the priest's words a mere declaration instead of an exhortation to behold the Lamb. This "beholding" is much deeper than just externally seeing the Host – it is recognizing in the Host the Lamb of God, it is having our eyes opened by faith and knowing Him in the breaking of the bread.

Preparing for the Lamb

This Lamb was prepared for starting back in the days of Abraham. As he led his beloved son Isaac up Mount Moriah (where the Temple would be built by King Solomon), Isaac asked his father where the lamb for the sacrifice was. Isaac, who carried the wood for the sacrifice on his back, was told, "God will provide himself the lamb." (Gen. 22:8) But at the top of the mountain, there was no lamb to be found, only a ram with its head crowned in thorns. (cf. Gen. 22:13) The descendents of Abraham would seek for centuries for the lamb that God would provide.

It was not found at the Passover, for each family had to provide an unblemished lamb for the sacrifice, and they could not break any of its bones. (cf. Ex. 12:3, 46) It was not found on *Yom Kippur*, the day of atonement, when two lambs or goats were set aside, one to be offered in sacrifice, the other to have the sins of Israel placed upon its head and be sent into the wilderness, outside the camp, to die. (cf. Lev. 16)

But when St. John the Baptist cried, "Behold, the Lamb of God!" it surely must have attracted the attention of any Israelite who heard him.

Can you behold on the altar at Mass the "Lamb standing, as though it had been slain" (Rev. 5:6) as the priest holds up the Host? This Lamb is God's beloved Son. (cf. Matt. 3:17) This Lamb bore the wood of sacrifice on His back. (cf. John 19:17) This Lamb was crowned with thorns. (cf. John 19:2) This Lamb was found to be without blemish by Pilate. (cf. John 18:38) Not a bone of this Lamb was broken. (cf. John 19:32-36) This Lamb was offered as a sacrifice (cf. Heb. 9:26) and bore our sins. (cf. 1 Pet. 2:24) This Lamb was sent outside the camp to die. (cf. Heb. 13:12) On the banks of the Jordan, St. John beheld this Lamb. Do you?

The Marriage Supper of the Lamb

Earlier in this chapter, I compared the Mass to a marriage banquet and a feast. This comparison is comes ultimately from the book of Revelation. St. John saw the new Jerusalem, the Bride of the Lamb, descending from Heaven. (cf. Rev. 21:9-10) Prior to this vision he heard the voice of a multitude in Heaven saying that "the marriage of the Lamb has come," and then an angel told him to write, "Blessed are those who are invited to the marriage supper of the Lamb." (Rev. 19:7, 9)

This line (with the exception of the word "marriage") was added to the *Ecce Agnus Dei* in the Ordinary Form of the Mass. The old translation ("Happy are those who are called to his supper") masked the scriptural origin somewhat, although we should have known that the "his" referred to "the Lamb." The old translation was also sometimes slightly altered by some priests to "Happy are *we* who are called to *this* supper." This variation, while it may have been an attempt to be more inclusive, falls short in two regards.

First, all of us present at Mass should not necessarily receive Holy Communion, and more than just those of us present at this particular celebration are being called. Second, it is not just to *this* supper, to this particular celebration of the Mass, that we are called, but to the eternal, heavenly marriage supper of the Lamb. The Eucharist unites us across space and time, so both of those (illicit) changes in the old translation, instead of being inclusive, rendered the invitation exclusive, focused only on those people at the local celebration.

The Mass is an act of love: the divine Husband offers Himself for His Bride, the Church, who offers herself back to Him. (cf. Eph. 5:25-27) Soon that Bride, in the faithful, will walk down the aisle to her Husband, to their marriage supper, and receive Him in Holy Communion.

The Priest's Communion

Now the priest, with great reverence, receives Communion.

"May the Body (Blood) of Christ..."

Facing the altar, he picks up the Host and prays quietly:

Corpus Christi custódiat me in vitam ætérnam.

May the Body of Christ keep me safe for eternal life.   *John 6:54; 12:25*

He consumes the Host and can pause for a moment of joyful meditation; then the priest picks up the chalice,[18] quietly praying:

Sanguis Christi custódiat me in vitam ætérnam.

May the Blood of Christ keep me safe for eternal life.   *John 6:54; 12:25*

---

[18] The celebrant is required to receive Communion under both forms.

By these prayers, the priest expresses a desire for the supreme benefit of Holy Communion: the salvation of his body and soul. Eternal life is not just a spiritual reward; it is enjoyed in our resurrected bodies as well.

In the Extraordinary Form, each of these prayers is preceded by another prayer evoking *todah* psalms. Before the priest picks up the Host, he would say "I will take the Bread of Heaven, and will call upon the name of the Lord." (cf. Ps. 105:40; 116:13, 17) Before picking up the chalice, he would say a longer prayer:

> How shall I make a return to the LORD for all the things He has given me? I will take the Chalice of Salvation, and call upon the name of the LORD. I will call upon the LORD and give praise: and I shall be saved from my enemies. (cf. Ps. 116:12-13; 18:3)

The question posed in Psalm 116:12 (what can we offer to the Lord for all He has given to us?) is answered by the Mass itself. The marvelous exchange is really just our good stewardship of the gifts God gives us, so all we have to offer God in return is what He has given us. Along with these, the priest offers his gratitude: thanksgiving for the Eucharist.[19] Even with these prayers absent from the Ordinary Form, the priest can adopt the same sentiment and attitude toward the mystical banquet set before him.

The Communion Antiphon

After the priest has completed his Communion, he administers it to the deacon, and then to any extraordinary ministers of Holy Communion.[20] At this time, the Communion antiphon begins. While this chant is often replaced by a hymn (much like the Introit and Offertory antiphons), its purpose is "to express the communicants' union in spirit by means of the unity of their voices, to show joy of heart, and to highlight more clearly the 'communitarian' nature of the procession to receive Communion." (GIRM 86)

The custom of singing at this time may come from the singing of the *Hallel* psalms during the Passover; Jesus and the Apostles were singing

---

[19] Psalm 116 also includes the verse "I will offer to you the *sacrifice of thanksgiving* and call on the name of the LORD." (Ps. 116:17)

[20] Priests are not to wait for the people's Communion to conclude before receiving Communion themselves. (cf. *Redemptionis Sacramentum* 97) Neither deacons nor extraordinary ministers of Holy Communion are to receive Communion in the manner of concelebrants, who consume the Host at the same time as the principal celebrant. (cf. *Ecclesiae de Mysterio* Art. 8, 2; GIRM 162)

these as they went to the Mount of Olives. (cf. Matt. 26:30) In the early centuries of the Church, this Communion chant would often incorporate Psalm 34, according to St. Ambrose and St. Cyril: "O taste and see that the LORD is good." (Ps. 34:8; cf. *De Mysteriis* IX, 58; *Catechesis* V, 20)

The People's Communion

The Communion Rite is about the Body of Christ (the Church) receiving the Body of Christ (the Eucharist). Through this sacrament, Christ feeds His Church with Himself.

"The Body (Blood) of Christ."

To each communicant, the minister of Holy Communion says:[21]

Corpus (Sanguis) Christi.

The Body (Blood) of Christ.   *1 Cor. 10:16*

This is an ancient formula for administering Communion, to which each communicant responds "Amen." In the Extraordinary Form, the prayer said by the priest for his own Communion ("May the Body of Christ...") is used, accompanying the distribution of Communion with a prayer for an effective reception.

Just as the phrase "the Body of Christ" identifies both the Church and the Eucharist, so too does "Communion." The names of the local bishop and the Pope are mentioned in the Eucharistic Prayer as a reminder that whoever receives Communion needs to be in communion with those successors of the Apostles. This is one very important reason why the Church does not ordinarily administer Holy Communion to non-Catholic Christians.[22] (*The Bible and the Mass*, p. 95) The Church encourages those who cannot receive Communion sacramentally (for any reason) to make an act of spiritual Communion.

---

[21] In distributing the Host, it is recommended that a Communion-plate be used, regardless of whether the person is receiving on the tongue or in the hand, to avoid, as far as possible, the Host falling. (cf. GIRM 287; *Redemptionis Sacramentum* 93)

[22] Canon 844 in the Code of Canon Law makes exceptions for members of the Eastern Churches not in communion with Rome, and for Protestants, under certain circumstances, one of which is that the person must manifest the Catholic faith about the Eucharist.

Holy Communion as an Exchange

As was said at the beginning of this chapter, Communion is bound up in sacrifice: there is no Holy Communion without the Consecration. Rev. Fulton Sheen expressed this in his book *Calvary and the Mass*. In the fifth chapter, on the Communion Rite, he wrote that Jesus Christ "made our very crime a happy fault;[23] He turned a Crucifixion into a Redemption; a Consecration into a Communion; a death into life everlasting."

We recognize that in Communion we are partaking in the life of the Trinity, but have you considered that there is more to Communion than just receiving? "Men may hunger for God, but God thirsts for men," wrote Rev. Sheen, referring to the "fifth word" of Christ from the cross: "I thirst." (John 19:28) He then asked a series of important questions:

> Is all the Life to pass from Christ to us and nothing to go back in return? Are we to drain the chalice and contribute nothing to its filling? Are we to receive the bread without giving wheat to be ground, to receive the wine and give no grapes to be crushed? If all we did during our lives was to go to Communion to receive Divine Life, to take it away, and leave nothing behind, we would be parasites on the Mystical Body of Christ.

In short: if the Mass is truly a mystical exchange between God and man, what do we give back as we receive the marvelous gift of the Eucharist?

Rev. Sheen provided the same answer as St. Paul: we must fill up in our bodies what is lacking in the suffering of Christ. (cf. Col. 1:24) We respond to Christ's sacrificial death by mortifying ourselves, voluntarily dying to ourselves, bearing in our bodies the death of Christ, so that He may give to us His life. (cf. 2 Cor. 4:10)

Ablutions

After the distribution of Communion is completed, the priest or deacon performs the ablutions of the sacred vessels.[24] The liturgical purification of the vessels developed between the eleventh and fourteenth centuries, although they certainly were cleansed before then, if only for practical reasons. A more careful cleansing of the vessels probably developed out

---

[23] Rev. Sheen was referring to the "happy fault" sung of in the Exsultet on the Easter Vigil: "O truly necessary sin of Adam … O happy fault that earned so great, so glorious a Redeemer."

[24] An instituted acolyte is also permitted to do so. The indult permitting other extraordinary ministers of Holy Communion to do so is no longer in force in the United States.

of reverence for the Blessed Sacrament and to better manifest the Church's teaching on the Real Presence of Christ in the Eucharist.

Christ is present in even the smallest recognizable fragment of the consecrated bread or a single drop of the consecrated wine, which is why we should pay close attention to the handling of the Eucharist. In the Extraordinary Form, for example, the priest's thumb and forefinger are joined to each other from the Consecration until the ablutions (except while distributing Communion). The Eucharist is not to be treated casually, let alone a portion of it be discarded, and our reverence for it extends to the sacred vessels that hold it. St. Cyril of Jerusalem went so far as to compare crumbs of the Eucharistic bread to gold dust:

> Partake of [the Holy Body]; giving heed lest you lose any portion thereof; for whatever you lose, is evidently a loss to you as it were from one of your own members. For tell me, if any one gave you grains of gold, would you not hold them with all carefulness, being on your guard against losing any of them, and suffering loss? Will you not then much more carefully keep watch, that not a crumb fall from you of what is more precious than gold and precious stones? (*Catechesis* V, 21)

"What has passed our lips..."

The ablutions take place at the altar or at a credence table off to the side; it is also permissible to do the ablutions immediately after Mass instead of at the end of the Communion Rite. (GIRM 163) The one doing the ablutions pours a bit of water into the patens and ciboria to collect fragments of the Host, and this water is carefully poured into the chalice. Then the chalice is purified in a similar manner while the minister prays this seventh century prayer quietly:

Quod ore súmpsimus, Dómine, pura mente capiámus, et de múnere temporáli fiat nobis remédium sempitérnum.

What has passed our lips as food, O Lord,	*Ps. 78:25*
may we possess in purity of heart,	*Ps. 73:1; Matt. 5:8; 1 Tim. 1:5*
that what has been given to us in time	
may be our healing for eternity.	*1 Pet. 2:24; Rev. 22:2*

He then drinks the contents of the chalice, and dries the sacred vessels with a purificator. After Mass, the purificator will first be washed in a special sink called the *sacrarium* which goes directly into the ground (and not into the local sewer system), so that any particles contained in it are sent into the earth; only then is it laundered normally.

The prayer's sentiment is common to the Post-Communion prayers. It speaks of the Eucharist as spiritual food, for what other sort of food do you hope to "possess in purity of heart"? It juxtaposes our temporal reception of the sacrament with Its eternal effects. The Eucharist is a temporal gift because we receive it in the days of our earthly pilgrimage. (*The Glories of the Catholic Church*, p. 269) Furthermore, the sacrament is with us only so long as the appearances of bread and wine remain, for however long our bodies take to break down food. But the grace and healing received in the Eucharist are not bound to the external form. They remain active in us so long as we abide in Christ.

In the Extraordinary Form, the priest purifies the chalice twice: once with wine, then again with water and wine. After he purifies the chalice once, he says the following prayer quietly:

> May your Body, O Lord, which I have eaten,
> and your Blood, which I have drunk, cleave to my soul,
> and grant that no trace of sin be found in me,
> who has celebrated these pure and holy mysteries.

This prayer is like the first, asking that the sacrament remain with the one who has received it, and for the effects (freedom from sin chief among them) to be long-lasting. Both of these prayers "can and should be made their own by the faithful." (*The Spirit of the Liturgy*, p. 214)

Post-Communion Prayer

There should be ample opportunity for the priest and the congregation to spend time in personal prayer before the Post-Communion prayer. After this period of silent meditation, reflection, and thanksgiving, the priest and the people stand. Then the priest summons the faithful to prayer once more: "Let us pray."[25]

The Post-Communion Prayer, like the Collect and the Prayer over the Offerings, directs our minds and hearts to the particular intention of this Mass, and it can either express our personal sentiments or help us to

---

[25] The Post-Communion is not the "closing prayer" of the Mass, so announcements are made after this prayer, not before it.

refocus if our minds have wandered. This prayer tends to be short in length but rich in doctrine. Here is the prayer from the Twenty-Seventh Sunday in Ordinary Time:

Concéde nobis, omnípotens Deus,
ut de percéptis sacraméntis inebriémur atque pascámur,
quátenus in id quod súmimus transeámus.

Per Christum…

Grant us, almighty God,	*Invocation*
that we may be refreshed and nourished	*Petition*
by the Sacrament which we have received,	
so as to be transformed into what we consume.	*Purpose*
Through Christ our Lord.	*Conclusion*

This particular prayer echoes the prayer at the mixing of the wine with water, and it appears inspired by a sermon of St. Augustine, in which he says to the congregation:

> If, therefore, you are the body of Christ and its members, your mystery is placed on the Lord's table: you receive your mystery. To that which you are [*or:* eat], you answer "Amen." … Therefore, be a member of the body of Christ, that the "Amen" may be true! (*Sermon* 272, Pentecost A.D. 408)

After this prayer, the Communion Rite comes to an end and the Mass draws to a close.

The Liturgy of the Eucharist has brought us through the five actions of Christ as the Last Supper: taking bread, giving thanks for it, blessing it, breaking it, and then giving it to His disciples. The actions of the priest have shown forth various mysteries: the Incarnation, the Crucifixion, the Resurrection, and our eventual sharing in Christ's divinity. We picked up our crosses and followed our Lord, uniting ourselves to His sacrifice as it was renewed on the altar and then given to us as spiritual food. We have gazed upon the Lamb of God and renewed our vow of commitment to the New Covenant made in His Blood.

The word "Eucharist" means "thanksgiving," and that is what we offer God for all He has given us; the whole time after Communion is meant to be spent in private and public thanksgiving. This spirit of gratitude continues through to the very end of the Mass, up to its very last words: "Thanks be to God."

Questions for Reflection: Priests

1) **Interpret:** Why is the consuming of part of the sacrifice such an important part of offering sacrifice?

2) **Interpret:** How does Jesus Christ perfect the revelation of God as Father?

3) **Interpret:** What connection did the Apostles see between peace and unity in the early Church?

4) **Explain:** Why are our prayers for peace specifically connected to the offering of the Eucharist?

5) **Explain:** What are you focused on (e.g. visually, mentally) as you pray the Communion Rite prayers addressed to Christ?

6) **Explain:** Why are there so many ritual elements in between the consecration of the Eucharist and its reception by the priest and the congregation in Holy Communion?

7) **Relate:** How does your celebration of the Mass *in persona Christi* effect your relationship with God the Father?

8) **Relate:** In what areas of your life do you pray for peace?

9) **Relate:** What is the state of your relationship with your superior, your pastor, or your bishop?

10) **Relate:** How does your preparation for meeting Christ in the Eucharist relate to your preparation for meeting Christ at the end of time?

11) **Relate:** What do you give to Jesus in return for the Eucharist?

12) **Relate:** How do you teach the faithful under your care about the connection between participation in Holy Communion and the other sacraments, such as Baptism and Reconciliation?

Questions for Reflection: Laity

1) **Interpret:** Why is Christ's second coming our "blessed hope"?

2) **Interpret:** How can we make peace with our brothers and sisters before offering our gift at the altar? (cf. Matt. 5:23-24)

3) **Interpet:** Christ is the "Lamb of God," but He is also the "Lion of Judah." (cf. Gen. 49:8-10; Rev. 5:5) How is Christ manifested as the Lion of Judah in the Mass?

4) **Explain:** How does the Communion Rite both prepare you for Communion in the Body of Christ and manifest the communion shared among the Body of Christ?

5) **Explain:** What can you learn doctrinally from the priest's quiet prayers of preparation?

6) **Explain:** How does the Fraction Rite represent our participation in the suffering of Christ?

7) **Explain:** What does "The Body of Christ" mean, in the context of receiving the sacrament? What does the response of "Amen" mean?

8) **Relate:** How soon after the Rite of Peace does your patience run out, or your temper flare up? How can you receive the peace of Christ in a lasting way?

9) **Relate:** What prayers of preparation do you use before receiving Communion? How do you pray afterward? Have you ever given thought to adapting the priest's prayers for your own use?

10) **Relate:** How do you receive Holy Communion? Do you have an assembly-line mentality, or is it a personal encounter with Christ?

11) **Relate:** Are you prepared to share with others your experience with Christ, like the two disciples returning from Emmaus?

I heard the voice of the Lord saying,
"Whom shall I send, and who will go for us?"
Then I said, "Here am I! Send me."
(Isaiah 6:8)

"Go therefore and make disciples of all nations, baptizing them
in the name of the Father and of the Son and of the Holy Spirit,
teaching them to observe all that I have commanded you."
(Matthew 28:19-20)

8

Concluding Rites

JESUS GAVE HIS APOSTLES the gift of peace when He came to them on the day of His Resurrection, and then He commissioned them: "As the Father has sent me, even so I send you." (John 20:21) The Apostles did not act upon this commission until after Jesus blessed them as He ascended into Heaven and the Holy Spirit emboldened them on the day of Pentecost. Following this pattern, the Mass ends with the priest blessing the congregation and sending them forth on an apostolic mission. By the power of the Holy Spirit, they go into the world to sanctify it and bring it to Christ.

If we have participated in the Mass well, we will leave changed; this goes for the priest as well as the congregation. The priest does not offer the Mass only for the people's benefit and not his own, like a math tutor going over the basics of algebra with a struggling student. As the priest's prayers make abundantly clear, he needs the fruits of the Mass just as much as anyone else. We all need to be re-converted, to recommit ourselves to this New Covenant, to undergo a profound spiritual change.

We cannot always perceive this change, but feelings are not the true measure of conversion or holiness; just ask St. John of the Cross or Bl. Mother Teresa about their "dark night of the soul." As imperceptible as this change might be, God's grace is slowly working in us to bring about greater goods than we could ever hope to accomplish on our own. Why do we need to be changed? Because, as the Latin proverb goes, *nemo dat quod non habet* – no one can give what he does not have. How can we be effective messengers of God's forgiveness if we have not been forgiven? And how can we offer the peace of Christ when we are not at peace with Him? The Mass, in addition to being the means by which the Church worships God, is also the means by which God equips His Church to go out and bring Christ to the world... and bring the world to Christ.

The Concluding Rites are succinct: important brief announcements can be made, the priest greets the people one final time, he blesses them, and then he (or the deacon) dismisses them. As the priest and deacon leave the sanctuary, they reverence the altar with a kiss and a profound bow, and then they process out with the other ministers. (GIRM 90)

Announcements

The making of announcements is not a liturgical act per se, but rather a practical means of relaying important news in the life of the parish, the community, the diocese, the Church, or the world. A simple guideline for their function and content comes from Rev. Thomas Margevičius: because the "parish is very much part of the world," the announcements should answer the question, "How can our Eucharistic faith be lived in our parish, our community, our world?"[1]

Greeting

It may seem odd that the Concluding Rites *begin* with a greeting, but the greeting is a common and important one: "The Lord be with you." This is potentially the fourth time this greeting is said during the Mass: first, at the beginning of the Introductory Rites; second, just before the Gospel; third, at the beginning of the Preface; and fourth, just before the blessing and dismissal.

Why do the priest and the congregation repeatedly pray for the Lord to be in their midst? The most ardent desire of the Church is the

---

[1] Quotes from Rev. Margevičius in this chapter are from his seven-part series on the Mass, found online here: **http://www.relevantradio.com/Page.aspx?pid=1681**

continual presence of her Lord, so she does not tire of asking it. Such a short and simple prayer may seem to pale in comparison with the long and complex orations that the Roman Rite has acquired over the centuries, but sometimes it is the shortest prayer that expresses the greatest urgency and the deepest need.

Pontifical Blessing

If a bishop celebrates Mass, the blessing is preceded by a brief antiphonal dialogue from the Psalms (like the Penitential Act, Form B). The bishop first says:

Sit nomen Dómini benedíctum.

Blessed be the name of the Lord. *Ps. 113:2*

to which the congregation responds "Now and forever." Then he says:

Adiutórium nostrum in nómine Dómini.

Our help is in the name of the Lord. *Ps. 124:8*

and the congregation responds "Who made heaven and earth."

The first half of this dialogue comes from one of the *Hallel* psalms, so called because they begin "*Hallelu Yah*" ("Praise the LORD"). This psalm goes on to say, "O servants of the LORD, praise the name of the LORD!" (Ps. 113:1) The second verse, which the bishop and people say, fulfills that command. It should remind us of the beginning petition of the Our Father, "Hallowed be thy name," which is followed by the petition "Thy kingdom come."

The second half of the dialogue comes from Psalm 124, a "Song of Ascents" according to its rubric. Fifteen psalms have this designation, which refers to their being prayed by pilgrims as they approached the city of Jerusalem, or perhaps by the priests as they ascended the steps in the Temple.[2] As we confess that "Our help is the name of the LORD, who made heaven and earth," we should think of the third petition of the Our Father, which is for His will to be done on earth as it is in Heaven.

---

[2] This might explain the use of Psalm 124:8 in the Extraordinary Form: it follows the *Judica me*, a prayer said by the priest at the beginning of Mass shortly before he goes "in to the altar of God." (Ps. 42:4, Douay-Rheims)

How can we hallow the Father's name? How can we bring about His Kingdom? How can we fulfill His will on earth as it is in Heaven? Only with the help of Him Who made Heaven and earth, Who provides us with our daily bread, Who forgives us our trespasses, Who leads us not into temptation, and Who delivers us from evil.

Final Blessing

As a sign that the Lord is truly with us and helping us to accomplish His will in the world, the priest or bishop calls God's blessing down upon the congregation. There are three forms of blessing that can be used.

Simple Blessing

The first option is probably the one you are most familiar with. It is very simple and straightforward:

Benedícat vos omnípotens Deus, Pater, et Fílius, + et Spíritus Sanctus.

May almighty God bless you,   *Jdth. 15:10; Ps. 29:11; 115:15; 1 Pet. 3:9*
the Father, and the Son, + and the Holy Spirit.   *Matt. 28:19*

The congregation responds "Amen." A priest blesses the people with one Sign of the Cross, but a bishop makes three, typically one in each of three directions.

At the end of the Penitential Act, the priest says "May almighty God have mercy on *us*," but in the blessing he says "May almighty God bless *you*." This is not a pious wish; it is a true priestly blessing. This blessing reminds us that priests participate in Christ's priesthood in a different way from the laity. Priests exercise the ministerial priesthood, and their vocation is to forgive sins, to offer sacrifice, and to bless. The hands with which he blesses the congregation are the same hands that hold Christ in the Eucharist; God blesses His people through the mouth and hand of His priests. (*The Holy Sacrifice of the Mass*, p. 806)

By making the Sign of the Cross over the congregation, the priest or bishop is blessing them with the same gesture used over the deacon who proclaims the Gospel, and over the bread and wine at the end of the epiclesis of the Eucharistic Prayer. The priest calls upon God – he does not bless us "in the name of…" but invokes the blessing of God directly. God is the source of every grace and blessing.

Solemn Blessing

The second form of the blessing is preceded by the priest (or deacon, if there is one) instructing the people:

Inclináte vos ad benedictiónem.

Bow down for the blessing.   *Ex. 4:31*

The *Apostolic Constitutions* contain a similar invitation to blessing:

> Now we have received the Precious Body and the Precious Blood of Christ. … And let the deacon say: "Bow down to God through His Christ, and receive the blessing." (*Apostolic Constitutions* VIII, XIV-XV)

The priest then extends his hands over the congregation, using the same gesture as in the Eucharisic Prayer at the epiclesis.

The Solemn Blessing is usually composed of three exhortations or petitions that speak of God but are directed to the congregation. After each petition, the people say "Amen." Here is a Solemn Blessing for use throughout the year, the Aaronic blessing from Numbers 6:23-27.

Benedícat vobis Dóminus, et custódiat vos. (Amen.)

May the Lord bless you and keep you.   *Num. 6:24*

Illúminet fáciem suam super vos, et misereátur vestri. (Amen.)

May he let his face shine upon you and show you his mercy.   *Num. 6:25*

Convértat vultum suum ad vos, et donet vobis suam pacem. (Amen.)

May he turn his countenance towards you and give you his peace. *Num. 6:26*

Prayer over the People

The Solemn Blessings are spoken to the congregation, but the Prayer over the People is addressed to God *about* the congregation. These prayers were once restricted to the season of Lent, but the third edition of the Roman Missal permits their use year-round.

Unlike the Solemn Blessing, which has multiple petitions to which the congregation says "Amen," the Prayer over the People is a single prayer. After the invitation to the people to bow their heads, the priest extends his hands over the people and says the prayer, and the people respond "Amen." Here is a Prayer over the People for general use:

Largíre, quaesumus, Dómine,
fidélibus tuis indulgéntiam placátus et pacem,
ut páriter ab ómnibus mundéntur offénsis,
et secúra tibi mente desérviant.

Bestow pardon and peace, O Lord, we pray, upon your faithful,   *Eph. 1:7-8*
that they may be cleansed from every offense   *Ps. 51:2; 1 John 1:7*
and serve you with untroubled hearts.   *Rom. 12:2,11; 1 Cor. 15:34*

Conclusion

The Solemn Blessing and the Prayer over the People end with different words of blessing than the simple blessing.

Et benedíctio Dei omnipoténtis,
Patris, et Filii, + et Spíritus Sancti,
descéndat super vos et máneat semper.

And may the blessing of almighty God,
the Father, and the Son, + and the Holy Spirit,
come down on you and remain with you for ever.   *John 1:32-33; Acts 2:2-3*

These words should evoke the movement of the Holy Spirit, descending from Heaven like a dove and remaining on Jesus after His baptism in the Jordan. They should also remind us of the Holy Spirit descending like tongues of fire and resting on the disciples on the day of Pentecost.

Whatever form the blessing takes, it is meant to remind us of the blessing that Jesus gave His Apostles as He ascended into Heaven:

> Then he led them out as far as Bethany, and lifting up his hands
> he blessed them. While he blessed them, he parted from them, and
> was carried up into heaven. (Luke 24:50-51)

The similarity between these two blessings was commented on by many medieval liturgists, who perceived the Mass to be a representation of the whole sacrificial life of Christ, or of salvation history from the beginning of the world to the end of time. From that eschatological perspective, they also saw the blessing at the end of Mass as prefiguring that blessing yet to be given: "Come, O blessed of my Father, inherit the kingdom prepared for you from the foundation of the world." (Matt. 25:34)

Dismissal

Jesus not only blessed His disciples before leaving them, but gave them a great commission to go out and make disciples, baptizing and teaching people all over the earth. At Mass, once the people have been blessed, the deacon dismisses them to carry out their Christian lives in the world.

There were once two dismissals in the ancient liturgies, and the first of these has been restored in the Ordinary Form, thanks to the Rite of Christian Initiation of Adults. The first dismissal is of the catechumens, those who are not yet baptized, and it occurs near the end of the Liturgy of the Word, after the homily and before the Creed. This was done in antiquity for reasons of secrecy and to inspire, in both the dismissed and the faithful who remained, an elevated appreciation for the holy mysteries being celebrated. These dismissals were not mere disciplinary measures, but were solemn liturgical rites, preceded by a prayer and a blessing, with a formal announcement by the deacon.

The word "dismissal" comes from the traditional Latin phrase used at this point of the Mass: *Ite, missa est.* The word *missa* in Latin is a form of the noun *missio*, which literally means "sending forth" or "dismissal." But the word also acquired a Christian meaning: "mission." It is this word *missa* that gave us the name "Mass" for the Divine Liturgy in the Roman Rite, "because the liturgy in which the mystery of salvation is accomplished concludes with the sending forth (*missio*) of the faithful, so that they may fulfill God's will in their daily lives." (*Catechism* 1332) The earliest written record of the word *missa* being used to refer to the Mass comes from a letter of St. Ambrose to his sister written around Easter in the year A.D. 385: "I, however, remained at my ministry, and began to celebrate Mass [*missam facere*]." (*Letters* XX, 4) This casual use of the term implies that it was an established name for the Divine Liturgy.

Whatever dismissal text is used, the congregation responds "Thanks be to God," not because they are glad the Mass is over, but because they are imitating the disciples who "returned to Jerusalem with *great joy*, and were continually in the temple blessing God" (Luke 24:52-53) after Jesus ascended to His Father.

"Go forth, the Mass is ended."

The first option for dismissal is to use the traditional Roman words:

Ite, missa est.

Go forth, the Mass is ended. *Heb. 13:13*

The Latin literally translates to "Go, it is the dismissal," but that fails to capture the spirit of the words; it seems rather flat and cold, and does not evoke the same reaction as "Lift up your hearts!" The new translation renders *ite* as "Go forth" and not just "Go." In doing so, this dismissal is less about going *out* of the church building and more about going *into* the world on a mission. We will consider what this mission is as we look at the other options for dismissal.

The other three texts for dismissal are new in the third edition of the Roman Missal. The bishops at the 2005 Synod on the Eucharist had proposed that, in order to "make more explicit the relationship between Eucharist and mission … new dismissal formulas be prepared … which underline the mission in the world of the faithful who have participated in the Eucharist." Pope Benedict XVI approved this suggestion and selected the three following formulas for dismissal.

"Go and announce the Gospel of the Lord."

The first new text gives us a clear idea of why we are being sent out:

Ite ad Evangélium Dómini annuntiándum.

Go and announce the Gospel of the Lord.   *Mark 16:15; Eph. 6:19*

The core of the Church's mission is evangelization, the preaching of the Gospel for the salvation of souls. This duty belongs to all the members of the Church, not just to the ordained and religious. The Concluding Rites are short so that "we can get to evangelizing right away," writes Rev. Margevičius. "If we rush out of the church doors, it should not be because we want to beat other cars out of the parking lot, but because we can't wait to tell others about Jesus."

Have you ever noticed the same people in church, week after week? Have you ever wondered why no one new was showing up? Perhaps the reason is that no one has asked them to go to Mass! It does not require a professional to ask someone, "Would you like to come to Mass?" Maybe there is a person in your neighborhood who is thinking about the Catholic Church but does not know where to start; maybe you are just the one to talk to them. The Mass itself is a good means of evangelizing, but it does not exhaust the Church's activity. (SC 9) The Eucharist is the source of all the Church's evangelical efforts, as well as their summit:

everything we do to preach the Gospel flows from our communion with Christ, and this preaching leads others to full communion with Him and His Church. But between the Concluding Rites and the Introductory Rites, we should be living the reality of the Mass in the world, making Christ present by our words and deeds. Rev. Margevičius explains that Mass "call[s] us out of our busy worlds … to worship the Father through Christ in the Spirit, so that this Spirit empowers us to bring people back to the Father through Jesus Christ, whom we have encountered in the Eucharist."

The example of the two disciples on the road to Emmaus serves us well. They had journeyed seven miles from Jerusalem to Emmaus, and the day was almost over. But they wasted no time after they recognized the Lord: "They rose that same hour and returned [seven miles] to Jerusalem; and they found the eleven… Then they told what had happened on the road, and how he was known to them in the breaking of the bread." (Luke 24:33, 35)

"Go in peace, glorifying the Lord by your life."

Living the Mass in our daily lives is what the second new dismissal text is about:

Ite in pace, glorificándo vita vestra Dóminum.

Go in peace, glorifying the Lord by your life.   *Luke 5:25; 1 Cor. 6:20*

As mentioned in earlier chapters, the lay faithful exercise their priesthood primarily by sanctifying the world from within. The laity have a vocation to holiness in their everyday lives, as the Second Vatican Council made clear in its document on the lay apostolate:

> They exercise the apostolate in fact by their activity directed to the evangelization and sanctification of men and to the penetrating and perfecting of the temporal order through the spirit of the Gospel. In this way, their temporal activity openly bears witness to Christ and promotes the salvation of men. Since the laity, in accordance with their state of life, live in the midst of the world and its concerns, they are called by God to exercise their apostolate in the world like leaven, with the ardor of the Spirit of Christ. (*Apostolicam Actuositatem* 2)

Jesus told His disciples not to do good deeds "before men in order to be seen by them." (Matt. 6:1) At the same time, He told them to let their light shine before men "that they may see your good works and give glory to your Father who is in heaven." (Matt. 5:16) These might sound contradictory: should others see our good deeds or not? The answer is that we should do our good deeds to glorify God and not worry about who sees them, so that if (and when) others see them, they too will glorify God and not us.

There is no "liturgy" in the world, at least not like there is in the Church. So we must go and live the liturgy: we must bring contrition, adoration, petition, and thanksgiving into the world. Our daily lives should be a witness to the love of God in Jesus Christ in every word and deed. This is how we can fulfill our apostolic and evangelical mission, glorifying the Lord. (*Apostolicam Actuositatem* 6)

"Go in peace."

The last option for the dismissal is not really new; it is the recovery of an ancient formula: "Depart in peace." (*Apostolic Constitutions* VIII, XV)

Ite in pace.

Go in peace. *Judg. 18:6; Isa. 55:12; Luke 2:29; 7:50; 8:48*

This recalls once more the peace that Christ gave to His Apostles on the day of His Resurrection. He gave them peace and told them that He was sending them as He had been sent by His Father. This means that the Church's mission is the Son's mission: to preach the Gospel, to call all men to repentance, and to lead them to salvation and eternal life.

This attitude of Christian peace is how we are sent out: "Whatever house you enter, first say, 'Peace be to this house!' And if a son of peace is there, your peace shall rest upon him; but if not, it shall return to you." (Luke 10:5-6)

Recessional

After the dismissal, the priest and deacon kiss the altar. At the foot of the altar, with the other ministers, they make a profound bow and depart. While this is happening, there is probably a hymn being sung, although a silent recessional can be appropriate especially in a penitential season.

A word of advice: unless some emergency compels you, do not leave Mass before the priest does! Consider the closing hymn to be a prayer: leaving before the hymn is over is like praying only half of a Hail Mary or an Our Father. Not only can it be distracting, but it is an irregular way to pray and it can be considered disrespectful.

Thanksgiving After Mass

Just as the Missal provides preparatory prayers for the priest before Mass, it also includes prayers of thanksgiving for after Mass. It may be harder for priests to spend time in thanksgiving between Masses nowadays, but it is said that those who cannot find a half hour for prayer need to find an hour.

After Jesus ascended into Heaven, the disciples were found to be "continually in the temple blessing God." (Luke 24: 53) This is a good example for priests (and laity) to follow. In addition to the prayers found in the Missal – among them the *Anima Christi*, a prayer of St. Thomas Aquinas, and the beautiful "Universal Prayer" of Pope Clement XI – the *Placeat tibi* prayer from the Extraordinary Form is an appropriate offering of thanksgiving. This prayer, said quietly by the priest as he kneels at the altar just before the final blessing, revisits the sentiments of several of the Offertory prayers:[3]

> May the tribute of my humble ministry be pleasing to You, Holy Trinity.
> Grant that the sacrifice which I, unworthy as I am,
> have offered in the presence of Your majesty may be acceptable to You.
> Through Your mercy may it bring forgiveness to me
> and to all for whom I have offered it, through Christ our Lord. Amen.

Whatever the priest decides to pray, the important thing is that he takes time outside the liturgy to offer personal thanksgiving to God. The more he can live in gratitude to God outside the liturgy, the more heartfelt and genuine the prayers that the Mass places on his lips will be, and then he will not only be saying the Mass, he will truly be praying the Mass.

It is my sincere hope that this book has revealed to you – whatever your vocation or state in life – that much more happens at Mass than meets the eye and ear. Every gesture and action carries great significance, and there is a great sense of "activity" in the Mass even in the deepest silence

---

[3] Specifically, the prayer to the Holy Trinity (found in the Extraordinary Form), the prayer *In spiritu humilitatis* ("With humble spirit"), and the prayer *Orate, fratres* ("Pray, brethren").

or stillness. That activity is not the busy-ness or noise of our daily lives, but the unseen work of the Holy Spirit to sanctify everything that happens at Mass for the greater glory of God the Father.

For the ordained, I hope that this book has reminded you of the importance and gravity of what you say and do at Mass. I am convinced that the closer you look at the prayers of the Mass, the more fervently and earnestly you will pray the Mass. While a proper celebration of the liturgy includes saying the right words and following the rubrics, it is also important to be deeply spiritually committed to the prayers. And if you celebrate the Mass from the heart, I believe that the faithful entrusted to your care will take notice and glorify God, and they too will participate in the Mass more aware of the mysteries unfolding before them.

The Mass is a wonderful gift and a marvelous prayer. It engages our whole being: heart, soul, strength, and mind. But for all that we can say and learn about the Mass, I think it is to the heart that all our catechetical efforts must ultimately be directed. We can only know so much and do so much, but there is no limit to love, because God is love and He is eternal and infinite. If this book has accomplished anything, may it be to show you that God's love for you is etched into every word and action in the Mass, and so inspire you to pray the Mass with all your heart.

Questions for Reflection: Priests

1) **Interpret:** Who did God send in the Old Testament to speak to His people? What does this say about the role of the Church in being sent out into the world to preach the Gospel?

2) **Interpret:** The priesthood of Christ is not Aaron's priesthood. Why does the Church use the Aaronic blessing (cf. Num 6:23-27) in her liturgy?

3) **Interpret:** Christ has not left His Church alone. What did He promise to send to us after His Ascension? How does this gift help the Church bring salvation to the world?

4) **Explain:** Why are the rites that conclude the Mass so similar to those that begin the Mass?

5) **Explain:** Why does the bishop make three crosses, while a priest makes only one?

6) **Relate:** How are announcements presented in your parish? Are they merely social rather than communal?

7) **Relate:** How do you offer thanksgiving to God after Mass? How do you find rest after Mass?

8) **Relate:** How can you keep a Eucharistic attitude between one celebration of the Mass and the next?

9) **Relate:** How can a more devout praying of the Mass help you to be a better priest for the people under your care?

Questions for Reflection: Laity

1) **Interpret:** How did Jesus send out His disciples to preach and to heal during His time on earth? (cf. Luke 9:1-6; 10:1-11) How does Jesus send you out into the world at the end of Mass?

2) **Interpret:** What did Jesus tell His disciples immediately after He gave them the Great Commission? (cf. Matt. 28:20) What does this mean for the Church today?

3) **Explain:** Rev. Romano Guardini wrote that standing is "the sign of vigilance and action" showing the respect "of the soldier on duty." (*Sacred Signs*, p. 22) Why do we stand for the dismissal?

4) **Explain:** Why do we bow our heads for the solemn blessing?

5) **Explain:** How are the four dismissal texts similar? How do they differ from one another? Why are there multiple texts?

6) **Relate:** How do the three new dismissal texts challenge you in your lay apostolate to sanctify the world?

7) **Relate:** The priest makes certain acts of reverence as he leaves the sanctuary. What do you do when you leave the church after Mass?

8) **Relate:** How do you offer thanks to God after Mass?

9) **Relate:** What do you talk about on your way home from Mass? Do you discuss the readings or the homily? Do you focus on things that brought you joy, or on things that irritated you?

10) **Relate:** How do you see the Mass differently now? What can you share with your family and friends?

Bibliography

Atchley, E. G. Cuthbert F. *Ordo Romanus Primus*. The De La More Press, 1905.

Braun, Joseph. "Vestments." *The Catholic Encyclopedia*. Vol. 15. New York: Robert Appleton Company, 1912.

Benedict XVI, Pope. *Compendium of the Catechism of the Catholic Church*. USCCB Publishing, 2005.

Challoner, Richard, et. al. *The Glories of the Catholic Church, Volume II*. John Duffy, 1895.

Clark, Stephen B. *Catholics and the Eucharist: A Scriptural Introduction*. Charis Books, 2000.

Danielou, Rev. Jean, SJ. *The Bible and the Liturgy*. University of Notre Dame Press, 1956.

Donovan, Rev. J., trans. *The Catechism of the Council of Trent*. Lucas Brothers, 1829.

Driscoll, Rev. Jeremy, OSB. *What Happens at Mass*. Gracewing Publishing & Liturgy Training Publications, 2005.

Dubruiel, Michael. *The How-To Book of the Mass*. Our Sunday Visitor, 2007.

Elliott, Msgr. Peter J. *Ceremonies of the Modern Roman Rite*. Revised Edition. Ignatius Press, 2005.

Galli, Mark. *Beyond Smells and Bells: The Wonder and Power of Christian Liturgy*. Paraclete Press, 2008.

Gihr, Rev. Nicholas. *The Holy Sacrifice of the Mass*. B. Herder, 1949.

Guardini, Rev. Romano. *Sacred Signs*. Pio Decimo Press, 1956.

Hahn, Scott. *The Lamb's Supper*. Doubleday, 1999.

Hahn, Scott. *Swear to God: The Promise and Power of the Sacraments*. Doubleday, 2004.

Hahn, Scott and Regis J. Flaherty, eds. *Catholic for a Reason III*. Emmaus Road Publishing, 2004.

John Paul II, Pope. *Catechism of the Catholic Church*. USCCB Publishing, 1997.

Jungmann, Rev. Josef A., S.J. *The Mass*. Liturgical Press, 1986.

Kocik, Rev. Thomas A. *Loving and Living the Mass*. Zaccheus Press, 2007.

Lukefahr, CM, Rev. Oscar. *We Worship: A Guide to the Catholic Mass.* Liguori Publications, 2004.

Mazza, Enrico. *The Eucharistic Prayers of the Roman Rite.* Trans. Matthew J. O'Connel. Liturgical Press, 1989.

Oury, Rev. Guy. *The Mass.* Catholic Book Publishing Co., 1988.

Ratzinger, Joseph Cardinal. *Feast of Faith: Approaches to a Theology of the Liturgy.* Trans. Graham Harrison. Ignatius Press, 1986.

Ratzinger, Joseph Cardinal. *The Spirit of the Liturgy.* Trans. John Saward. Ignatius Press, 2000.

Sheen, Rev. Fulton J. *Calvary and the Mass.* P.J. Kenedy & Sons, 1936.

Soubigou, Msgr. Louis. *A Commentary on the Prefaces and the Eucharistic Prayers of the Roman Missal.* Trans. Rev. John Otto. Liturgical Press, 1969.

Stravinskas, Rev. Peter M. J. *The Bible and the Mass.* Newman House Press, 2001.

Tuberville, DD, Henry. *The Douay Catechism.* Excelsior Catholic Publishing House, 1649.

United States Conference of Catholic Bishops. *General Instruction of the Roman Missal.* USCCB Publishing, 2002.

Zundel, Maurice. *The Splendour of the Liturgy.* Sheed & Ward, 1939.

10505273R0

Made in the USA
Lexington, KY
30 July 2011